kosher by d

picture-perfect food for the holidays & every day

SUSIE FISHBEIN

Photographs by John Uher

Event Planning by Renee S. Erreich

Design Styling by Larry Sexton

Food Styling by Jill Raff

Graphic Design by Eli Kroen

Recipe Testing by Sandra Blank

Recipe Editing by Sarah Brueggemann

Judaic Writing by Charlotte Friedland

Wine Consulting by Miriam Morgenstern-Laufer

Published by

Mesorah Publications, ltd

Published by ARTSCROLL / SHAAR PRESS
4401 Second Avenue / Brooklyn, NY 11232 / (718) 921-9000
www.artscroll.com • www.kosherbydesign.com

Distributed in Israel by SIFRIATI / A. GITLER
6 Hayarkon Street / Bnei Brak 51127 / Israel

Distributed in Europe by LEHMANNS
Unit E, Viking Industrial Park, Rolling Mill Road
Jarrow, Tyne and Wear, NE32 3DP / England

Distributed in Australia and New Zealand by GOLDS WORLD OF JUDAICA
3-13 William Street / Balaclava, Melbourne 3183, Victoria / Australia

Distributed in South Africa by KOLLEL BOOKSHOP
Shop 8A Norwood Hypermarket/ Norwood 2196 / Johannesburg, South Africa

ISBN: 1-57819-707-4

Printed in Canada by Noble Book Press

kosher by design

by Susie Fishbein, editor of *The Kosher Palette*

We spend year after year gathering those we love around the holiday table, week after week savoring the life-enhancing magic of Shabbat, and night after night conversing and reflecting upon the day's events. These memorable meals provide an unmatched pleasure.

Over time, there's been a shift away from formal meals loaded with rich choices to simpler, well-planned menus. Although many of us enjoy watching chefs prepare intriguing dishes, when we're in our own kitchens we want easy-to-read recipes. We look for fresh ingredients that can be prepared with a minimal amount of fuss, but yield a maximum amount of aesthetic impact.

The recipes in this book offer abundant directions to help walk you through them. The selected dishes mix modern and traditional styles. I always try to include a clever twist on the traditional wherever possible. You will find tips, hints, menus, and wine recommendations to round out your meals.

During the photo shoots for this book, my food stylist taught me that when we cook, we cook with all of our senses. Listen for the sizzle as meat hits the pan, feel the food to determine its doneness, smell the nutty aroma of grains as they toast, behold with your eyes the plate's appeal, taste with your palate the delight of your creations.

This is true about entertaining, too. It is not only what you serve, but how you serve it. A simple garnish, a beautiful table, an unusual floral arrangement, a colorful plate filled with assorted delicacies-all of these things elevate the mundane to the magnificent.

We hope that our tables will inspire you for the Holidays and every day. Look around your house for things that can be used to achieve the ideas shown in this book. Mix and match concepts and adapt them to the various events of your lives.

You may have noticed that our title, *Kosher by Design,* carries a double meaning: this book is for you — the cook who *chooses* to cook kosher and who wants to present beautifully designed dishes with style and grace. I hope you'll find using it a joy for you as well as for those lucky enough to be invited to your table.

Above all, have fun. Let each meal be a wonderful journey-the sharing of something special with people you care about.

Susie Fishbein

Thank You

Kalman
My helpmate and soulmate.
The one man I know who knows where to find phyllo, shallots, quinoa or any other ingredient on any supermarket shelf. Your never-ending support gives me one more reason to adore you.

Kate, Danielle, Jodi and Eli
You are the main ingredients in my recipe for a happy life. You are the highlights of my every day. Having you cook and bake right alongside me made writing this book so much fun.

Mom and Dad
Thank you for your love and encouragement. Your kindness and endless energy set a constant example for all of our family.
I love you.

Muth
You are always there for our family, with love, care and a home cooked meal. Thank you for sharing your trademark recipes.

Rabbi Meir Zlotowitz
Thank you for giving the go ahead on this project and allowing me to be part of the Artscroll family.

Gedaliah Zlotowitz
Working with you has exceeded my every high expectation. You have been a true mensch.

Estee Berman
for shamelessly bragging about me and for believing in me long before I did.

Tuvia Rotberg
Thank you for making the shidduch.

The pleasure of doing this book was greatly enhanced by the people who participated in its creation.

Renee Erreich
Your charm and amazing attitude opened doors for this book, while your attention to detail made it everything I dreamed it could be. Your heart, commitment and enthusiasm are unequaled.

Larry Sexton
You were a scream and a dream to work with. You ooze talent and style. I was lucky to have you involved with this book.
Thank you for playing such a big role.

John Uher
Your tireless, egoless perfectionism is what made this book "picture perfect".

And to your team;

Bob, Paul and Chris
an easygoing, talented, accommodating group, I am grateful.

Sandra Blank
Whose "plate" is never too full for a friend.

Eli Kroen
Thank you for being totally committed to excellence.

Menucha Mitnick
Thank you for your sharp eye and patience.

Jill Raff
Thank you for transforming paper dreams into edible reality. Your styling prowess elevated this book to a higher level.

Miriam Morgenstern-Laufer
Your excitement for kosher wines is palpable. I raise my glass to you.

Charlotte Friedland
Thanks for stepping into this project like Cinderella into the glass slipper.
You added just the right tone to the Judaic writing.

Thank you to the following businesses and people that opened their doors to Kosher by Design.

Elliot and Larry Atlas and Atlas Florists
It is easy to see why you are the pinnacle of the Manhattan flower world. The generosity with which you gave and the quality of your flowers are quite the combination.

Randy Zablo & Foremost Caterers
Thank you for getting me on the right track and for the private tutoring session with Wali Alidad, chef extraordinaire.

Michael Strauss Silversmith
for all of the gorgeous Judaic pieces that grace our photo spreads.

Ruth Fischl
for the stunning tablecloths.

The Finished Room, Crate & Barrel, Avventura, and McKenzie Childs
for the spectacular table decor and accessories.

Skyview Wine & Liquors and McCabe's Wine & Spirits
for providing assistance and the wine

Michael Kane and Park East Kosher Butcher
for providing all of the meat for the photo shoots.

Elliott Strauss & Aaron Rothberg and Supersol
for providing all of the groceries for the photo shoots.

Barbara Fogel and Food for Thought
for the shalach manot basket

Howard Bodner & Party Source
for providing the chairs

Manischewitz
for the off-season Pesach ingredients.

Yakov Salczer & West Side Judaica
for the Judaica items.

To my friends and family who sensed me drowning in my own cake batter and tossed me an oven mitt. Thank you for sharing your recipes and for talking me through them.

Shari Alter	*Erica Freilich*	*Irene Laub*
Dovid Bendory	*Robin Fried*	*Judy Listhaus*
Atara Blumenthal	*Rina Fuchs*	*Lauren Mayer*
Ann Conte	*Debbie Golubtchik*	*Darbie Rabinowitz*
Limor Decter	*Rachel Green*	*Helen Ratzker*
Beth Eidman	*Elisa Greenbaum*	*Malkie Ratzker*
Yael Eisenberg	*Aline Grossman*	*Amy Schwartz*
Sarah & Steven Epstein	*Donald Hevaghan*	*Meira Silver*
Donna & Walter Epstein	*Robyn Krieger*	*Jessica Spector*
Mindie Erreich	*Seryl Kushner*	*Dena Wruble*
Karen Finkelstein	*Ellie Langer*	*Daniella Zlotowitz*

To the following people who welcomed the Kosher by Design crew into their magnificent homes for the photo shoots:

Arlene & Harvey Blau	*Rikki & Mendy Gross*	*Ellen & David Korn*
Jewel & Ted Edelman	*Lolly Daskal & Red Katz*	*Marcia Raff*
Sharon & Sinclair Haberman	*Phyllis & Joseph Korff*	*Ruth & Jerry Turk*

contents

c o n t e n t s

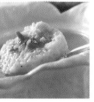

the kosher kitchen

Kosher cooks today have advantages undreamed of by their grandmothers: meat and poultry come from the butcher already koshered; kosher wines have taken top awards in international competitions; and most importantly, thousands upon thousands of food products now have reliable rabbinic supervision — and the number of kosher certified products is constantly growing!

Below is a summary of rules about kosher cooking. If your kitchen is not yet kosher (including your appliances), or if you have questions concerning kosher cooking, contact a qualified rabbi for guidance.

- Meat and dairy are cooked and eaten separately, using separate utensils, including dishes and flatware. The utensils are also washed separately.
- All meat must be slaughtered by trained, certified kosher slaughterers; the blood is then removed in accordance with Jewish law. In many places, the butcher "koshers" the meat (removes the blood) using the prescribed salting and soaking process. If you need to "kosher" your own meat, consult a rabbi (in advance) about the proper procedure.
- Liver is "koshered" by salting and broiling.
- Foods that are neither meat nor dairy (such as vegetables, eggs, grains) are called parve. They may be eaten with meat or dairy, but to retain their parve status they must be cooked in designated parve utensils.
- Fish is parve and does not require special koshering. Only fish with fins and scales are kosher. All other seafood is prohibited.
- Eggs with bloodspots are discarded.
- All processed food products, including wine and cheese, require kosher certification.
- Produce must be well washed and checked for insects.
- Passover requires its own set of meat, dairy and parve utensils as well as Passover certified foods.

While these rules may sound complicated, they are not difficult to keep once your kitchen is set up correctly. A well-arranged kosher kitchen just hums along – meat, dairy and parve dishes and utensils are well marked (usually by color coding). A rabbi's phone number is kept handy for consultation if a mistake occurs. And the cook knows that both family and guests are eating food prepared in accordance with Jewish law, ensuring their spiritual, as well as physical, well being.

shabbat

If you were told that your home had been chosen to host a queen visiting this country, how would you prepare for her arrival? No doubt, every corner of your house would sparkle, everyone in your family would be dressed in his or her finest clothing, and you would serve the most lavish cuisine in honor of your royal guest.

This is how we greet Shabbat, known in sacred Jewish literature as the Sabbath Queen. The ambience at the Shabbat table is elegant, yet relaxed — for the queen is not only a special guest, but an old friend as well. It is our privilege to honor her every week.

There are numerous ways to honor Shabbat, and many of them revolve around our three Shabbat meals. The first meal on Friday night has a glow all its own, as the warmth of candlelight brings out the mellow shine of challah and the sparkle of wine. Lighting the Shabbat candles is a *mitzvah* performed by the wife/mother of the household eighteen minutes before sundown. As we light the Shabbat candles, we absorb the tranquil mood that helps turn our thoughts from the mundane to the spiritual.

Our candles are also symbolic of God's creation of the physical and spiritual universes, as the Torah records that the universe began with the Divine declaration "Let there be light." The creation of the world is prominently featured in the words of Kiddush, the prayer over wine that begins our meal.

The challah on the table is a reminder of the manna that fell in the desert to feed our ancestors after their Exodus from Egypt. It fell six days a week, but not on Shabbat. On Fridays, each household received a double portion. And that is why we place two challot on our Shabbat table — recalling the double portion of food lovingly sent by Heaven for every Jew every *erev Shabbat* for nearly 40 years.

When Shabbat is over, the Havdalah blessings are said over wine, a multi-wick candle and spices. Havdalah marks the separation between Shabbat and the weekday, between the holy and the mundane. The emptiness we feel at the departure of the Sabbath Queen is offset only by her assurance that she will surely return in just six days.

shabbat dinner menu

Challah Napkin Rings
page 17

SOUP:
Porcini Mushroom and
Caramelized Onion Soup
page 56

SALAD:
Asian Steak Salad
page 72

ENTREE:
Honey Mustard Cornish Hens
page 110

SIDE DISHES:
Sun-dried Tomato & Portabello Rissoto
page 204

Green Beans with Crispy Shallots
page 201

DESSERT:
Chocolate Lovers Truffle Brownie
page 264

Strawberry Lemon Tart
page 280

The aroma of freshly baked challah and the fragrance of flowers fill the air on Shabbat, the high point of the Jewish week. Each week, we are blessed with the invaluable chance to stop rushing and make time for our spouse, children, relatives, friends and ourselves. And we strengthen one more vital relationship — our personal connection with God.

Shabbat dinner has not changed over the years and its importance has never diminished. Our radiant table represents the way Shabbat dinners have been for generations. To reflect the elegance of Shabbat itself, we placed a breathtaking cascade of hydrangeas as a centerpiece. Challah Napkin Rings hold floral napkins while also providing a challah roll for each guest.

All of the Shabbat finery, including crystal, silver Kiddush cups, silverware, our challah board and knife are polished to a magnificent shine. A sparkling candelabrum, which is lit before sundown to usher in Shabbat, is the focal point of the table. It's amazing how something as simple as using tapers instead of traditional Shabbat candles will add to the grandeur of your table.

Since all cooking must cease by the time Shabbat begins, the menu is comprised of foods that can be prepared in advance. The delicious Porcini Mushroom and Caramelized Onion Soup offers a nice change from traditional chicken soup. A colorful Asian Steak Salad is hearty enough to be considered an appetizer. Honey Mustard Cornish Hens — just a bit more unusual than chicken — make for a beautiful presentation. Our two colorful side dishes round out the hues of the plate. A Chocolate-lovers Truffle Brownie serves as a perfect foil for the Strawberry Lemon Tart. We paired a rich, sweet dessert with a light fruity one — so there's something for everyone!

wine list

TIO PEPE SHERRY

This Spanish Sherry complements the Porcini Mushroom and Caramelized Onion soup.

ABARBANEL GEWURZTRAMINER

This aromatic wine from Alsace possesses floral aromas
and is a traditional accompaniment to Asian Cuisine.
We recommend it for the Asian Steak Salad.

BARON HERZOG RESERVE CHARDONNAY

This full-bodied rich Chardonnay with lots of fruit
will pair well with the Honey Mustard Cornish Hens.

PORT
BARON HERZOG LATE HARVEST RIESLING

Port is the perfect match for chocolate and would enhance
the rich Chocolate Lovers Truffle Brownie.

For the Strawberrry Tart we recommend the Late Harvest Riesling.
The ripe fruit in the wine pairs well with most fruit desserts.

Challah

The *mitzvah* of challah addresses our relationship with the fundamental staff of life. In Judaism, the mundane process of baking bread is elevated to holiness by a ritual that recalls the days of ancient Jewish glory.

In the days of the Holy Temple in Jerusalem, the *Kohanim* were not apportioned farmland for they were required to devote themselves entirely to the study of Torah and to the Temple service. Their relationship with the rest of the Jewish nation was defined by their role as spiritual mentors.

A system of tithes and gifts of food was mandated by the Torah for their support. One of these gifts was "challah." By Jewish law, anyone who baked bread was required to give a small portion of the dough to a *Kohen*. Of course, in bringing the dough to the *Kohen*, the individual would strengthen their mutual bond – kind words would be exchanged, family inquiries made, a lesson in Torah learned. One's personal link with those who serve God was reinforced.

Today, we do not have the Temple and Jewish law does not permit *Kohanim* to accept the separated dough. Yet the *mitzvah* of *hafrashat challah* remains. The obligation begins when at least 2 lbs., 10 ounces of dough is kneaded, if it is made of one or more of five grains: wheat, barley, oats, rye or spelt. A piece of dough the size of an olive is removed and burned. (You can wrap it in foil and put it in the oven until it is too charred to be edible.) If the batch is larger (legal opinions of the minimum amount range from 3 lbs, 10.7 ozs. to 4 lbs. 15.2 ozs.), a blessing is made before pulling off the dough: Blessed are You, Hashem, our God, King of the universe, Who has sanctified us with His commandments and has commanded us to separate challah from the dough.

Few people realize that the name for our special Shabbat bread derives from the *mitzvah* associated with it. By sanctifying our loaves, we demonstrate that we appreciate God's blessings; and in keeping alive the practice of reserving this portion of our food, we express our faith that someday the Jewish people will be able to return to the Temple and to the spiritual level that once was ours.

challah

I love the ease of baking challah in my bread machine. However, there are times that I love the experience of spending a Thursday night in the kitchen with my three daughters baking challah the old-fashioned way, the way its been done by mothers and daughters for generations. The kneading and mixing become a group effort with lots of giggling to go around. The anticipation of Shabbat fills the air. This is my family's favorite recipe. It produces light and chewy challot and the aroma makes our house smell great for days.

½ cup warm water	4 cups boiling water
4 (¼-ounce) packages active dry yeast	1 (5-pound) bag unbleached all-purpose flour or high gluten bread flour, plus extra for kneading
1 tablespoon sugar	
7 large eggs	
2 cups sugar	1 large egg, lightly beaten
1½ cups vegetable oil	sesame seeds
7 teaspoons salt	poppy seeds

Place the warm water, yeast, and 1 tablespoon sugar into a large glass measuring cup or bowl. Set aside in a warm place. (If your kitchen is cold, put it on your opened oven door with the oven temperature set at 300 degrees.)

Crack 7 large eggs into an 8-quart pot and mix. In a separate large bowl, combine the 2 cups sugar, oil, salt, and boiling water. Mix with a wooden spoon.

When yeast is bubbly (proofed) add the yeast mixture into the egg mixture. (If the yeast does not get bubbly then it is dead and you must discard it and make the yeast mixture again with new yeast.)

Add the sugar/oil mixture into the pot. Stir. Add the flour into the pot in 3 additions, mixing well with wooden spoon between additions.

Sprinkle ½ cup flour on your kneading surface. Knead the dough for 10-15 minutes, adding flour to the surface as needed. Try not to add too much. It is easier to add more to a sticky dough than to restore a dough once too much flour has been added.

Put the dough back into the original 8-quart pot. Wet a kitchen dishtowel, wring it out well, and use it to cover the top of the pot. Try not to lift the towel, as air will dry out the dough.

Let the dough rise for 2-3 hours. Turn the dough out onto a floured surface. This is the point where you separate challah for the mitzvah. Make the blessing, then take off a piece of dough. Preheat oven to 350 degrees.

Using a dough cutter or sharp knife, divide the dough into 6-7 equal sized pieces. Divide each piece into 3 sections. Roll each section into a long strand. Lay the three strands in front of you. Pinch the top ends together. Braid the dough and pinch the bottom ends together. Place on parchment-lined or lightly greased baking sheets. Repeat with remaining dough. At this point you may freeze some of the challot. I place them on the baking sheet in the freezer to ensure that they freeze flat. When dough is frozen, remove and wrap each challah in a heavy-duty zip-lock bag. When ready to use, remove from freezer, place on baking sheet, and leave out to thaw completely. Proceed with recipe.

Let rise covered, for 30 minutes.

Brush challot with 1 beaten egg. Sprinkle with sesame or poppy seeds. Bake for 30 minutes or until golden brown and challah sounds hollow when tapped on bottom.

Yield: 6-7 challahs

challah napkin rings

Parve

My sister-in-law's aunts are famous in both Brooklyn and Queens for this fabulous creation. Could there be a cuter accent on a Shabbos table than challah napkin rings? They serve a dual purpose by holding the napkins and providing each dinner guests with their own challah roll. The amount of dough you need depends on the number of your guests. For 5 rings use the amount of dough needed for 1 challah. In a pinch, you can even buy challah dough from your local bakery.

1 batch any challah dough, prepared according to recipe directions
1 large egg, lightly beaten
  poppy seeds
  sesame seeds

Preheat oven to 350 degrees. Cover one large or 2 smaller baking sheets with parchment paper.

Take 2 empty paper towel rolls. Smoothly cover them with a double layer of aluminum foil. Cover the foil with a sheet of parchment paper. (Tape won't stick to keep the parchment layer sealed. Instead, use a small strip of foil like a rubber band around the center of the tube.) Set aside.

Cut the dough into 5 sections. Divide each section into 3 equal pieces. Roll each piece into a rope. Place the 3 ropes side by side on a piece of parchment paper. Pinch the top ends together loosely. Braid the dough and loosely pinch the bottom ends together (you don't want the ends too tapered). Place the braid over the prepared wrapped tube. Wrap it around so the top and bottom ends meet. Pinch the ends together to make a complete circle. Repeat this process with all 5 sections, placing up to 3 rings on each tube.

Brush each ring with the beaten egg and sprinkle with both poppy and sesame seeds. Set the tubes down lightly on the prepared baking sheets. Bake for 30 minutes or until golden.

Yield: Dough for 1 challah = 5 challah napkin rings

the best bread machine challah

This recipe yields 2 pounds of dough or 2 medium-size challahs. They are the best I have ever had. My machine calls for the wet ingredients and salt to be placed in the pan first, followed by the remaining dry ingredients. Using a finger, make a well in the dry ingredients and add the yeast. Press dough cycle.

1½ cups water	½ cup plus 1 generous tablespoon
5 large egg yolks	sugar
1⅛ teaspoon salt	1 tablespoon active dry yeast
⅓ cup oil	1 large egg, lightly beaten
4¼ cups all-purpose or bread flour	sesame seeds or poppy seeds

Place the water, egg yolks, salt, oil, flour, sugar, and yeast in the bread machine pan, according to manufacturer's directions. Process the ingredients in the dough cycle. Remove immediately when the machine beeps.

Preheat oven to 350 degrees. Divide the dough in half. Divide each piece into 3 sections. Roll each section into a long strand. Lay the three strands in front of you. Pinch the top ends together. Braid the dough and pinch the bottom ends together. Place on parchment-lined or lightly greased baking sheets. Repeat with remaining dough. Let the challot rise covered, for 30 minutes

Brush the challah with beaten egg. Sprinkle with sesame seeds, poppy seeds, or a mixture of both. Bake for 30 minutes. Cool on a wire rack.

Yield: 2 challahs

honey whole wheat challah

2 (¼-ounce) packets active dry yeast
1 teaspoon sugar
2 cups lukewarm water
½ cup honey
½ cup sugar
2 large eggs

1 tablespoon vegetable oil
2½ cups whole wheat flour
3½-4 cups bread flour or all-purpose flour
1 large egg, lightly beaten
sunflower seeds or sesame seeds

Place the yeast, 1 teaspoon sugar, and warm water into a large glass measuring cup or bowl. Set aside in a warm place for 5-10 minutes. (If your kitchen is cold, put it on your opened oven door with the oven temperature set at 300 degrees.)

Place the honey, ½ cup sugar, 2 eggs, and oil into the bowl of a standing mixer fitted with a dough blade. (This can also be mixed by hand with a wooden spoon in a large bowl or pot.)

When yeast is bubbly (proofed) add the yeast mixture into the egg mixture. (If the yeast does not get bubbly then it is dead and you must discard it and make the yeast mixture again with new yeast.)

Add the whole wheat flour into the bowl a little at a time. Mix well with the dough hook or wooden spoon. Slowly add in the 3½ cups bread flour. If the dough is sticky, slowly add in the additional ½ cup bread flour as necessary until it is no longer sticky.

Remove from bowl and knead until smooth. Place back in original bowl. Wet a kitchen dishtowel, wring it out well, and use it to cover the top of the pot. Try not to lift the towel, as air will dry out the dough.

Let the dough rise for 2-3 hours. Punch down for 10 minutes and shape (see challah recipe for directions).

Preheat oven to 350 degrees. Brush with 1 beaten egg. Sprinkle with sunflower or sesame seeds. Bake for 30 minutes. Remove to racks to cool.

Yield: 4 challahs

cinnamon-sugar challah

Parve

On Rosh Hashana we eat sweet foods and round challot. What could be better than combining these traditions into sweet, doughy, fresh challah sprinkled with cinnamon and sugar?

1   batch challah dough, prepared according to recipe directions

    cinnamon/sugar
    raisins (optional)
1   large egg, lightly beaten

Preheat oven to 350 degrees. Once your dough is prepared and has risen, cut it into equal pieces. (Each recipe will determine how many loaves it will yield.) Roll each piece into a long snakelike strand. Sprinkle each strand with cinnamon/sugar. If using raisins, press them in along the strand. Roll up by coiling the strip around itself. Place on parchment-lined or lightly greased baking sheet. Brush with beaten egg. Sprinkle with more cinnamon/sugar. Bake for 30 minutes or until golden and challah sounds hollow when tapped on the bottom.

chicken negemaki with red pepper chutney

appetizers

chicken negemaki with red pepper chutney Meat

The sauce is much better when prepared the day before so the flavors have a chance to mingle. When it comes time to sauté the negemaki, use peanut oil because it can reach high temperatures and not burn. This dish is best served right away, but if you prepare it in advance make sure not to sauté it for too long or the chicken will dry out when reheated.

Red Pepper Chutney:

- 1 red bell pepper, seeded
- 1 clove garlic
- ½ cup rice vinegar
- ½ cup light brown sugar
- ½ teaspoon dried red hot pepper flakes

Chicken Negemaki:

- 8 boneless, skinless chicken breasts, tenders removed
- 2 bunches scallions, separated into individual strips with roots trimmed
- 1 red bell pepper, sliced into very long, thin strips
- 2 cloves garlic, minced
- ¼ cup soy sauce
- 2 tablespoons rice vinegar
- 2 teaspoons toasted sesame oil sesame seeds
- 3 tablespoons peanut oil

Red Pepper Chutney:

In the container of a food processor fitted with a metal blade, process the red pepper, garlic, and vinegar. Place the mixture in a small saucepan over a medium heat. Add the brown sugar and red pepper flakes. Simmer the sauce about 10 minutes or until reduced. Store sauce in the refrigerator until ready to use.

Chicken Negemaki:

Using a rolling pin or meat mallet, pound the chicken breasts between 2 pieces of parchment or waxed paper until they are an even thickness.

Take 8 of the scallions and trim them to be the same length as the red pepper strips. Place the rest of the long scallions in a pot of hot water to blanch them so they will soften a little.

In the center of each cutlet place 1 strip of the red pepper and 1 trimmed scallion. Roll the chicken around the pepper and scallion. Take 2 of the blanched scallions and use them to tie the chicken rolls about an inch from each end. It's okay if the knot doesn't hold perfectly. If your scallions are too long you may trim them a little after you've tied them. Make 7 more rolls in this way.

Place the chicken rolls in a zip-lock bag. In a small bowl combine the garlic, soy sauce, vinegar, and sesame oil. Add mixture to the chicken rolls. Seal the bag and turn it over a few times to coat each chicken roll. Marinate in the refrigerator for 6 hours or overnight, turning the bag occasionally.

Spread the sesame seeds on a piece of wax or parchment paper. Remove the chicken rolls from the marinade and roll each one in sesame seeds. Heat the peanut oil in a large skillet over medium heat until hot but not smoking. Cover the pan and cook the chicken about 10 minutes or until cooked through, shaking the pan and turning occasionally to brown on all sides, adding more oil if necessary.

Transfer the chicken to a cutting board. Using a sharp knife, trim the edges of each roll so they are flat. Slice each negemaki roll on the diagonal. To serve, stand the two pieces up on a plate and spoon the red pepper chutney around it.

Yield: 8 servings

chopped liver

My father is a huge chopped liver fan. It isn't Shabbos in my house until the chopped liver is served. He breaks his fast on chopped liver. At my wedding the caterer surprised him with his name spelled out in chopped liver. My Mom has even been known to grind his favorite dish by hand. But even for a connoisseur like my Dad, packaged chopped liver is really excellent. Here's a quick recipe to make the purchased liver taste a bit more homemade.

2-3 large eggs, hard cooked
2-3 tablespoons vegetable oil
1 medium onion, chopped
 salt
 pepper
1 (12-ounce) container chopped liver spread
1 teaspoon honey

For perfect hard-cooked eggs, use eggs that are a few days old. This gives the air a chance to separate the shell from the membrane a little.

Place eggs in a single layer in a saucepan. Add water to cover by at least an inch. Cover. Quickly bring to a boil. Turn off the heat and remove from stove. Let stand 15 minutes for large eggs, 18 minutes for extra large eggs.

In their shell, hard cooked eggs can keep for a week in the refrigerator.

Using a box grater, coarsely grate the eggs. Set aside.

Heat the oil in a medium skillet over medium high heat. Add the onions; sauté 7-9 minutes or until brown and caramelized. Season with salt and pepper.

Empty the chopped liver spread into a large bowl. Mix in the eggs, onions, and honey. Serve in scooped out tomatoes, cucumbers, or on a lettuce leaf, if desired.

Yield: 8-10 servings

unstuffed cabbage

This recipe was created specifically to help all my fellow cooks avoid the following true, but hard-to-believe scenario.

A newlywed preparing her first Yom Tov meal for her mother-in-law slaved for hours over stuffed cabbage. When she tasted one she was horrified to see how dried out they were. She called her husband at work in hysterics and pleaded with him to help her. He responded "Honey, I am a physician, not a cook, what can I do?" But knowing how hard she had worked he rummaged through his drawers and medicine cabinets and rushed home. They spent the next hour injecting the stuffed cabbage rolls with sauce-filled syringes. As their company showered her with compliments, the couple smiled at each other knowingly.

Betty, this one's for you.

3	pounds ground beef	1	head green cabbage, shredded
2	large eggs, lightly beaten	1½	tablespoons Kosher Salt
¼	cup water	1½	cups tomato juice
¾	cup uncooked long grain white rice	4	(8-ounce) cans tomato sauce
1	onion, finely chopped	½	cup brown sugar
	salt	1½	cups sugar
	black pepper	3	lemons
	garlic powder	½	cup raisins
1	tablespoon vegetable oil		

In a large mixing bowl combine the ground beef, eggs, water, rice, and onion. Season with salt, pepper, and garlic powder. Gently mix by hand. Set aside.

Heat the oil in a large pot over medium heat. Add the cabbage and the kosher salt. Simmer for 10 minutes. Add the tomato juice, tomato sauce, brown sugar, sugar, juice from the lemons, and the raisins.

Gently form meatballs out of the meat mixture. Do not handle them too much or the meat will toughen. Add to cabbage mixture.

Lower the heat to medium-low and simmer, covered, for 1 hour.

Yield: 12 servings

stuffed zucchini

This is a warm, wonderful, and filling first course. Don't use zucchini that are too small; they will be hard to stuff. For the nicest presentation, choose medium-size ones. Serve two on a plate, one angled on the other over a bed of sauce.

10-12 green medium zucchini, unpeeled, trimmed on both ends and cut in center (not lengthwise) to form 2 equal pieces

2 pounds ground beef
salt
black pepper

garlic powder

1 cup uncooked enriched long-grain white rice

3 tablespoons vegetable or olive oil

2 medium onions, finely chopped

3 (8-ounce) cans tomato sauce

3 cans water

Preheat oven to 350 degrees. Using the tip of a vegetable peeler or an apple corer, cut a round tunnel through each piece of zucchini. Set aside.

In a large mixing bowl, generously season the ground beef with salt, pepper, and garlic powder. Mix in the rice. Stir until well combined.

Stuff the meat mixture into the scooped out zucchini, completely fill end to end; but do not pack too densely. The filling will expand during cooking. Lay the zucchini in a single layer in a shallow baking pan; you may need 2 or 3 pans; don't pack them in too tightly. Set aside.

Heat the oil in a large pot over medium-high heat. Sauté the onion about 10 minutes or until a deep golden brown, stirring often.

Add the tomato sauce and water. Season the sauce with salt, pepper, and garlic powder. Ladle the sauce over the stuffed zucchinis. Cover very tightly. Cook in the oven for 2 hours, turning zucchinis over after 1 hour.

Yield: 10 servings

tri-color gefilte fish

This easy spin on traditional gefilte fish has three different colored layers for a sophisticated look. It takes only 5 minutes to prepare. The recipe is based on a 9-inch springform pan with a removable bottom. If you are using a larger springform pan you may need to use 1-2 loaves per layer. Playing with the amounts won't affect the cooking method, but you may need to increase the cooking time by 10-15 minutes.

2   (22-ounce) loaves plain gefilte fish, defrosted in wrapper
1   (22-ounce) loaf salmon gefilte fish, defrosted in wrapper
2   tablespoons fresh dill, chopped
1   lemon
6   cucumbers for horseradish wells, plus one extra long cucumber for top garnish (optional)
    prepared red horseradish (optional)
    mayonnaise (optional)
    yellow pepper (optional)

Preheat oven to 350 degrees. Spray a 9-inch springform pan with nonstick vegetable spray. Give it a heavy even coat. Open each of the 3 gefilte fish wrappers.

Add the dill and juice from lemon into one of the plain gefilte fish loaves. Mix thoroughly so the dill is dispersed evenly. Set aside.

Using a thin spatula, spread the plain gefilte fish into an even layer in the bottom of the springform pan. Top with an even layer of the salmon. On top of the salmon, spread an even layer of the lemon dill fish mixture.

Cover the pan with foil. Bake for 1 hour. If the fish does not look set in the center, remove the foil and bake 5 minutes longer.

Let cool and refrigerate overnight. Can be made a few days in advance. As an optional garnish, slice a long unpeeled cucumber by hand or by mandoline into paper thin slices. Lay the slices in concentric circles around the top of the fish.

Release the sides of the springform pan. To serve as individual servings, cut into wedges, like a pie. Trim any brown edges.

Cut the cucumbers into 2- to 3-inch pieces. Hollow out the center. Mix a few tablespoons of the prepared horseradish with a little mayonnaise to make a pretty pink sauce. Fill the cucumber wells.

Serve a slice of fish on a piece of leafy lettuce with a cucumber well. You can decorate each plate with tiny squares of yellow pepper.

Yield: 10-12 servings

grilled chicken over sesame noodles

The sesame noodles are parve and a fabulous side dish by themselves.

This recipe came to me from a friend who is a chef at the La Provence restaurant in Bloomingdales Short Hills. He prepares these every day as part of a salad bar. They are so loved that the restaurant goes through 65 to 70 pounds of the noodles at each lunch service!

Sesame Noodles:

1 pound box spaghetti
½ cup dark soy sauce
½ cup toasted or roasted sesame oil

⅓ cup sugar
3 scallions, thinly sliced
¼ cup or more sesame seeds

Grilled Chicken:

¼ cup soy sauce
¼ cup teriyaki sauce
2 cloves garlic, minced
¼ cup dark brown sugar

1 teaspoon fresh ginger, chopped, or
   ¼ teaspoon dried ginger
4-5 boneless, skinless chicken breasts
   teaspoon sesame oil

Sesame Noodles:

Prepare the spaghetti according to package directions. Drain. In a cruet or jar, shake together the soy sauce, sesame oil, and sugar. Pour over the pasta. Toss with scallions and sprinkle with sesame seeds. Set aside.

Grilled Chicken:

In a small bowl, mix the soy sauce, teriyaki, garlic, brown sugar, and ginger. Add chicken, tossing to coat. Cover and refrigerate 2-3 hours.

Remove the chicken from marinade, discarding marinade. Heat sesame oil in a large nonstick skillet over medium-high heat. Add chicken in batches and sauté 10 minutes or until done, adding drops of sesame oil as needed. Remove from the pan; cool slightly. Slice chicken diagonally into thin strips; keep warm. Serve chicken over the sesame noodles.

Yield: 8-10 servings

☞ *In place of the chicken you can use London broil or Minute Steak fillet. Brush both sides with bottled barbecue sauce and broil 6 inches from the heat for 10 minutes per side. Slice thinly on the diagonal.*

mediterranean chicken and
orzo salad in red pepper boats

Dressing:

1 tablespoon Dijon mustard
¼ cup red wine vinegar
¾ teaspoon salt
¼ teaspoon black pepper

1 tablespoon fresh oregano leaves or
1 teaspoon dried oregano
¾ cup olive oil
½ teaspoon dried Italian seasoning

Chicken Salad:

5 boneless, skinless chicken breasts
¾ cup bottled Italian dressing
1 tablespoon dried oregano
5 large sweet red peppers, halved
lengthwise, cored, and seeded

1 pound box orzo, uncooked
1 cup halved grape tomatoes
½ cup pitted black olives, coarsely
chopped

Dressing:

Mix the mustard, vinegar, salt, pepper, and oregano in a cruet or jar. Add the olive oil, shaking vigorously so the mixture emulsifies. Add the Italian seasoning and shake again. Can be made in advance. Refrigerate until ready to use. Bring to room temperature before using and shake well before pouring.

Chicken Salad:

Place the chicken breasts in a baking dish. Pour the bottled Italian dressing over the cutlets and sprinkle on the oregano. Turn the cutlets to ensure both sides are seasoned. Cover and marinate in the refrigerator for at least 15 minutes. This can be done the night before.

Preheat the broiler to high. Remove the chicken from the marinade and place in a single layer on a lightly olive-oiled baking sheet. Discard marinade. Broil 6-7 inches from the heat for 8 minutes per side. After the chicken is cooked, dice each breast. Set aside.

In batches, place the red peppers, cut side up, in a large pot and add water to come up halfway on the peppers. Turn the heat to medium and cover. Simmer the peppers for 6-8 minutes, until slightly softened. Do not overcook or the peppers will fall apart. Remove peppers from the pot. Let cool and pat dry. Set aside.

Cook orzo according to package directions. Do not overcook. In a large bowl mix the orzo, tomatoes, olives, and chicken pieces. Pour on the dressing while gently folding so that all the ingredients are coated with the dressing.

To serve, fill each pepper halfway with the orzo filing.

Yield: 10 servings

won ton wrapped chicken with apricot dipping sauce

Meat

I know another product on the market has already coined the phrase "Bet you can't eat just one." But even someone who could stick with a single potato chip could not stop at just one of these outstanding appetizers.

Won ton wrappers are available at most supermarkets. They are usually kept with the produce, near the Asian vegetables. The ones called for in this recipe are the smaller 3½-inch square ones. The larger won ton wrappers are really for egg rolls.

Marinated Chicken:

3 teaspoons brown sugar
2 teaspoons salt
4 cloves garlic, minced
4 teaspoons dry sherry
2 teaspoons cornstarch

6 tablespoons vegetable oil
1 teaspoon soy sauce
1 pound boneless, skinless chicken breasts (about 3 cutlets), cut into approximately 32 (1-inch) squares

Wrappers:

1 (12-ounce) package won ton wrappers
2 cups peanut oil

Apricot Dipping Sauce:

12 ounces apricot preserves
4 teaspoons yellow mustard
4 tablespoons teriyaki sauce

Marinated Chicken:

In a small bowl combine the brown sugar, salt, garlic, sherry, cornstarch, vegetable oil, and soy sauce. Mix the chicken squares with the marinade; cover and refrigerate for 8 hours or overnight.

Wrappers:

Lay the won ton wrappers in a single layer. Place 1 square of the marinated chicken in the center of the won ton wrapper. Dab a small amount of marinade on each of the corners. Fold the won ton over the chicken by bringing each of the corners to the center of the square, overlapping slightly, like a squared envelope.

Heat the peanut oil in a large skillet until hot. Cook the won ton wrapped chicken for about 2 minutes per side, turning once.

Apricot Dipping Sauce:

In a small bowl, blend the apricot preserves, mustard, and teriyaki sauce. Serve 4 won tons on each plate with the dipping sauce in the center.

☞ *Won tons may be fully prepared and frozen flat in a single layer and then put in plastic baggies for storage. To reheat, bake at 475 degrees for 10 minutes.*

Yield: 8 servings

penne with grilled chicken

Grilled Chicken:

- 2-3 boneless, skinless chicken breasts
- ¾ cup favorite bottled barbecue sauce
- 2 tablespoons olive oil
- 1 medium red onion, finely chopped
- 10 ounces portobello or cremini mushrooms, diced
- 3 ounces sun-dried tomatoes, not packed in oil, sliced (stack them when slicing to go faster)
- 1 pound box penne pasta, uncooked
- 1 head radicchio lettuce

Dressing:

- 1 cup olive oil
- ½ cup fresh basil leaves
- 4 teaspoons red wine vinegar
- 1 teaspoon salt
- 1 teaspoon garlic powder or 1 clove fresh garlic

Grilled Chicken:

Marinate the chicken in the barbecue sauce for 15 minutes. Grill or broil chicken, 8 minutes per side. Remove chicken and cut in half lengthwise. Cut each half horizontally into bite-size strips.

Heat the olive oil in a large sauté pan over medium heat. Sauté the onion and mushrooms 6-7 minutes. Remove from heat and add the sun-dried tomatoes. Toss in the chicken.

Place the pasta, prepared according to package directions, in a very large bowl. Add in the chicken mixture and toss until completely mixed.

Dressing:

In the bowl of a food processor fitted with a metal blade, process the olive oil, basil, vinegar, salt, and garlic.

Pour the dressing over the chicken and penne mixture, making sure to thoroughly combine. Separate the radicchio leaves. Add a serving of the penne salad to each leaf.

Yield: 10 servings

pistachio chicken skewers
with blackberry sauce

Meat

The chicken tenders are the perfect size for these skewers. If your cutlets have them attached, you will need more cutlets. Just cut the tenders off and reserve the cutlets for another use. If the cutlets have had the tenders removed, follow the directions below.

Chicken Skewers:

4 boneless, skinless chicken breasts
salt
black pepper
1 cup white wine

1 cup shelled pistachio nuts, roughly chopped
bamboo skewers, soaked in water for 15 minutes

Blackberry Sauce:

1 (15-ounce can) blackberries in heavy syrup (or substitute blueberries)

2 tablespoons sugar
1 tablespoon cornstarch dissolved in 1 tablespoon water

Chicken Skewers:

Place the chicken breasts in a plastic zip-lock bag. Slightly flatten by banging with the bottom of a saucepan. Cut each cutlet into 3 strips.

Season the chicken strips with salt and pepper. Place them in a bowl. Add the wine. Marinate for 1 hour. Preheat oven to 350 degrees.

Remove the chicken from the wine. Roll each strip in the chopped pistachios, pressing them into the chicken so they adhere. Thread the strips accordian-style onto the bamboo skewers. Bake on a cookie sheet for 13-15 minutes, turning once.

Blackberry Sauce:

Drain liquid from the blackberries, reserving liquid and blackberries.

Combine the blackberry liquid with the sugar and dissolved cornstarch in a small saucepan over medium heat, whisking until smooth. Bring mixture to a boil; boil for 1 minute or until thickened and bubbly. Remove from heat. Stir in reserved blackberries.

Drizzle sauce over the chicken skewers and serve with remaining sauce on the side.

Yield: 4 servings

chicken livers with caramelized onions and red wine

Meat

1¼ pounds kashered chicken livers (see note)
2 tablespoons vegetable oil
3 large onions, thinly sliced
¼ teaspoon black pepper

½ cup red wine, port, Madeira, or sherry
1 large egg, hard cooked and chopped
2 tablespoons fresh parsley, chopped

Cut chicken livers into bite-size pieces. Set aside.

Heat the oil in a large skillet over medium heat. Add the onions and pepper. Cook, stirring frequently, about 15 minutes or until the onions are well browned. Add the wine and simmer for 5 minutes.

Remove from heat. Add in the chopped chicken livers. Place on serving dishes and top with the egg and parsley.

Yield: 4 servings

☞ *This can also be served over barley or in baked puff pastry shells.*

☞ *Kashering Chicken Livers*

How to Kasher Liver

The laws of kashruth permit the flesh of certain species of animals and fowl, but only after the animal or bird has been ritually slaughtered and its meat has been kashered (prepared). As a practical matter, in today's market most kosher meat and poultry is kashered before reaching the consumer. The major exception is liver. If your butcher does not sell kashered liver, here are the directions for kashering raw liver:

1. *Utensils that have been used for kashering liver may not be used for any food or its preparation except for kashering other liver.*
2. *The only way to kasher liver is by broiling it over an open flame (or, if that is not possible, by the red-hot coils of an electric stove). The broiling is described below.*
3. *Inspect the liver to ascertain that all the fat has been trimmed away.*
4. *Rinse the liver under running water — three times on each side.*
5. *Salt the liver lightly with Kosher Salt.*
6. *Place the liver on a grate that will allow its juices to run or drip away from it.*
7. *Broil thoroughly — five minutes on each side.*
8. *Break open a few pieces to ascertain that the liver is well done on the inside. If it is not, broil a little longer.*
9. *Rinse the liver under running water – three times on each side.*

veal loaf

This is a simple yet elegant first course. Anyone that knows me can tell you that I am freezer phobic, but even I must admit this one freezes beautifully. You can also double or triple the recipe with ease. I usually make a few of these at a time and freeze them.

If you don't have time to chop each of the vegetables, throw the celery, onions, garlic, mushrooms, parsley, and spinach together into the food processor and pulse a few times. This makes the preparation a snap.

Veal Loaf:

3 tablespoons vegetable oil
2 stalks celery, chopped
2 large onions, chopped
2 cloves garlic, chopped
1 (10-ounce) box mushrooms, chopped
¼ cup fresh parsley

1 (10-ounce) package frozen chopped spinach, thawed and squeezed dry
2 pounds ground veal
1 cup seasoned bread crumbs
2 large eggs
¼ teaspoon black pepper

Glaze:

1 cup dark brown sugar
1 tablespoon red wine vinegar

5 tablespoons ketchup

Veal Loaf:

Preheat oven to 375 degrees. Lightly spray two loaf pans with nonstick cooking spray.

Heat the oil in a large skillet over medium-high heat. Add the celery, onions, garlic, mushrooms, parsley, and spinach. Remove from heat and cool for 5 minutes.

Add the veal, bread crumbs, eggs, and pepper, mixing thoroughly. Divide the meat mixture in half and place in the prepared loaf pans.

Glaze:

In a small saucepan over low heat, combine the brown sugar, vinegar, and ketchup. Stir until smooth. Pour the glaze over the two veal loaves.

Bake uncovered for 1-1½ hours. To serve, place a slice of veal loaf over pretty greens.

Yield: 14 servings

salmon wellington
with cucumber sauce

This is a beautiful first course. The chive-wrapped packets look very appealing. I have included two different sauces, one parve and one dairy, so that the recipe isn't limited to a single kind of meal. Choose whichever fits your meal and serve the sauce in a scooped out cucumber well or a scooped out lemon half.

Salmon Wellington:

- 3 tablespoons margarine or butter
- 1½ shallots, chopped
- 12 ounces mushrooms, coarsely chopped
- 2 cloves garlic, minced
- 3 tablespoons dry Vermouth
- 2 teaspoons fresh thyme leaves
- ¾ teaspoons salt, divided
- ½ teaspoon black pepper, divided
- 6 (4- to 5-ounce) 2-inch-wide salmon fillets, cut in half to make 12 (3- by 2-inch) rectangles
- 1 (17.3-ounce) package frozen puff pastry sheets, thawed

Cucumber Sauce: Parve

- 1 large cucumber, peeled, seeded, and diced
- ¾ cup mayonnaise
- ½ cup water
- 1 tablespoon chopped fresh dill
- 3 tablespoons chopped onion

Cucumber Sauce: Dairy

- 1 large cucumber, peeled, seeded, and diced
- 1 (8-ounce) container sour cream
- 2 teaspoons chopped fresh dill
- salt and black pepper to taste

Garnish:

fresh chives

Salmon Wellington:

Preheat oven to 450 degrees. Melt the margarine or butter in a large skillet over medium-high heat. Sauté the shallots for 2 minutes. Add the mushrooms and garlic. Cook for 5 minutes or until the liquid evaporates. Add the Vermouth. Cook for a few minutes longer, until the liquid evaporates.

Remove from heat. Stir in thyme, ¼ teaspoon salt, and ¼ teaspoon pepper. Remove mixture from pan. Set aside.

Sprinkle the salmon rectangles with remaining ½ teaspoon salt and ¼ teaspoon pepper. Coat the skillet with nonstick cooking spray. Cook the salmon over high heat for 2 minutes per side.

Roll out the puff pastry sheets and cut into 12 (8-inch) squares. Spread ¼ cup of the mushroom mixture into the center of each square. Top with a piece of salmon. Wrap pastry over each fillet, tucking edges under to make packets. Place seam side down in a broiler pan.

Bake for 15 minutes or until golden. Wrap each packet with a chive to garnish, if desired.

Cucumber Sauce:

Combine all ingredients for either parve or dairy cucumber sauce, chill. Serve with salmon.

Yield: 12 servings

ॐ

brie cups

This is a sweet-looking mini hors d'oeuvre that is a snap to make. The phyllo (FEE-lo) dough cups come prebaked in the frozen food section where they keep puff pastry and phyllo dough. You can store them in the refrigerator for a few days in advance or defrost them for a few hours on the day of use. I like to make some topped with a single fresh blackberry, some topped with 2-3 blueberries, some topped with 2-3 raspberries, and some I leave plain. The assortment of color looks beautiful when combined on the same plate.

You can assemble the whole recipe in advance and then just pop it in the oven to melt the cheese.

2 (2.1-ounce) boxes mini phyllo
dough shells (30 mini cups in total)
9 ounces brie, rind removed, cut into
30 small chunks
fresh raspberries

fresh blueberries
fresh blackberries

Heat oven to 350 degrees. Place the mini phyllo cups on a cookie sheet. Place a chunk of the brie into each cup. Top with berries. Bake 10-12 minutes or until cheese is melted. Serve immediately.

Yield: 30 brie cups

ॐ

☞ *Pour a mixture of dried black and white beans on a plate or platter that has a rim. Arrange small hors d'oeuvres on this eye-catching bed.*

potato latkes

This recipe combines lacy grated potatoes with smooth potato batter. The latkes are flecked with green from the scallions and are just beautiful when fried. Peanut oil works well, because no matter how hot the oil gets it won't burn.

2 pounds Yukon gold or Russet potatoes, peeled	1½ teaspoons salt
1 medium yellow onion, quartered	black pepper
4 medium scallions	3 tablespoons fresh parsley (optional)
1 large egg	1 cup peanut oil

Using the grating disc of a food processor, grate the potatoes. Remove half of the grated potatoes to a large strainer set over a large bowl. Replace the food processor disc with the metal blade. Add the onion and scallions. Pulse until mixture is smooth.

Add the potato/onion mixture to the grated potatoes in the strainer. Push down to strain out as much liquid as possible. Let this liquid sit in the bowl for 5 minutes. Pour off the liquid, reserving the potato starch at the bottom of the bowl.

Add the potatoes to bowl with potato starch. Mix in the egg, salt, pepper, and parsley, if desired.

In a large skillet, heat the peanut oil until very hot but not smoking. Add the potato mixture 1 heaping tablespoon at a time. Fry until golden, flip and fry until golden on the other side. Drain on paper bags or paper towels. Do this until all the batter is used.

You can make the latkes up to 4 hours ahead. When ready to serve, bake at 375 degrees for 5 minutes. Can also be frozen and reheated at 375 degrees for 8 minutes per side.

Serve with applesauce and/or sour cream for dairy meals.

Yield: 14-18 latkes

focaccia bread three ways

Focaccia:

3-4 tablespoons olive oil, divided
1 pound frozen pizza or bread dough, thawed, or 1 pound fresh pizza dough

¼ teaspoon kosher salt

Tomato Garlic Focaccia:

3-4 tablespoons tomato paste
1 teaspoon dried oregano, crumbled by hand

1 clove garlic, minced
4 plum tomatoes, thinly sliced

Olive Rosemary Garlic Focaccia:

½ cup sliced black olive
2 cloves garlic, minced

2 teaspoons rosemary, chopped

Artichoke Onion Focaccia:

3-4 tablespoons tomato paste
1 (6-ounce) jar marinated artichokes, thinly sliced

½ red onion, thinly sliced

Brush 1-2 tablespoons olive oil onto a baking sheet. Press pizza dough into an 8- by 15-inch rectangle. Let dough rise in a warm place for 30 minutes to 1 hour.

Preheat oven to 400 degrees. Make shallow indentations all over the dough with your fingertips, then brush dough with remaining olive oil. Sprinkle with ¼ teaspoon kosher salt. Top with any of the ingredients listed above.

Bake for 20-25 minutes until the bottom is golden brown.

Yield: 8-10 servings

✒ *Tomato Paste Tip*
I find it so annoying when a recipe calls for 1 tablespoon of tomato paste and the rest goes in the garbage. A solution is to spoon 1-tablespoon portions of tomato paste onto a piece of plastic wrap. Freeze until firm. Place into zip-lock freezer bag. Store in freezer until the next time you need a tablespoon or two.

portobello pesto stacks

Marinade:

½ cup olive oil
¼ cup balsamic vinegar
2 cloves garlic, minced

1 lemon
  freshly ground black pepper
  salt

Portobello:

8 (2½- to 3-inch in diameter)
  portobello mushroom caps
2 red bell peppers, halved and seeded
  olive oil
1 thin, unpeeled eggplant, cut into
  1-inch slices

2 ripe plum tomatoes, ends trimmed,
  each cut into 2 thick slices

  shredded mozzarella (optional for
  dairy)

Pesto:

2 cups fresh basil leaves, stems
  removed
2 cloves garlic
¼ cup walnuts
⅛ cup pine nuts or pistachio nuts

¾ cup olive oil
4 (5-inch) sprigs fresh rosemary,
  bottom leaves removed to expose
  the stick

Preheat the oven to broil with rack 5 inches from heat.

Marinade:

In a cruet or in a bowl with a whisk, combine the olive oil, vinegar, garlic, juice from lemon, pepper, and salt. Whisk or shake until it forms an emulsion.

Portobello:

Pour the marinade over the mushrooms and marinate while you prepare the rest.

Place red peppers on an aluminum-foil lined baking sheet, cut side down. Brush with olive oil. Broil (with oven door partially opened) about 8-10 minutes or until peppers look blistered and blackened.

Place peppers in a paper bag; seal and let stand 10 minutes to loosen skin. Peel peppers; it's okay if a little black remains. Set aside.

Place the eggplant and tomato slices on the baking sheet and brush with olive oil. Broil for 5-8

minutes. Remove the tomatoes and set aside. Flip the eggplant and broil 3-4 minutes on the second side. Remove from baking sheet. Set aside.

Remove the mushrooms from the marinade. Place on the baking sheet and place under broiler for 7-8 minutes. Set aside.

Pesto:

In a food processor fitted with a steel blade, combine the basil, garlic, walnuts, pinenuts, and olive oil. Process until smooth.

To assemble the stacks:

Place 1 portobello rounded side down, top with a layer of pesto, 1 piece of pepper, 1 eggplant slice, and 1 grilled tomato slice.

If using for dairy, top with some shredded mozzarella and run under the broiler for 3-4 minutes, until cheese melts.

Top with a second portobello cap, rounded side up. Skewer each stack with a sprig of rosemary through all the layers.

Drizzle the plate with pesto, if desired.

Yield: 4 servings

Edible Breadstick Holders

Preheat the oven to 325 degrees. Wrap aluminum foil around 2- to 3-inch diameter empty vegetable cans. Spray with nonstick cooking spray. Cut 12-inch tortillas in half (or use strips of lavash bread). Brush one side with olive oil; if it's a dairy meal you can sprinkle with Parmesan cheese. Roll uncoated side around the can. Place the wrapped cans, rolled-edge down, on a baking sheet. Bake 10 minutes. While still warm, remove the can from tortilla; let cool. Repeat with remaining tortilla. Fill with breadsticks and place one at each setting.

savory goat cheese strudel

12	thin asparagus spears (only the top 3- to 4-inches)	1	sprig fresh thyme, stem removed
2	portobello mushroom caps, cleaned with gills scooped out	4	tablespoons sugar
	olive oil	1	cup white wine vinegar or red wine vinegar
	salt	14	ounces goat cheese
	freshly ground black pepper	2	sticks of unsalted butter, melted
1	tablespoon olive oil	1	package phyllo dough sheets, defrosted
1	large Vidalia or Spanish onion, sliced into thin rings	2	cups Merlot
		1	teaspoon cornstarch

Preheat oven to 425 degrees. Place the asparagus and mushrooms on a baking sheet. Brush with olive oil, sprinkle with salt and pepper. Roast for 12-15 minutes. Remove from oven. Slice the mushrooms into very thin slices; set aside.

Heat the one tablespoon of olive oil in a medium pot over medium heat. Add the sliced onion and cook for 6-8 minutes, until translucent. Add the leaves from the sprig of thyme and the sugar. Cook for 6-7 minutes; the onions should be caramelized. Add the vinegar. Bring to a boil then reduce to a simmer; cook about 12-15 minutes or until the vinegar is almost all gone. Make sure not to burn the onions and stir occasionally. You should have a soft nest of golden sweet onions. Season with salt and pepper.

While the onions are still hot, place them in the bowl of a food processor fitted with a metal blade. Add the goat cheese and pulse until thoroughly combined. Remove and reserve at room temperature.

The dish can be made in advance up until this point and brought back to room temperature, assembled, and cooked before serving.

Preheat oven to 425 degrees. Line a baking sheet with parchment paper. Unfold the sheets of phyllo dough so you have a large horizontal rectangle in front of you. Using a sharp, not serrated knife, make a vertical cut down the middle so you are left with two stacks of vertical rectangles.

Take one sheet of phyllo, brush with melted butter, and top with another sheet of phyllo. Do this again so you have a stack of four buttered sheets. Form an even log-shaped mound of the cheese mixture along the bottom shorter edge of the pastry.

Top with 3 asparagus spears and a few slices of portobello. Roll once to cover filling. Fold the right and left sides over the center and roll, jelly-roll style, until completely closed. (Like a blintze).

Brush with melted butter. Place on prepared baking sheet. Repeat 3 more times. Bake uncovered for 6-8 minutes or until golden brown.

Place the Merlot in a small saucepan. Dissolve the cornstarch in 1 teaspoon water. Whisk into Merlot. Bring to a boil, sauce will thicken.

Drizzle over the strudels, or place in a squeeze bottle and decorate the plate with the syrup.

Yield: 4 servings

antipasto platter

2 boneless, skinless chicken breasts
Italian dressing, bottled
12 thin asparagus spears
10 ounces button mushrooms
olive oil
Kosher or coarse salt
freshly ground black pepper

1 whole salami, cut into large cubes
2 roasted red bell peppers, (see roasting red peppers page 99) or can be jarred, sliced
1 (6.5-ounce) jar marinated artichoke hearts, drained
assorted olives

Pour the Italian dressing over the chicken breasts. Marinate 15 minutes.

Preheat oven to 425 degrees. Place the asparagus and mushrooms on a baking sheet. Brush with olive oil, sprinkle with salt and pepper. Roast for 12-15 minutes. Remove from oven; set aside.

Turn your oven to broil and broil the chicken cutlets for 8 minutes on each side or until no longer pink. This can be done on a grill as well. Cut the chicken into large cubes and set aside.

To Arrange Your Platter:

Select a sectioned dish or a large platter. Skewer the salami cubes with 6-8 inch thin wooden skewers. Do the same with the chicken cubes and the mushrooms. Place on the platter. In separate piles or sections arrange the asparagus, roasted red peppers, artichoke hearts, and olives.

Yield: 6-8 Servings

☞ *A Vase Within a Vase*

For this versatile idea, set a tall cylindrical glass vase into a larger cylindrical glass vase. Fill the center vase with water and a bouquet of flowers. Fill the larger, surrounding vase with whatever is appropriate for the event: chocolate kisses, nuts, seeds, shells, dried oranges, coffee beans. I once got this arrangement of flowers as a gift-the outside vase contained water and a happy, swimming fish.

sun-dried tomato pinwheels

If you don't have sun-dried tomatoes packed in oil, you can use 15 dried sun-dried tomatoes. Place them in a bowl of boiling water and let sit for 15 minutes. Drain them. Place them in a food processor fitted with a metal blade and process them with 3 tablespoons olive oil.

30 sun-dried tomato halves, packed in oil
1 (17.3-ounce) package frozen puff pastry, thawed

12 tablespoons ricotta cheese
2 cups grated Parmesan cheese

Remove the tomatoes from the oil they are packed in. Place the tomatoes in the bowl of a food processor fitted with a metal blade. Process until they form a paste.

On a piece of parchment or plastic wrap, roll out the sheets of puff pastry. Spread the ricotta evenly over the pastry sheets. Spread the sun-dried tomatoes on top. Sprinkle each with Parmesan.

Roll each long edge of the pastry sheets, jelly-roll fashion, pressing to seal the seams. Wrap in plastic wrap. Freeze for 30 minutes so the rolls will keep their shape when cutting. Rolls can be frozen at this point for up to 1 month. When ready to bake, remove from freezer, let stand at room temperature about 10 minutes or until a sharp knife can slice through it without compressing the shape.

Preheat the oven to 400 degrees. Using a sharp knife, cut pinwheels into ½-inch-thick slices. Place on a parchment lined baking sheet. Bake for 20 minutes or until puffed and golden.

Yield: 2 dozen pinwheels

artichoke and spinach palmiers

Dairy

1 (10-ounce) package frozen chopped spinach, thawed
1 (14-ounce) can artichoke hearts, drained and chopped
½ cup mayonnaise
½ cup grated Parmesan cheese
1 teaspoon onion powder
1 teaspoon garlic powder
½ teaspoon black pepper
1 (17.3-ounce) package frozen puff pastry, thawed

Squeeze the water out of the spinach. In a medium bowl, mix the spinach, artichoke hearts, mayonnaise, Parmesan, onion powder, garlic powder, and pepper.

Unfold the puff pastry sheets. Place each one on a sheet of plastic wrap. Spread half of the artichoke mixture evenly on each pastry sheet.

Roll each long edge of the pastry into the center of the rectangle, making sure the pastry is even and tight. Wrap each roll with the plastic wrap.

Freeze for 30 minutes so the roll will keep its shape when cutting. The roll can be frozen at this point for up to 1 month. When ready to bake, remove from freezer, let stand at room temperature about 10 minutes or until a sharp knife can slice through it without compressing the shape.

Preheat the oven to 400 degrees. Using a sharp knife, cut roll into ½-inch-thick slices. Place on a parchment-lined baking sheet. Bake for 20 minutes or until puffed and golden.

Yields: 2 dozen palmiers

braised artichoke bottoms

Most people either love artichokes or haven't tried them yet. They are very healthy, contain no fat, and are high in fiber. Artichoke bottoms are simply artichoke hearts cleaned of the leaves. The first time will take a little longer, but once you get the hang of the trimming process it is actually quite fun to prepare. Give this Italian-style recipe a try: It is a celebration of vegetables and herbs that comes together in a real delicacy.

2 lemons, cut in half	2 carrots, sliced thinly on the bias
8 large artichokes	1 stalk celery, sliced thinly on the bias
⅓ cup olive oil	¼ teaspoon Kosher salt
3 cloves garlic, crushed	¼ teaspoon freshly ground black
7-8 stems curly parsley, leaves	pepper
separated from stems	1 cup white Zinfandel wine
1 medium onion, thinly sliced	2½ cups chicken or vegetable broth
1 bay leaf	

Fill a medium bowl with cold water and squeeze the juice from one of the lemon halves into the water. Set aside.

Keep artichoke stems attached. Lay each artichoke on its side and cut 1 inch off the top of each one with a sharp knife. Working with one artichoke at a time, bend back the outer leaves until they snap off close to the base. Discard all the leaves as you go around layer by layer.

Using a paring knife, trim the perimeter of the artichoke bottom to get rid of any dark green fibrous parts, being careful not to break off stem. Scoop out the fuzzy choke with a melon baller. Rub all of the exposed surfaces with cut lemon.

Cut ¼ inch from the end of the stem to expose the inner core. Using a vegetable peeler, trim the sides of the stem (still attached to the artichoke bottom) all the way down to the pale inner core. Rub exposed surfaces with lemon. Plunge artichoke into the cold lemon water, leaving them there until all of the artichokes are trimmed. Set aside.

Heat the oil in a large skillet or pot that has a lid over medium-low heat. Add the garlic, parsley stems, onion, bay leaf, carrots, and celery. Season with Kosher salt and pepper.

Gently cook the vegetables until translucent, but not brown, stirring frequently about 10 minutes. Add wine and cook until reduced by ¾.

Add the artichokes to the skillet and pour broth over them. Bring to a boil, then reduce heat; simmer, covered, about 35 minutes or until artichokes are tender. Taste and add seasonings if necessary. Discard bay leaf and parsley stems.

On each plate arrange 2 artichokes in the center. Top with cooked vegetables. Drizzle with cooking sauce. Garnish with reserved parsley leaves.

Yield: 4 servings

Acquiring something new always gives us as sense of freshness. Whether it's a new house, a new job or just a new hairstyle, we see possibilities open before us that we didn't have before.

Rosh Hashanah, the start of the new Jewish year, gives us all that and more — a chance for total rejuvenation. Tradition teaches us that on this day our actions and motivations are reviewed and judged by God. Because our lives are at risk, this is a solemn day. Yet when we reflect on our shortcomings of the past year and firmly resolve to do better in the future, we liberate ourselves from our mistakes. Nothing is more uplifting.

Jewish tradition stresses this newness and the hope that it brings. We wear new clothing and eat unusual foods, after we've given thanks for the opportunity to enjoy these new experiences. This is why there is a custom to eat exotic fruits that we have not tasted in the past year.

There are many reasons for eating apples dipped in honey. In King Solomon's *Song of Songs*, the moving allegory describing the mutual love between God and the Jews, the Jewish nation is compared to the unique and lovely apple tree. To the Jews enslaved in ancient Egypt, the apple symbolized affection between husbands and wives, connoting family harmony and the promise of future generations.

Honey, of course, expresses our hopes for a sweet year, and it also symbolizes our beloved Land of Israel that "flows with milk and honey." Although that Biblical passage refers to date palm honey, we customarily use bee's honey. While we savor its sweetness, it reminds us of the beautiful world of pleasures God created for mankind on the first Rosh Hashanah.

Other fascinating food traditions abound. Because the Diaspora is worldwide, different Jewish communities developed unique customs based on the names of foods. In the Ukraine, for instance, Jewish parents would give their children broiled chicken livers to eat because the Yiddish word for livers, *leberlach* sounds like *leb erlich*, meaning "live honestly."

Based on their meaningful names, special foods are consumed at the evening meal (whether it's done only on the first night or on both nights depends on family custom). These are preceded by prayerful expressions that begin, "*Yehi ratzon* — May it be Your will..." followed by the symbolic meaning of the particular food. These recitations are not magic formulae, but a means of "internalizing" our awareness that we depend on God for everything.

A few examples: As the Yiddish term for carrots is *mehren*, which can also mean "to increase," the eating of this food (often in the form of a honey-sweetened *tzimmes*) is preceded by "May it be Your will, *Hashem*, our God and God of our fathers, that our merits increase." What are these "merits"? They are the *mitzvot* and other commendable acts we do, and we pray that they will influence the Heavenly court to grant us blessings in the year ahead. The Aramaic word for beets is *silka*, similar in spelling to the Hebrew word *yistalku*, which means 'they should be removed." How would Jewish tradition turn this into a blessing? "May it be Your will...that our adversaries should be removed!"Is it strange to combine a day of spiritual growth with the mundane act of eating new and exciting foods? Not really. The goal of Judaism is to elevate physical acts to a spiritual plane. The food we eat on Rosh Hashanah, with its implied prayer for a sweet, fulfilling year, is a perfect example of this connection.

rosh hashanah menu

Cinnamon / Sugar Round Challah
page 20

APPETIZER:
Tri-color Gefilte Fish
page 26

ENTREE:
Pomegranate Chicken
page 107

Sweet and Sour Brisket
page 131

SIDE DISHES:
Cranberry-Apple Torte
page 215

Spinach Rice
page 214

DESSERT:
Sunken Apples and Honey Tart
page 270 and book cover

The symbols of Rosh Hashanah play an integral part in choosing table décor. Green orchids interspersed with bunches of green apples add a monochromatic flair. Honey straws, with a slice of apple, await guests at each place setting. Gilded goblets and fine china reflect the importance of the day. In recreating this look in your home, feel free to add your grandmother's crystal to your own china place setting. The mix provides a charming fusion of old and new, creating layers of textures and patterns.

On a side table, we set up a honey-tasting station. Use assorted dishes, bowls, and bottles to serve selected varieties of honey — from the mundane to the exotic. Provide sliced apples or pieces of challah to go with the honey. Then invite your family and guests to sample and enjoy.

The menu reflects symbolic holiday foods as well. Start with Cinnamon/Sugar Round Challah to suggest sweetness for the new year. Round challot are traditionally used on our Shabbat and holiday tables from Rosh Hashanah through Sukkot. Several reasons have been advanced to explain its symbolism: Since Rosh Hashanah is deemed the day of coronation of God as the universal King, the challah resembles a crown. We may also view the cycle of the year as round, and the round challah represents the continuation of that cycle.

We've also included easy and elegant Tri-color Gefilte Fish. Fish, particularly the heads, are used symbolically on this holiday, reminding diners that they should stand in the forefront of all good things, like the head and not the tail. At the ceremony of Tashlich, performed during the Rosh Hashanah season, we say prayers and symbolically cast off our sins near a body of water containing fish. This is to remind us that just as fish eyes are always open, so too God's "eyes" watch over us at all times.

Pomegranates, with their 613 seeds representing the 613 *mitzvot* of the Torah, appear on this menu in the form of Pomegranate Chicken. For those who would prefer meat, the brisket is an excellent option.

The Cranberry Apple Torte, a warm and filling sweet side dish, calls upon our special fruit of the day. The Spinach Rice adds bold color to the plate. For dessert, what could better symbolize the day than our round, sweet, apple-laden Sunken Apples and Honey Tart?

wine list

Hagafen Sauvignon Blanc

A chilled, crisp, California Sauvignon Blanc like this gold-medal winner
has a refreshing acidity that complements the Tri-Color Gefilte Fish.

Baron Herzog Chenin Blanc

Tishbi Merlot or Weinstock Merlot Reserve (Chile)

The intense fruity notes of peach and nectarine in the Chenin Blanc goes well with
poultry and a variety of flavorful foods such as our Pomegranate Chicken.
A fruity Merlot would be a lovely choice as well.

Abarbanel Gewurztraminer

The spice and fruit in this wine shows off the flavors in the Sweet and Sour Brisket.
Gewurztraminer is a classic choice for a tangy dish.

Chateau Peroudier Cotes de Bergerac Blanc

This sweet wine will echo the flavors in the Sunken Apples and Honey Tart.
It pairs well with cooked or fresh fruit.
Another choice would be a calvados, which is an apple brandy.

two-tone sweet pea
& carrot soup

soups

meatball minestrone

The credit for this fabulous and filling soup goes to someone who posted it on the Internet years ago. I can't trace its origin, but thanks Ron, wherever you are. This recipe is a gem that's warmed up my family on many cold nights.

1 (10-ounce) package frozen chopped spinach, thawed
1½ pounds lean ground beef
1 large egg
1 teaspoon salt
⅓ cup dry Italian-style bread crumbs or flavored dry bread crumbs
¼ teaspoon freshly ground black pepper
4 tablespoons olive oil
1 large onion, coarsely chopped
8 cups or 64 ounces beef broth (can use 4 beef bouillon cubes in 8 cups water)

1 (28-ounce) can diced tomatoes, with its liquid
1 (1-pound) can red kidney beans, with its liquid
½ teaspoon dried oregano
½ teaspoon dried basil
2 carrots, peeled and sliced into thin rounds
2 stalks celery, sliced
1 garlic clove, chopped
1 cup elbow or rotini pasta, uncooked

Preheat the oven to 350 degrees. Squeeze the water out of the spinach. Place it in a large bowl and add the ground beef, egg, salt, bread crumbs, and pepper. Knead and mix together. Shape into 1-inch meatballs.

Pour the olive oil directly onto a cookie sheet; do not line with tin foil, you will want to be able to scrape the surface later. Place the meatballs on the oiled cookie sheet and bake for 20 minutes.

Remove the meatballs from the sheet; set aside. Using a metal spatula or spoon, scrape the drippings and oil from the cookie sheet into a soup pot.

Sauté the onion in these drippings over medium-high heat for 6-8 minutes or until the onion gets soft, stirring occasionally. Stir in the broth, tomatoes with their liquid, kidney beans with their liquid, oregano, and basil. Cover. Reduce the heat. You want it to simmer but not reach a full boil.

Add the carrots and the celery. Cover and simmer another 10 minutes. Stir in the pasta. Re-cover and simmer 10 minutes. Stir once or twice to make sure the pasta is not sticking to the bottom of the pot.

Place the meatballs into the soup and heat through. If you are making this soup in advance, some of the liquid may get soaked up into the meatballs and pasta. If this happens, just add another cup or two of beef broth when reheating.

Yield: 8-10 servings

cream of asparagus soup

1 pound asparagus
2 tablespoons vegetable oil
1 medium onion, chopped
1 leek, white and pale green parts thinly sliced, discarding the rest
4 cups chicken stock
1 medium potato, peeled and diced
½ teaspoon marjoram

⅛ teaspoon nutmeg
½ cup nondairy creamer or soy milk
2 teaspoons lemon juice
¼ teaspoon freshly ground white pepper
2 tablespoons sherry or Marsala wine

Thoroughly wash the asparagus and snap or cut off the tough ends. Cut off and reserve the tips. Cut the stalks into ½-inch pieces. Set aside.

In a soup pot, heat the oil over medium heat. Add the onion and the leeks; sauté for 5-7 minutes or until leeks start to shine.

Add the chicken stock, potato, marjoram, and nutmeg. Bring to a boil. Add the chopped asparagus stalks. Reduce the heat; cover and simmer for 35-40 minutes.

Pureé the soup in a food processor or blender. It can be done right in the pot with an immersion blender as well, but it will be a little thicker.

Return the soup to the pot and add the creamer, lemon juice, pepper, and sherry. Bring to a simmer. Add the asparagus tips; simmer for 10 minutes. Serve immediately.

Yield: 6 servings

creamy tomato soup

This very simple favorite takes no time to prepare. I'm usually a big fan of the immersion blender that purees soup right in the pot, but for this recipe you should puree the soup in a blender or food processor fitted with a metal blade. You will be rewarded with an incredibly smooth, creamy, family-pleasing treasure. The best tomatoes for this soup are the whole peeled ones, sometimes called Italian or plum tomatoes. The cans usually have basil in them even when not listed in the title. Check the ingredient list; the basil just adds to the flavor.

3 tablespoons olive oil	2 (28-ounce) cans whole Italian
½ large onion or 1 medium onion, chopped	peeled tomatoes
1 shallot, thinly sliced	2 tablespoons butter
½ leek, white and pale green parts thinly sliced, discarding the rest	½-¾ cup heavy cream

In a large soup pot, heat the oil over medium heat. Add the onion, shallot, and leek. Sauté for 5-7 minutes or until they soften. Add the tomatoes and let the soup simmer, covered, for 15-20 minutes.

Add the butter; once butter melts add the cream. Remove from heat.

Transfer in batches to a food processor or blender. Run the machine for a full 40-50 seconds on each batch. This soup can be made in advance, but if you are going to freeze it, don't add the butter and cream until you are ready to serve it.

Yield: 10-12 servings

emerald soup

The color of this healthy soup is just beautiful. It is a bright emerald green, hence the name. I like using precut fresh spinach from the bag. I grab a handful at a time, gather it together, and coarsely chop it with a knife. It takes no time at all to prepare.

1 tablespoon olive oil
2 leeks, white and light green parts thinly sliced, discarding the rest
2 garlic cloves, chopped
3 cups vegetable or chicken stock
1½ pounds fresh spinach, stems removed and coarsely chopped
1 cup loosely packed fresh dill, stems removed
½ teaspoon salt
¼ teaspoon freshly ground white pepper
1 cup nondairy creamer or soy milk cayenne pepper

In a large soup pot, heat the oil over medium-high heat. Sauté the leeks and garlic for 2-3 minutes, stirring frequently. Add the stock and bring to a boil.

Add the spinach, dill, salt, and white pepper. Cover and cook 5-6 minutes or until the spinach is very soft.

Transfer to a food processor or blender and process until smooth. You can also use an immersion blender in the pot. Return to the pot and bring to a gentle boil over medium heat for 5 minutes. Reduce the heat and add the creamer or soy milk. Heat thoroughly, gently stirring. Do not bring to a boil.

After you ladle out each portion, sprinkle each bowl with the cayenne for flavor and color.

Yield: 6-8 servings

☞ *The Scoop on Soup*

A BISQUE is a rich, thick, and smooth soup.

A CHOWDER is a thick, chunky soup often made with fish.

A STOCK or BROTH is a thin, clear, strained liquid made by simmering meat, chicken, or fish with herbs and vegetables.

BOUILLON is a dehydrated version of stock or broth. It is sold as cubes or granules and needs to be reconstituted in liquid.

CONSOMMÉ is a strong flavorful broth that has been clarified.

porcini mushroom & onion soup

Parve

½ ounce dried porcini or shiitake mushrooms

2 cups boiling water

8 ounces (½ box) orzo, uncooked

drop of olive oil

2 tablespoons olive oil

2 tablespoons margarine

2 yellow onions, halved and thinly sliced

1 sweet or Vidalia onion, halved and thinly sliced

1 garlic clove, minced

1 teaspoon dried thyme

8 ounces cremini mushrooms, cleaned and thinly sliced

2 tablespoons dry sherry

2 (½-ounce) beef bouillon cubes dissolved in 4 cups water

2 (15-ounce) cans chicken stock or broth

4 tablespoons chopped flat leaf parsley

2 teaspoons salt

dash freshly ground black pepper

dash cayenne pepper

½ teaspoon sugar

In a small bowl, place the porcini or shiitake mushrooms and the boiling water; let soak for about 20 minutes. Lift the mushrooms out of the liquid and squeeze mushrooms to remove as much of the liquid as possible, strain the liquid and reserve. Dice the mushrooms; set aside.

In a large soup pot, add the dry orzo with a drop of olive oil. Sauté the orzo over medium heat until light golden; it will release a nutty aroma. Add enough water to cover by 5-6 inches. Turn up the heat and bring to a boil. Cook about 10 minutes or until the orzo is tender. Drain and set aside.

In the same stockpot, heat the 2 tablespoons of olive oil and margarine over low heat until foaming. Add onions, garlic, and thyme. Cook about 45 minutes or until the onions are soft and golden brown, stirring occasionally. Add cremini mushrooms and cook for 8-10 minutes, stirring occasionally. Add the sherry, porcini mushrooms, reserved mushroom liquid, beef bouillon, and chicken broth. Raise the heat and bring to a full boil. Lower to medium heat and simmer for 5 minutes. Add the orzo and cook until heated through, about 2 minutes. Stir in parsley, salt, black pepper, cayenne pepper, and sugar.

Yield: 10-12 servings

red lentil soup

This recipe is quick, easy, healthy, and delicious—-and cooks all in one pot.

2 onions, finely chopped
3 tablespoons olive oil
6 portobello mushroom caps, finely chopped

12 cups chicken or vegetable bouillon
2⅔ cups red lentils
2 (6-ounce) cans tomato paste

In a large soup pot, sauté the onions in the oil over medium heat about 5-7 minutes or until they become translucent. Add the mushrooms and sauté for 5 minutes longer. Add the bouillon, lentils, and tomato paste. Bring to a boil. Reduce heat and simmer for 15-20 minutes or until lentils are soft but not mushy.

Yield: 12-14 servings

vegetable soup with sweet potato

"Soup-erb!" Chock-full of vegetables and easy to make, this soup and a loaf of crusty bread make a great and healthy meal. This soup has received accolades from eaters of all ages. When reheating leftovers add more stock.

¼ cup olive oil
2 small onions, finely chopped
4 garlic cloves, minced
1 (28-ounce) can crushed tomatoes
6 cups vegetable stock, can use bouillon dissolved in water
2 large sweet potatoes, peeled and cut into ½-inch cubes

1 (15-ounce) can white kidney beans, also called cannellini
2 cups frozen green beans
1 teaspoon salt
1 teaspoon freshly ground black pepper
1 tablespoon fresh basil (about 4-5 leaves), minced
1 (20-ounce) box frozen corn kernels

In a large soup pot, heat oil over medium heat. Add the onions and sauté about 6-7 minutes or until translucent. Add the garlic and sauté 2-3 minutes longer.

Add the tomatoes, stock, and sweet potatoes. Bring to a boil. Add the white beans, green beans, salt, pepper, and basil. Return to a boil. Lower the heat and cook for 30 minutes. Stir in the corn and heat through.

Yield: 6 servings

two-tone sweet pea & carrot soup Meat or Parve

Either soup can be made on its own, but the colors and flavors of this two-toned combination are fabulous. Try serving the soup in half a baby pumpkin if the season is right. Have the produce department halve the pumpkins for you; they can be difficult to cut. This pea soup is very different from split-pea soup, which most people are used to. It is thin, smooth, and a gorgeous green. Float 1-2 sweet pea kreplach (see page 63) for a real show-stopper.

Carrot Soup:

- 6 cups vegetable or chicken stock or bouillon dissolved in water
- 7 tablespoons margarine, divided
- 4 tablespoons all-purpose flour
- 1 large onion, chopped
- 1 leek, white and light green parts thinly sliced, discarding the rest
- 2 pounds carrots, peeled and cut into chunks

Green Pea Soup:

- 6 cups vegetable or chicken stock or bouillon dissolved in water
- 7 tablespoons margarine, divided
- 4 tablespoons all-purpose flour
- 1 large onion, chopped
- 1 leek, white and light green parts only, thinly sliced
- 1 (20-ounce) bag frozen green peas

Bring the stock or bouillon to a boil. Reduce heat and simmer to keep warm.

To make either the carrot or sweet pea soup: Prepare a roux. In a large pot, heat four tablespoons of the margarine over low heat. Add the flour, whisking until smooth. Cook for 1 minute, whisking constantly. It will thicken. Add 1 tablespoon of margarine. Add the onion and leek; sauté 5-7 minutes or until translucent.

Add remaining 2 tablespoons margarine to the pot. Add vegetables (either the carrots or the peas). Sauté about 5-10 minutes; the carrots will take longer.

Stir hot stock into the vegetables. Bring mixture to a boil; reduce heat. Simmer, covered, 30 minutes.

Transfer soup in batches to the container of a blender; process until smooth. You may also use an immersion blender right in the pot. If the carrot soup is too thick, thin with a little stock, soy milk, or nondairy creamer. The pea soup must be poured through a strainer to get all of the shells out; press with back of a spoon to release all of the liquid.

Yield: 6 servings of single vegetable batch   *Yield: 10-12 servings of two-tone batch*

☞ *If using as a two tone, try this shortcut to avoid making each batch from scratch. In a large pot, make the roux as directed above, but prepare both batches in the pot at once. That means, 8 tablespoons margarine, 8 tablespoons flour, 2 large onions, and 2 leeks. Also, in another large pot, heat 12 cups of vegetable broth.*

Remove half of the roux to a third pot to which you will add your peas. Add the carrots to the pot that has the remaining first half of the roux; sauté. When the vegetables are ready, use a measuring cup to carefully pour 6 cups of the warmed stock into the carrots and 6 cups into the peas.

When ready to serve, use 2 measuring cups or teacups to scoop out a serving of each soup. Slowly pour the two soups at the same time, starting at the outer rim of the bowl so each soup meets in the center.

zucchini soup

This soup can be served hot or cold.

3 tablespoons canola oil
3 large onions, chopped
3 garlic cloves, roughly chopped
6-8 medium zucchini, with skin, ends
trimmed, and cut into chunks
1 tablespoon fresh parsley, chopped
1 tablespoon fresh dill, chopped

1 tablespoon fresh basil, chopped
(about 3-4 leaves)
7 cups chicken broth, can use parve
bouillon dissolved in water
salt
freshly ground black pepper

In a large pot, heat oil over a medium-high heat. Add the onions and garlic. Sauté until translucent, about 5-7 minutes.

Add the zucchini; sauté 3-5 minutes. Add the parsley, dill, and basil; sauté 2-3 minutes longer. Add the broth; bring to a boil. Simmer, covered, for 25 minutes.

Transfer soup in batches to the container of a blender; process until smooth. You may also use an immersion blender right in the pot. Season with salt and pepper to taste.

Yield: 8 servings

☞ *Potato Shape Garnish*

A great garnish for a bowl of creamy soup is a potato shape. Thinly slice a white potato. Use small cookie cutters, canapé cutters, or hors d'oeuvre cutters to cut out pretty shapes. Fry these shapes in a small amount of canola oil until golden brown and crisp and float one or two in each bowl of soup.

roasted chestnut butternut squash soup Meat or Dairy

For an eyepopping treat, serve this soup in cooked acorn squash halves. I have the produce department at the supermarket cut them in half for me, as they are hard and dangerous to cut at home. Have them cut them around the "waist" so you get two rounded cups, as opposed to cutting them lengthwise and getting shallower ovals. I also ask them to take a small sliver off the bottom so the bowl will sit flat. Don't worry about the stems, once the squash is cooked, the stem can be pulled right off. Place the squash halves cut side down in a roasting pan and fill with water, coming up the sides of the squash by 2 inches. Cook in 350 degree oven for 45 minutes.

1 tablespoon walnut oil or cooking oil
3 tablespoons margarine or butter
2 (20 ounce) bags frozen butternut squash cubes, defrosted
1 cup chestnuts, roasted and peeled, see note, or 1 (15-ounce) can whole chestnuts, drained, extra for garnish

6 cups chicken or vegetable broth, separated
⅛ teaspoon ground nutmeg, optional
½ teaspoon salt
1 cup nondairy cream, or 1 cup light cream
chopped roasted chestnuts, for garnish

In a large pot heat the oil and margarine. Add the squash cubes. Roughly break up the chestnuts with your fingers and add to the pot. Sauté for 8-10 minutes, stirring often.

Add the broth and heat to boiling. Reduce heat. Add nutmeg if using, and salt. Simmer for 10 minutes.

Transfer the soup in batches to the container of a blender; process until smooth. Return to pot. You can use an immersion blender and process directly in the soup pot.

Stir in the cream.

Ladle into bowl or acorn squash prepared as noted above. Garnish with a sprinkle of chopped roasted chestnuts.

Yield: 8 servings

☞ Roasting Chestnuts

To shell the chestnuts, use the tip of a knife to carefully carve an "x" on the flat side of each chestnut. Place on a baking sheet and roast at 400 degrees for 15-20 minutes or until corners of the x's curl up. Peel while warm. Roll peeled chestnuts in a towel to remove any papery skin. The chestnut season is November-January, but they keep for several months in the refrigerator.

chicken soup

1 chicken, cut in ⅛ths, with skin on
4-6 chicken thighs or legs, with skin on
2 large parsnips, peeled
2 large carrots, peeled
2 celery stalks, cut into large pieces
1-2 large leeks, sliced in half and
cleaned thoroughly
1 onion, skin removed

1 turnip, peeled and quartered
1 bouquet garni of 10 parsley sprigs,
10 dill sprigs, 1 bay leaf, 10
peppercorns (see page 155)
1 tablespoon Kosher salt
2 teaspoons freshly ground black
pepper

Place the chicken in a large pot and cover with cold water. Add an additional 4-5 inches of cold water. Bring to a boil. Using a small strainer, skim the fat and impurities off the top of the soup as it rises.

Add the parsnips, carrots, celery, leeks, onion, turnip, bouquet garni, salt, and pepper. Lower the heat and simmer, uncovered, for 1½-2 hours. Strain the foam and impurities off as needed. Season with salt and pepper to taste. Turn off the heat.

When soup is room temperature, pour it through a strainer. This will sift out any chicken bones or stray skin. Return the vegetables and chicken pieces from the bones, discarding bones, to the pot. This also allows you to transfer to a smaller pot so that it will fit in your refrigerator, if desired.

Yield: 12 servings

Always let a hot pot of soup come to room temperature before putting the pot in the refrigerator. This prevents raising the internal temperature of your refrigerator and everything else in it.

sweet pea kreplach

Parve

These can also be fried in vegetable oil as pictured and served as an appetizer.

salt
2 (4-ounce) jars sweet pea baby food
freshly ground black pepper

½ (12-ounce) package won ton
wrappers

Pour water into a medium pot. Add salt. Bring to a low boil. Empty the peas into a small bowl. Season with salt and pepper. Stir. Place a teaspoon of the filling in the center of each won ton wrapper. Dip a finger or brush in water and run it around the edges of the square. Take a corner of the square and fold it diagonally over the filling to form a triangle. Seal the edges by pressing firmly together with fingers or the tines of a fork. Drop the kreplach into the water for 45 seconds-1 minute. Remove, and serve in soup.

traditional kreplach dough

Parve

This dough is traditionally filled with ground beef that has been sautéed with onion.

2 large eggs
¼ teaspoon salt

1½-2 cups sifted all-purpose flour

In a medium bowl, beat the eggs until frothy. Add the salt. Gradually work in the flour to make form a stiff dough. Knead for about 5 minutes until soft and elastic. Can also be done in a mixer with a dough hook.

Roll the dough out on a floured surface until very thin. Cut into 3-inch squares.

Place a teaspoon of desired filling in the center of each square. Dip a finger in water and run it around the edges of the square. Take a corner of the square and fold it diagonally over the filling to form a triangle. Seal the edges by pressing firmly together with fingers or the tines of a fork. Let dry for at least 1 hour. Drop the kreplach into boiling salted water and cook for 15 minutes. Drain well and serve in soup.

Yield: 12-15 kreplach

tortellini spinach & tomato soup

This is the #1 requested soup at my house. The pasta appeals to my kids and cooking the complete dinner in one pot appeals to me.

1 tablespoon olive oil	6 ounces cheese tortellini, frozen
2 tablespoons butter	1 (28-ounce) can crushed tomatoes,
6 garlic cloves, minced	and their liquid
5 cups vegetable broth	salt
5-8 ounces fresh spinach	freshly ground black pepper
8-10 fresh basil leaves	½ cup grated Parmesan cheese

In a large pot, heat the olive oil over medium-low heat. Add the butter. When the butter melts, add the garlic and sauté for 2-3 minutes. Add the broth and bring to a boil.

Meanwhile, prepare the spinach using a method known as chiffonade. Start by removing the stems. Grab a pile of the leaves and roll like a log. Cut this log into quarter-inch slices, so when unraveled, the spinach looks like ribbons. Repeat process with all of the spinach. Use the same procedure for cutting the basil; set spinach and basil aside.

Add the frozen tortellini to the boiling broth and cook for 5 minutes (if using fresh tortellini cook for 3 minutes). Add the tomatoes with their liquid. Cook for 5 minutes.

Stir in the prepared spinach and basil. Cook 1-2 minutes or until wilted. Season with salt and pepper. Stir in the Parmesan.

Yield: 6 servings

☞ *Edible Bread Bowl*

Use bread bowls to serve soup or salads. Be sure to place the bread bowl in a regular bowl or plate, in case of leaks.

1 pound store-bought pizza dough, cut into 4-equal pieces
nonstick cooking spray

Preheat oven to 425 degrees. Coat the outside of 4 small, stainless steel bowls with nonstick cooking spray. Stretch a piece of dough over the outside of each bowl; prick all over with a fork. Bake for 10 minutes or until lightly brown. Remove from oven; carefully remove the crusts from the bowls and place on a wire rack to cool.

Yield: 4 bread bowls

parsnip bisque

This comforting soup's velvety texture and beautiful creamy color are sure to warm your family on any cold winter night. If the soup gets too thick, which it usually does overnight in the refrigerator, thin with a little stock. Thanks for this recipe goes to Damian Sansonetti, chef of Shallots NY.

2 tablespoons olive oil	2 Idaho potatoes, peeled and diced
½ Spanish onion, diced	8 cups chicken or vegetable stock
¾ celery stalk, diced	salt
1-2 garlic clove, minced	freshly ground black pepper
6 medium parsnips, peeled and diced	fresh chives, optional

In a large pot, heat the oil over medium heat. Add the onions and sauté about 6-7 minutes or until translucent. Add the celery and garlic; sauté 2 minutes longer.

Add the parsnips, potatoes, and chicken or vegetable stock. Bring to a boil. Cover and reduce heat to low; simmer about 30-35 minutes or until the vegetables are very tender.

Let cool. Transfer the soup in batches to a blender and puree. You can also use a handheld immersion blender to puree the mixture until smooth. Season with salt and pepper.

For extra smoothness, you can strain the soup through a fine chinois. Garnish with fresh chopped chives in the center of each bowl, if desired.

Yield: 8-10 servings

☞ *Pastry Covered Soup Crocks*

To add a great rustic touch to any creamy or thick soup, serve it in a pastry case. Pour the soup into oven-proof crocks. Cover with circles of puff pastry dough, making sure the pastry adheres to the edges of each crock. Brush the pastry with beaten egg. Cook in a preheated 300 degree oven for about 20 minutes or until puffed and golden.

roasted garlic & potato soup

This soup is a garlic-lover's delight. Make sure the garlic is very fresh and well roasted, even if it takes longer than the recipe states. The garlic heads should be soft and easy to squeeze. This recipe makes a big batch; you can halve the ingredients or freeze half of it, just don't add the cream or soy milk until ready to serve.

8 medium red potatoes, 4 peeled
2 medium onions, coarsely chopped
3 teaspoons fresh snipped rosemary (about 3 stems) or 1½ teaspoons dried rosemary
2 tablespoons olive oil
2 garlic heads

5 cups or 40-ounces chicken or vegetable stock, divided
2 tablespoons all-purpose flour
½ teaspoon black pepper, additional for seasoning
2 cups soy milk, nondairy creamer, or light cream
   salt

Preheat oven to 400 degrees. Cut the potatoes, both peeled and non-peeled, into cubes, no larger than one-inch thick.

Place the potatoes into a large baking pan. Sprinkle the onions and rosemary over the potatoes. Drizzle with olive oil.

Peel the dry outer leaves away from the heads of garlic. Hold the head on its side and cut a slice off the top, exposing the cloves. Wrap each head in aluminum foil. Place the wrapped garlic on top of the potatoes, cut side up.

Cover and bake for 50-60 minutes or until the garlic is soft and the potatoes are tender when pierced with a fork. Set aside to cool slightly.

Squeeze the garlic from the cloves into the container of a blender or a food processor. Add the potatoes, onion, 4 cups stock, flour, and pepper. Process or blend until smooth. You may need to do this in batches.

Pour the mixture into a large pot. Add the remaining 1 cup stock. Cook over a low- medium flame until heated through. Add the soy milk or cream. Simmer for 5 minutes. Season with salt and black pepper.

Yield: 12-14 servings

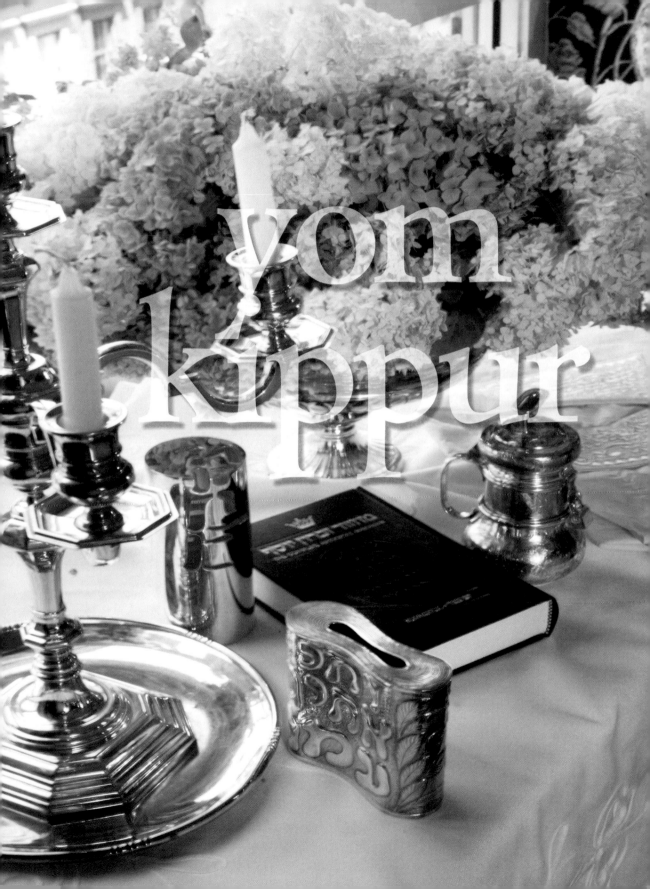

Contrary to popular belief, Yom Kippur is not a day of sadness or mourning. Of course it is intense and serious, as it is the Day of Judgment; but it is also a day of serene confidence in the goodness of God, Who forgives our sins on this holiest of days.

But there's a catch: we cannot expect divine forgiveness until we've mended our relationships with our fellow human beings. In the days prior to Yom Kippur and on Yom Kippur itself, conscientious Jews sincerely apologize to anyone they may have offended in the past year. It's not always easy. Long-standing feuds and emotional pain often prevent us from asking forgiveness or granting it.

This is where the wisdom of Jewish law and tradition play a role. In directing us to overcome these emotional barriers, Yom Kippur makes it possible for us to renew friendships and unify the Jewish nation. For this reason, it should also be a day of rejoicing.

To achieve all this, we try to elevate ourselves above our human limitations. The restrictions of Yom Kippur — prohibitions on eating, drinking, bathing, marital relations and wearing leather shoes (a sign of comfort and luxury) — are designed to focus us on our spiritual needs and aspirations. We live as angels for one day a year.

White is worn for numerous reasons. It is a symbol of purity and reminiscent of the Yom Kippur clothing worn by the High Priest in the Holy Temple of Jerusalem. It is also a sober reminder that we are all mortal, for we will someday be interred in white shrouds. Contemplating that fact usually helps us appreciate life that much more and makes it easier to resolve to live uprightly.

Tradition teaches that in addition to prayer and repentance, we should give charity prior to Yom Kippur. By sharing with others, we cement our bond with mankind and exhibit the compassion we hope to receive from God.

Going into Yom Kippur knowing that we have righted wrongdoings and healed strained relationships brings inner peace. Prior to this holy day we feed ourselves well, both physically and spiritually, and we are ready to begin anew.

erev yom kippur menu

SOUP:
Chicken Soup with Sweet Pea Kreplach
and Julienne of Vegetables
page 62

SALAD:
Shredded Endive, Radicchio,
Baby Spinach and Tomato
in a Lemon Zest Olive Oil Vinaigrette
page 87

ENTREE:
Poached Chicken in Leek Broth on Puree
of Carrots and Cauliflower
pages 108 and 211

SIDE DISH:
Asparagus Tivoli
page 210

DESSERT:
Sorbet in Martini Glasses
store purchased

Yom Kippur is not about food. However, eating before the fasting begins is as much of a *mitzvah* as the fast itself. It should be a full holiday meal.

Spend a few minutes setting a beautiful table to help put you in the proper frame of mind for this holy day. We selected a simple white tablecloth because white is a symbol of Yom Kippur. Pin up the table's sheer overlay between place settings to create scallops. They can be accented with a small corsage of vintage white flowers. Pin these same flowers to the back of each person's chair, which also has a sheer overlay tied in a bow.

Although the candles are not lit until after the meal, we have flanked them with charity boxes next to the dining table as a reminder of the impending holiday.

The simple menu omits salty and spicy foods because they cause thirst. Begin with homemade Chicken Soup; add Sweet Pea Kreplach for a twist on the traditional. Serve the salad as its own course or with the entree. The lightly flavored Poached Chicken and vegetable purees are healthy and filling. Time can run short, so we suggest store-purchased sorbets for dessert. Serving them in crystal martini glasses will elevate them to holiday elegance.

asian steak salad

salads

asian steak salad

I learned this outrageous recipe from Chris Hollis at a cooking class. It's great warm, but it's also nice at room temperature for a Shabbos lunch. Don't reheat the steak; just bring it to room temperature. This substantial salad can serve as a main dish or appetizer. Skirt steak is salty, so you must soak it in water for a few hours or overnight before slicing it. Be sure to use low-sodium soy sauce.

Dressing:

olive oil
3 tablespoons minced fresh ginger
3 garlic cloves, minced
¼ cup low-sodium soy sauce

¼ cup olive oil
⅛ cup sesame oil
⅛ cup balsamic vinegar
2 tablespoons Dijon mustard

Salad:

3-4 tablespoons peanut or olive oil
1½ pounds skirt steak, soaked, cut into ½-inch thick slices against the grain, and visible fat trimmed
½ red onion, thinly sliced

½ yellow pepper, thinly sliced
½ red bell pepper, thinly sliced
mixed greens
1 teaspoon sesame seeds

Dressing:

In a nonstick skillet, place a drop of olive oil. Brown the ginger and garlic over medium heat, making sure not to burn.

In a blender or food processor fitted with a metal blade, combine the soy sauce, olive oil, sesame oil, vinegar, and mustard. Add the ginger and garlic. Pulse 2-3 times. Set aside.

Salad:

In a large skillet, heat the peanut oil. Add the steak; it should sizzle when it hits the skillet or your oil is not yet hot enough. Cook steak about 6 minutes or until medium doneness. Remove the steak from the skillet and set aside.

Add the red onion, yellow pepper, and red pepper to the skillet. Cook about 5-6 minutes or until vegetables are nearly done; add 2-3 tablespoons of the dressing. Mix and remove from heat.

To serve, lightly dress the greens. Save any extra dressing for another use. Place the greens in the center of the plate. Put the steak and vegetables in the center of the greens. Sprinkle sesame seeds on top.

Yield: 4 servings

oriental spinach salad

Dressing:

6 tablespoons olive oil

3 tablespoons rice vinegar

3 tablespoons sugar

3 tablespoons soy sauce

Salad:

1 tablespoons olive oil

1½ cups or 1 (2.8-ounce-package) Ramen noodles, discard the spice pack

¼ cup sesame seeds

½ cup sliced almonds

12 ounces fresh baby spinach leaves

Dressing:

In a jar or cruet, mix the 6 tablespoons of olive oil, vinegar, sugar, and soy sauce. Shake until thoroughly emulsified. Set aside.

Salad:

In a sauté pan, heat 1 tablespoon of olive oil over medium heat. Add the noodles, sesame seeds, and almonds. Sauté until toasted, stirring constantly, making sure not to burn. If making this salad in advance, store the noodle mixture in an airtight container in the refrigerator.

Before serving, toss the spinach with the dressing and sprinkle with the noodle mixture.

Yield: 8 servings

bruschetta salad

Fresh garlic croutons add a lot of flavor and texture to this salad, but in a pinch you can just use good quality packaged croutons. You can also serve this salad over a bed of mixed greens.

1 loaf French bread
2 large garlic cloves, minced
¼ cup olive oil, plus extra for brushing on bread
12 medium-large tomatoes, cut into chunks

½ medium onion, finely chopped
½ medium red onion, finely chopped
5 tablespoons fresh basil, coarsely chopped
¼ cup balsamic vinegar

Preheat oven to 300 degrees. Cut the French bread in half lengthwise. Rub the garlic into the bread and brush with the olive oil. Cut each half of the bread in half lengthwise again and then cut into ¾-inch pieces. Place the pieces, crust side down, on a baking sheet. Bake about 45-55 minutes or until bread is golden brown. Set aside. Alternatively, you can brush the bread with the oil and garlic, grill the bread, and then cut it into cubes.

Place the tomatoes in a bowl. Add the onions and basil. In a separate bowl, whisk the vinegar and ¼ cup olive oil.

Pour over the salad and toss. Add the croutons right before serving.

Yield: 10-12 servings

candied almond, pear, and
goat cheese salad with shallot vinaigrette Dairy

Right now it is difficult to find Kosher bleu or gorgonzola cheese. But it is produced Kosher in Denmark, so there is a chance it will be available in the United States soon. In the meantime goat cheese works very well.

Vinaigrette:

- 2 tablespoons balsamic vinegar
- 1 teaspoon minced shallot
- ¼ cup plus 2 tablespoons good quality olive oil
- salt
- freshly ground black pepper

Candied Almonds:

- 1½ cups slivered almonds
- ⅔ cup sugar

Salad:

- 5 cups mesclun mix
- 2 cups arugula, torn
- 2 pears, cored and cubed
- 1 cup red grapes, halved
- 1 handful sweetened dried cranberries, like Craisins
- 1½ ounces goat cheese, bleu cheese, or gorgonzola, crumbled
- salt
- freshly ground black pepper

Vinaigrette:

Place the vinegar, shallot, olive oil, salt, and pepper in a jar or cruet. Shake until emulsified. Set aside.

Candied Almonds:

Cover a baking sheet with tin foil. In a nonstick skillet sprayed with nonstick cooking spray, heat the almonds over medium heat. Cook 2-3 minutes to toast the almonds, gently shaking the skillet.

Slowly add the sugar; cook about 8-9 minutes, stirring constantly, to keep the almonds separated as the sugar caramelizes. The sugar will turn a deep amber color; make sure not to burn the sugar.

Remove from heat immediately and quickly spread the almonds onto the prepared baking sheet. Separate them to prevent clumping. If making the almonds in advance keep them in an airtight container.

Salad:

In a large bowl toss the mesclun, arugula, pears, grapes, cranberries, and cheese. Sprinkle over the candied almonds and coat with the vinaigrette. Season with salt and pepper to taste.

Yield: 6 servings

layered chopped salad

This recipe is my favorite incarnation of an old classic. As its name implies, the salad is layered in a glass or trifle bowl. Each layer shows through for a stunning and colorful presentation. The amounts given are for a large bowl; if you only have a small one, use about ⅔rds the amount of the peas, purple cabbage, and shredded carrots. You will not need all of the dressing; use your eye to judge.

Dressing:

4 tablespoons mayonnaise
⅔ cup red wine vinegar

2 (0.7-ounce) packets dried Italian seasonings

Salad:

1 (16-ounce) bag petite frozen peas
1 (15-ounce) can chickpeas or garbanzo beans, drained
3 cups or 1 (10-ounce) bag shredded purple cabbage
1 head iceburg lettuce, shredded
1 red bell pepper, sliced
1 (11-ounce) can corn niblets, drained

1 bunch scallions, chopped
1 (10-ounce) bag shredded carrots or 4-5 medium carrots, shredded
3-4 cucumbers, peeled and sliced
3-4 Roma tomatoes, sliced; or 2 cups grape tomatoes
1½-2 (15-ounce) cans French fried onions

Dressing:

Prepare the dressing at least 2 hours in advance. Mix the mayonnaise, vinegar, and Italian seasonings. Cover and refrigerate.

Salad:

Place the peas in the bottom of the trifle bowl in an even layer. Carefully add an even layer of chickpeas, cabbage, lettuce, red pepper, corn, scallions, carrots, cucumbers, and tomatoes.

Before serving, pour the dressing over the tomato layer, it will seep down through the layers. Sprinkle with the French fried onions.

Yield: 10-12 servings

🐚 *Pepper Pointers*

To slice a bell pepper, hold the pepper by the stem. Cutting along the inside of the curves, slice into fourths. Lay the pepper sections skin side down. With knife almost parallel, cut off the white membrane. With the skin side still down, cut each section into thin, long strips.

health salad

This salad has found its way onto the tables of many delis and restaurants. Simple to make in advance, the dish pairs nicely with barbecue.

Salad:

- 4 carrots, peeled and sliced
- 2 cucumbers, peeled and sliced
- 1 red bell pepper, seeded and cut into small cubes or thin slices
- 1 green bell pepper, seeded and cut into small cubes or thin slices
- 1 head green cabbage, coarsely shredded

Dressing:

- ½ cup vegetable oil
- ½ cup white vinegar
- ½ cup honey
- 1 tablespoon salt

In a large bowl, combine the carrots, cucumbers, red bell pepper, green bell pepper, and cabbage. In a jar or cruet, mix the oil, vinegar, honey, and salt. Shake well to mix. Pour over salad. Allow to sit for at least ½ hour. Mix well before serving.

Yield: 10-12 servings

crunchy cole slaw

This alternative to the traditional creamy slaw is best made at least ½ hour in advance.

- ½ cup margarine
- 6 ounces Ramen noodles (if using Ramen noodle soup mix, discard the spice packets)
- 1 (16-ounce) bag shredded green cabbage
- 3-4 scallions, thinly sliced
- ½ cup sesame seeds
- ½ cup slivered almonds
- ½ cup sunflower seeds
- 1 cup vegetable or canola oil
- 2 tablespoons soy sauce
- ¾ cup sugar
- ½ cup red wine vinegar

In a large skillet, melt the margarine over medium heat. Break the Ramen noodles into small pieces and add to the pan. Brown the noodles and remove from heat.

In a large bowl, combine the cabbage, scallions, sesame seeds, almonds, and sunflower seeds. Add the Ramen noodles. Toss to combine.

In a jar or cruet, mix the oil, soy sauce, sugar, and vinegar. Shake to emulsify. Add most of the dressing to the slaw, tossing to combine. Add the rest of the dressing, if desired. This salad can be made in advance and refrigerated.

Yield: 8-10 servings

asparagus spinach salad

Parve

Dressing:

- 2 tablespoons sesame seeds
- 1 tablespoon poppy seeds
- ½ cup sugar
- 2 teaspoons dried minced onion
- ¼ teaspoon paprika
- ¼ cup white-wine vinegar
- ¼ cup apple-cider vinegar
- ½ cup vegetable oil

Salad:

- 12 asparagus spears, blanched in boiling water for 2-3 minutes and cut into 1-inch pieces
- 1 pound fresh baby spinach leaves
- ¾ cup slivered almonds

Dressing:

In a jar or cruet, mix the sesame seeds, poppy seeds, sugar, onion, paprika, white-wine vinegar, apple-cider vinegar, and vegetable oil. Shake until emulsified.

Salad:

In a large bowl, toss the asparagus and spinach with the dressing. Sprinkle with the slivered almonds.

Yield: 8 servings

purple cabbage salad

This salad also makes a wonderful side dish. It is a beautiful combination of colors and textures. Many men tell me they don't like fruit on their salad, but for some reason this salad is an exception to that rule.

Salad:

16 ounces shredded purple cabbage
⅓ cup chopped scallions
⅓ cup pine nuts
3 carrots, julienned, or 1 (8-ounce) bag shredded carrots

1 (11-ounce) can mandarin oranges, reserving juice
1-2 handfuls dried cranberries (can be the sweetened kind)

Dressing:

4 tablespoons brown sugar
½ teaspoon freshly ground black pepper
¼ teaspoon salt
4 tablespoons red or white wine vinegar
1 tablespoon reserved mandarin orange juice

½ cup vegetable oil
1 vegetable or parve chicken flavor bouillon cube, or 1 teaspoon dried consomme powder
garlic powder

Place the cabbage, scallions, pine nuts, carrots, oranges, and cranberries into a large zip-lock bag. Set aside.

In a jar or cruet, mix the brown sugar, pepper, salt, vinegar, reserved orange juice, oil, bouillon cube, and garlic powder. Close and shake until thoroughly mixed.

Pour over the salad. Refrigerate to let the flavors mix for at least 1 hour. Can prepare early in the day.

Yield: 8-10 servings

chef's salad

Dressing:

- 3 tablespoons mayonnaise
- ¼ cup olive oil
- 1½ teaspoons sugar
- ¼ teaspoon freshly ground black pepper
- 1 tablespoon fresh parsley, chopped
- 1 tablespoon scallions, thinly sliced
- 1 teaspoon Dijon mustard or ½ teaspoon dry mustard powder
- 2 garlic cloves, minced
  juice of 1 lemon

Salad:

- ¼ pound pastrami, sliced into thin strips
- ¼ pound smoked turkey breast, sliced into thin strips
- ¼ pound salami, sliced into thin strips
- 1 small red onion, thinly sliced
- 1 cup cherry tomatoes
- 1 pound mixed salad greens

In a jar or cruet, mix the mayonnaise, oil, sugar, pepper, parsley, scallions, mustard, garlic, and lemon juice. Shake or whisk until emulsified.

Toss the pastrami, turkey, salami, red onion, and tomatoes with the salad greens. Lightly coat with dressing.

Yield: 8-10 servings

☞ *Herbed Bagel Chips*

These pair nicely with any soup or salad. Cut a bagel (can be a day or two old) crosswise into four slices. Place the slices cut side up on a baking sheet in a single layer. Lightly spray with cooking spray. Sprinkle with onion powder, garlic powder, and Italian seasonings. In a preheated 375 degree oven, bake for 10-12 minutes or until golden and crisp. Can be kept in an airtight container for 4-5 days.

strawberry fields salad

Dressing:

¼ cup sugar
¼ cup red wine vinegar
¼ cup honey
¼ cup warm water

½ teaspoon freshly ground black pepper
½ teaspoon dry mustard powder
½ cup canola oil

Sugared Almonds:

6-7 tablespoons sugar
2 cups slivered almonds

Salad:

1 pound mixed salad greens
1 cup sprouts
8 ounces strawberries, stems removed and cut into chunks

2 handfuls pine nuts
½ red onion, thinly sliced

Dressing:

In a jar or cruet, combine the sugar, vinegar, honey, water, pepper, mustard, and oil. Shake or whisk until emulsified.

Sugared Almonds:

Heat a nonstick skillet over medium-high heat. Place the sugar and almonds into the warm skillet. Stir constantly until the sugar melts and coats the almonds. Make sure the sugar does not burn. Remove from heat and lay the almonds onto a sheet of parchment or tin foil. Break up any large clumps. If making almonds in advance store them in an airtight container.

Salad:

In a large bowl, combine the salad greens, sprouts, strawberries, pine nuts, and red onions. Lightly coat with dressing. Make sure some strawberries remain on the top. Sprinkle with sugared almonds.

Yield: 8 servings

hearts of palm salad

This salad is a perfect complement to barbecued food.

5-6 ripe Haas avocados, peeled, pitted, and diced
1 (17-ounce) can hearts of palm, drained and sliced
½ cup red onion, chopped
2 cups grape or cherry tomatoes, halved

1 heaping tablespoon mayonnaise
salt
freshly ground black pepper
juice from ½ lemon

In a large bowl combine the avocado, hearts of palm, onion, and tomatoes. Toss with the mayonnaise. Season with salt, pepper, and lemon juice.

Yield: 10-12 servings

☞ *Lemon juice never seems to do the trick of keeping cut avocado halves green and firm. The key is keeping light and air away. To achieve this, lightly spray the exposed flesh with cooking spray. Wrap in foil and refrigerate.*

arugula salad with pomegranate-raspberry vinaigrette

This salad is perfect for a fall holiday table, when pomegranates are in season. The green, orange, and red colors combine for a gorgeous display. Pomegranate are full of vitamins and anti-oxidants, low in calories and have a healthy dose of fiber. A large pomegranate will yield about 1 cup of seeds known as arils.

1 pomegranate
⅓ cup olive oil
2 tablespoons raspberry vinegar
1 teaspoon sugar
½ teaspoon salt

freshly ground black pepper
3 bunches arugula, stems removed
1 small red onion, cut into thin rings
1 (8-ounce) can mandarin orange slices, drained

Cut the "crown" end off the fruit exposing the seeds. Score the rind 4-5 times. Submerge the pomegranate in a large bowl of cool water for 5 minutes. Working underwater, break the fruit apart into sections, freeing the seeds from the membranes. The seeds will sink to the bottom and the membranes will float to the top. Drain the seeds into a sieve or strainer.

Reserve ⅛ cup seeds for garnish. Press the remaining seeds with the back of a spoon to release the juices. Collect 2 tablespoons of juice, discarding the crushed seeds.

Pour the juice into a jar or cruet. Add the oil, vinegar, sugar, salt and black pepper. Shake or whisk until blended.

Place the arugula into a large bowl. Add the red onion, separating the slices into rings. Drizzle with the dressing and toss to coat evenly.

Arrange a handful of salad on each plate. Distribute the oranges evenly. Garnish with the reserved pomegranate seeds.

Yield: 6 servings

endive salad with shallot vinaigrette

Parve

If you make the vinaigrette in advance, bring it to room temperature before using.

Salad:

- 2 endives, separated into individual leaves
- 4 plum tomatoes, chopped
- 1-2 avocados, peeled and diced
- 1 (14-ounce) can hearts of palm, cut into ½-inch slices
- 1 (7-ounce) can corn niblets, drained
- 25 nicoise or 1 (2.25-ounce) can sliced black olives, drained

Shallot Vinaigrette:

- ½ cup olive oil
- 1 large shallot, minced
- ¼ cup balsamic vinegar
- 1 tablespoon Dijon mustard
- ¼ teaspoon dried dill
- ½ teaspoon salt
- ⅛ teaspoon freshly ground black pepper

Arrange the largest and prettiest endive leaves on the individual plates or large platter in a sunburst fashion. Discard the small leaves.

In the center, mix the tomatoes, avocados, hearts of palm, corn, and olives. In a jar or cruet, mix the olive oil, shallot, vinegar, mustard, dill, salt, and pepper. Shake to mix. Drizzle dressing over salad.

Yield: 6-8 servings

greek pasta salad

- 1 pound bow tie pasta, uncooked
- ½ cup olive oil plus 1 teaspoon olive oil
- 2 garlic cloves, minced
  juice from 2 lemons
- 3 tablespoons red wine vinegar
- 1 teaspoon dried oregano
- ½ teaspoon salt
- ⅛ teaspoon freshly ground black pepper
- 1 red bell pepper, seeded and diced
- 1 yellow bell pepper, seeded and diced
- 2 scallions, chopped
- 1 large seedless English cucumber, cut in half lengthwise and chopped
- 8 ounces Greek olives or 1 (6-ounce) can pitted black olives, drained
- 2 tomatoes, cut into wedges
- 2 tablespoons capers (optional)
- 8 ounces feta cheese, crumbled

Cook pasta according to package directions until al denté. Drain. Place in a large salad bowl. Mix with 1 teaspoon olive oil.

In a jar or cruet, mix the ½ cup olive oil, garlic, lemon juice, vinegar, oregano, salt, and pepper.

Add the red pepper, yellow pepper, scallions, cucumber, olives, tomatoes, capers, if desired, and feta cheese to the pasta. Toss with the dressing to coat.

Yield: 8-10 servings

roasted portobello salad with basil vinaigrette Parve

As a meat option, add grilled London broil strips to this salad. It makes for a memorable meal.

Vinaigrette:

- 1 cup olive oil
- ½ cup balsamic vinegar
- 1 garlic clove, chopped
- 1 teaspoon sugar

- 1 cup fresh basil leaves, chopped
- juice of 1 lemon
- salt
- freshly ground black pepper

Salad:

- 6 large portobello mushroom caps
- 1 tablespoon olive oil

- 1 pound mesclun or other mixed salad greens
- 1 bunch watercress

Vinaigrette:

In a cruet or a jar, combine the olive oil, vinegar, garlic, sugar, basil, lemon juice, salt, and pepper. Shake until emulsified and thoroughly combined.

Salad:

Preheat oven to 450 degrees. Using a teaspoon, scrape the gills from the underside of each mushroom cap and discard. Sprinkle the caps with salt and pepper. Brush with oil. Place gill side down on a baking sheet and roast for 15-20 minutes or until soft.

Remove the mushrooms from oven and slice. Mix the salad greens and watercress. Top with sliced mushrooms. Drizzle with the vinaigrette.

Yield: 6 servings

grilled London broil Meat

- 2 pounds London broil
- ½ cup olive oil
- ½ cup low-sodium soy sauce
- ¼ cup honey

- 1 tablespoon coarsely ground black pepper
- 1 teaspoon salt
- 6 garlic cloves, minced

Score the meat on both sides by making diagonal cuts ¼-inch deep at 1-inch intervals to form a diamond pattern. Place it in a zip-lock bag.

In a bowl, whisk together the oil, soy sauce, honey, pepper, salt, and garlic. Add the marinade to the bag. Seal and marinate in refrigerator for up to 1 hour.

Remove meat from marinade and grill 10 minutes per side. Let stand 5 minutes. Slice thinly and toss with mushrooms and salad.

shredded endive, radicchio, baby spinach and tomato in a lemon zest olive oil vinaigrette

Parve

¼ cup balsamic vinegar
1 tablespoon Dijon mustard
¼ teaspoon salt
⅛ teaspoon freshly ground black pepper
  pinch of sugar
2 teaspoons finely grated lemon zest, just yellow, not the white pith

¾ cup olive oil
1 head Belgium endive, thinly sliced
2 cups radicchio (about ¾ head), thinly sliced
1 cup fresh baby spinach leaves
1 cup grape tomatoes

In a jar or cruet whisk or shake together the vinegar, mustard, salt, pepper, a pinch of sugar, and the lemon zest. Slowly add the olive oil Whisk or shake until combined.

In a large mixing bowl combine the endive, radicchio, and spinach. Drizzle with the dressing and toss to combine. Add in the tomatoes.

Yield: 4 servings

🐚 *The Microplane*

One of my favorite tools in the kitchen is the microplane. This easy-to-use grater produces a cloud of lemon or orange zest so fine that it melts away into your cakes and cookies, leaving only the delicate flavor.

🐚 *To get the most juice from a lemon, roll it firmly between your palm and a hard work surface before squeezing. The pressure will crush the lemon's membranes, releasing more liquid.*

red bliss potato salad

Parve

This is one picnic table favorite you will never tire of. You'll welcome skipping the tedious task of peeling potatoes. I like to serve this dish while its still warm, but it can also be made in advance and refrigerated.

6 medium red potatoes, unpeeled	salt
3 eggs	freshly ground black pepper
¾ red bell pepper, seeded and diced	garlic salt
8 heaping tablespoons mayonnaise	onion powder

Boil potatoes and eggs, in water to cover, over medium-high heat about 40-50 or until the potatoes until tender. Drain; cover the potatoes and eggs with cold water. Let sit until eggs are cool enough to handle.

Peel the eggs and cut them into small pieces. Cut the potatoes into small pieces. Mix the potatoes and eggs in a large bowl. Add the red pepper and the mayonnaise. Season to taste with the salt, pepper, garlic salt, and onion powder.

Yield: 8-10 servings

couscous salad

This light grain salad can easily be made a day or two in advance. This gives the flavors a chance to mix.

- 2 cups water
- ½ teaspoon salt
- ¼ teaspoon freshly ground black pepper
- 10 ounces couscous, uncooked
- 2 tablespoons lemon juice
- 3 tablespoons olive oil

- 2 large tomatoes, chopped
- 1 medium green zucchini, unpeeled, halved, and thinly sliced
- 18 fresh basil leaves, cut into strips
- ⅓ cup scallions, thinly sliced
- ¾ cup feta cheese, crumbled

In a pot, boil the water, salt, and pepper over high heat. Add the dry couscous and stir; remove from heat. Cover and let stand for 5 minutes.

Pour the couscous into a bowl. Add the lemon juice, olive oil, tomatoes, zucchini, basil, and scallions. Chill 4-6 hours. Before serving, stir and sprinkle with the feta cheese.

Yield: 10 servings

new millennium waldorf salad

Until I tried this recipe, I never understood the appeal of Waldorf salad. Globs of mayonnaise with apple pieces floating in it is not my idea of haute cuisine. Try this incredible updated version, which substitutes heavy cream, for a salad even your kids will love. Serve it plain or on a bed of lettuce.

- 3 cups heavy whipping cream
- 8 ounces confectioner's sugar
- 5 red Delicious apples, cored and diced with skin on

- ½-¾ cup raisins
- ¾ cup chopped walnuts

Whip the cream and sugar until stiff peaks form. Fold in the apples and raisins. Sprinkle with walnuts.

Yields: 12-15 servings

fandango salad

This recipe makes more than enough dressing to use at multiple meals. My guests fight over who gets to take home the extra! As of now, it is difficult to find Kosher bleu or gorgonzola cheese. But it is produced Kosher in Denmark, so there is a chance it will be available in the United States soon. Keep this salad with cheese in mind for dairy meals.

Raspberry Dressing:

⅔ cup frozen raspberries, thawed
½ cup sugar
¼ cup red wine vinegar
2 tablespoons minced red onion

1 tablespoon dry mustard powder
½ teaspoon salt
½ teaspoon lemon juice
1 cup olive oil

Salad:

1 head Romaine lettuce, torn into bite-size pieces
1 (8-ounce) can mandarin oranges, drained

½ cup chopped walnuts
handful of crumbled bleu or gorgonzola cheese, optional for dairy meals

Raspberry Dressing:

In the container of a food processor fitted with a metal blade, blend the raspberries, sugar, vinegar, onion, dry mustard, salt, and lemon juice. With the motor running, slowly drizzle in the olive oil. Mix until emulsified.

Salad:

Place the lettuce in a bowl and add enough dressing to coat; you will have extra. Sprinkle with the oranges, walnuts, and cheese, if desired.

Yield: 6 servings

Sukkot

he Torah records that following the exodus from Egyptian bondage the Children of Israel lived in "booths" — *sukkot* — in the desert. But the holiday of Sukkot is not merely commemorative: its message is as contemporary as today's newspaper. In leaving the security and comfort of our home to reside in a fragile structure, we are expressing our trust in God as our only Protector. It's an eternal lesson — and we pass it on to our children in this wonderful, memorable way.

Even if you do not normally love the great outdoors, you will find that your sukkah has a magnetic pull. It was built and decorated by your own family, and it expresses your collective tone and taste. And its mood is ever changing. The same little room that sparkles in the morning sunlight becomes tranquil as evening shadows appear. At night, after you've lit the holiday candles, their warm glow invites family and friends to gather for a cozy meal.

Sukkot is one of the *Shalosh Regalim*, the holidays on which Jews gathered in the Holy Temple in Jerusalem in ancient times. It was a huge, joyous reunion, with thousands of families pouring into the holy city from every part of the country.

Today, Sukkot is still about Jewish brotherhood. Our sukkot remind us of the solidarity of the Jews when they lived in the desert and during the peaceful times of the Jewish commonwealth in Israel. The "Four Species" — the collective term for the *etrog* (citron), *lulav* (date palm branch), *hadassim* (myrtle branches) and *aravot* (willow branches) — used during the holiday service symbolize harmony on several levels. The Sages teach that they represent different parts of the body and different types of people. Bound together and blessed as one entity, they represent the harmony within each of us, the unity of the Jewish people, and our national bond with our Creator.

Sukkot is the only holiday called "the time of our joy," for it caps the High Holidays during which we acquired divine forgiveness. The harvest season at this time of the year is symbolic of the spiritual harvest that is ours to enjoy in its abundance. We reach the door of our sukkah confident that the year is off to a great start.

sukkot menu

APPETIZER:
Stuffed Zucchini
page 25

SOUP:
Two-tone Sweet Pea and Carrot Soup
in half a Mini Pumpkin
page 58

SALAD:
Arugula Salad with
Pomegranate-Raspberry Vinaigrette
page 83

ENTREE:
Herb Crusted Silver Tip Roast
page 131

SIDE DISHES:
Roasted Garlic Mashed Potato Galette
page 208
Acorn Squash with
Sugar-Coated Cranberries
page 221

DESSERT:
Nut Coffee Layer Cake
page 284

As the cool fall evening envelops us, families and friends gather in the sukkah to enjoy a hearty holiday meal. It is a *mitzvah* to share your sukkah with others, especially those who do not have their own. In many communities, "sukkah hopping" is a popular activity.

The whole family helps decorate the sukkah; the possibilities stretch as far as the imagination. Since Sukkot is also known as "the harvest festival," we designed our sukkah to convey the feeling of bountiful fields. The painted lattice has an outside lining of green canvas. The lattice is completely covered by leaves, bunches of grapes, and huge sunflowers woven into the crosshatches. The green and gold motif is vibrant against the backdrop of the autumn sun.

The right table decor can coax friends to linger in your sukkah. Our sage green and pale yellow dishes enhance the outdoor feel. Instead of glasses for water or soda, use large hurricane globes as oversized cups. A rustic tablecloth and napkins evoke a harvest theme. As a finishing touch, accent each chair with a giant sunflower.

Many people serve stuffed foods on this holiday; our spin on this is the meat-and- rice Stuffed Zucchini. The Two-tone Sweet Pea and Carrot Soup served in a mini pumpkin provides a riot of color. To showcase nature's bounty, the rest of our menu is laden with an array of seasonal fruits and vegetables. The Herb Crusted Silver Tip Roast offers an impressive, but simple, centerpiece to this menu. For dessert, the Nut Coffee Layer Cake is large enough to feed any unexpected guests who drop by.

wine list

CONTOUR
DOMAINE TORTUE CHABLIS
ABARBANEL CHARDONNAY

Contour wine hails from California. The lovely fruit in
this medium bodied blend of Chenin Blanc and Chardonnay grapes
will offer an interesting counterpoint to the peppery yet fruity arugula salad.

A classic Chablis/Chardonnay from France
would also stand up well to the dressing in this salad.

BARON HERZOG RESERVE CABERNET
CHATEAU FIGEAC ST. EMILION 99
CHATEAU GISCOURS MARGAUX 97
CHATEAU LEOVILLE POYFERRE ST. JULIEN
YARDEN CABERNET SAUVIGNON
TIERRA SALVAJE MALBEC

The Herb-Crusted Silver Tip Roast is classically paired with
Cabernet from California, or a Bordeaux from France.
For good value and for something different, try a Malbec from Argentina.

CHATEAU PIADA SAUTERNE 2000

The honeyed richness of this wine will be a perfect complement
to the Nut Layer Coffee Cake.
A good cognac or brandy would be a fine choice, as well.

roast turkey with
caramelized onion-balsamic gravy

poultry

hickory-smoked chicken
smothered in onions

The smoky flavor of this chicken is great, especially in winter after barbecue season. Hickory Seasoning can be found in the dry spice section of your supermarket. You can use any dried barbecue seasoning spice blend. Just check the ingredient list and make sure it includes hickory or smoke flavor.

1 chicken, cut into ⅛ths	⅛ cup Worcestershire sauce (see note)
Hickory Seasoning	½ cup ketchup
4 tablespoons margarine	½ cup pure maple syrup
3 onions, sliced into rings	4 tablespoons apple-cider vinegar
1 cup dark brown sugar	2 tablespoons Dijon mustard

Preheat the broiler to high. Spread the chicken pieces skin side up in a single layer in a baking pan. Sprinkle both sides of chicken pieces with the hickory seasoning. Broil for 7-8 minutes.

While the chicken broils, prepare the onions. In a large skillet, melt the margarine over high heat. Add the onions, brown sugar, and Worcestershire sauce. Cover and cook for 7-8 minutes over high heat, stirring every few minutes. Remove the chicken and preheat the oven to bake at 350 degrees.

In a small bowl, combine the ketchup, maple syrup, vinegar, and mustard. Stir to combine. Pour the onions over the chicken. Pour the ketchup mixture over the chicken and onions. Bake uncovered for 1½ hours.

Yield: 4 servings

☞ A note about Worcestershire sauce
All Worcestershire sauce contains anchovies. If the kosher certification marks stands alone, then the percentage of anchovies is less than 1.6% of the whole product. Many rabbinical authorities say that this is okay to use with meat.
If the kosher certification on the label has a fish notation next to it, the level exceeds the 1.6% and you should refrain from using it in meat dishes.

pesto chicken with roasted red pepper sauce

Pesto Chicken:

8 boneless, skinless chicken breasts	⅛ cup pistachio nuts, shelled
3 cups fresh basil leaves	4½ tablespoons lemon juice
2¼ cups fresh flat leaf parsley	¾ cup olive oil
4 garlic cloves	salt
¼ cup pine nuts or walnuts	freshly ground black pepper

Roasted Red Pepper Sauce:

1 roasted red pepper or 1 (7-ounce) jar red peppers, drained	1 tablespoon lemon juice
3 garlic cloves	dash red pepper sauce
2 tablespoons olive oil	1 cup mayonnaise

Pesto Chicken:

Lay the chicken breasts in a glass baking dish or zip-lock bag. Set aside.

In the bowl of a food processor fitted with a metal blade, process the basil, parsley, garlic, nuts, and lemon juice. Process until a thick paste is formed. With the motor running, slowly add the olive oil. Season with salt and pepper.

Pour the pesto over the chicken and let marinate for 1 hour.

Roasted Red Pepper Sauce:

In the bowl of a food processor fitted with a metal blade, process the roasted red pepper, garlic, olive oil, lemon juice, and red pepper sauce. Pulse a few times until smooth. Add the mayonnaise and pulse a few times until combined. Refrigerate until ready to use.

Grill or broil the chicken until cooked through, about 8-10 minutes per side. Cool the chicken and refrigerate. An hour before serving, remove the chicken and bring to room temperature. Serve with the roasted red pepper sauce.

Yield: 8 servings

Roasting a Red Bell Pepper
Preheat the broiler with racks 5 inches from the heat. Cut your peppers in half and remove the seeds. Place the peppers skin side up on a foil lined baking sheet. Broil about 5 minutes or until peppers look blistered and blackened. Place peppers in a paper bag; seal and let stand 10 minutes to loosen skin. Remove skin. It is okay if some of the black pieces remain, they add to the flavor.

chicken oporto

1 tablespoon margarine	2 large shallots, chopped
1 tablespoon olive oil	3 garlic cloves, roughly chopped
1 chicken, cut into ⅛ths	½ pound mushrooms, sliced
⅛ teaspoon salt	⅓ cup Port wine
⅛ teaspoon freshly ground black pepper	1 small can Italian plum tomatoes

In a large skillet, heat the margarine and olive oil over high heat. Season the chicken with the salt and pepper. Place the chicken in the skillet, skin side down. Sauté for 10 minutes, shaking pan occasionally to prevent chicken from sticking. The skin should look nice and brown. Turn the chicken over and sauté for 10 more minutes.

Remove the chicken from the pan, discarding all but 1 tablespoon of the fat. Try to leave the brown bits in the pan as well.

At this point, the skin will look brown but won't be crisp. If you like crisp skin, run the chicken under the broiler for 2-3 minutes; set aside.

Add the shallots, garlic, and mushrooms to the pan; sauté over medium-high heat for 3-4 minutes, scraping up the brown bits from the bottom of the pan.

Return the chicken to the pan. Add the wine. Remove 4 of the tomatoes from the can, shaking off any liquid and discarding any basil leaves. Chop the tomatoes and add them to the pan. Cover the chicken and cook for 25 minutes.

To serve, remove the chicken from the pan and cover with the mushrooms and shallots.

Yield: 4 servings

sombrero chicken

This interesting chicken dish gets its name from its Mexican flavor. The spices and the tomatoes mix to form a pretty color. It tastes great with a side of yellow rice and a bag of tortilla chips.

¼ cup all-purpose flour
   pinch freshly ground black pepper
6 boneless, skinless chicken breasts
3 tablespoons margarine
1 (14.5-ounce) can stewed tomatoes,
   Italian-seasoning flavored, with liquid
½ cup red wine
2 tablespoons dark brown sugar
1 tablespoon white vinegar

1 tablespoon balsamic vinegar
2 tablespoons Worcestershire sauce
   (see note page 98)
1 teaspoon salt
1 teaspoon chili powder
1 teaspoon dry mustard powder
½ teaspoon celery seed
1 garlic clove, minced
⅛ teaspoon hot red pepper sauce

In a plate, combine the flour with the pinch of pepper. Dredge the chicken in the flour, coating both sides.

In a large skillet, melt the margarine over medium heat. Brown the chicken on both sides. Remove the chicken from the skillet; set aside.

Into the same skillet, pour the tomatoes with their liquid, wine, brown sugar, white vinegar, balsamic vinegar, and Worcestershire sauce. Stir to combine. Sprinkle in the salt, chili powder, mustard powder, celery seed, garlic, and hot red pepper sauce.

Bring the sauce to a boil and return the chicken to the skillet. Cover, reduce heat, and simmer for 35-40 minutes or until chicken is cooked through.

Yield: 6 servings

pine nut crusted chicken

This dish is great served hot or at room temperature.

3½ slices white bread	¼ teaspoon salt
½ cup pine nuts	1 egg white
2 tablespoons yellow cornmeal	3 tablespoons Dijon mustard
2 tablespoons fresh parsley	1½ teaspoons water
1 garlic clove	8 boneless, skinless chicken breasts
½ teaspoon cayenne pepper	

Preheat oven to 375 degrees. Spray a large baking pan with nonstick cooking spray.

In the bowl of a food processor fitted with a metal blade, combine the bread, pine nuts, cornmeal, parsley, garlic, cayenne pepper, and salt. Process to fine crumbs. Add the egg white and pulse 2-3 times. Transfer the mixture to a shallow dish.

In a small bowl, combine the mustard and water. Evenly brush the mustard mixture over both sides of each chicken breast. Roll the chicken into the bread crumb mixture, pressing to coat evenly.

Arrange in the prepared pan. Bake, uncovered about 30 minutes or until coating is crisp and brown.

Yield: 8 servings

balsamic-herb rubbed chicken

½ cup firmly packed basil leaves	¼ cup olive oil
½ cup chopped fresh parsley	2 tablespoons Dijon mustard
2 tablespoons chopped fresh rosemary	¾ teaspoon salt
2 tablespoons chopped fresh thyme	¼ teaspoon red pepper flakes
¼ cup balsamic vinegar	2 chickens, cut into ⅛ths

In the bowl of a food processor fitted with a metal blade, place the basil, parsley, rosemary, thyme, vinegar, oil, mustard, salt, and red pepper flakes. Pulse until it forms a coarse herb paste.

Place the chicken pieces in a baking pan and rub each piece with the paste, coating the chicken completely. Cover and refrigerate at least 4 hours or overnight.

Preheat oven to 350 degrees. Bake uncovered for 1 ½ hours. If skin doesn't look crisp, run the chicken under the hot broiler for 1-2 minutes. This dish can also be cooked on an outdoor grill.

Yield: 8 servings

olive chicken

4 tablespoons olive oil, divided
2 garlic cloves, minced, divided
   juice of 1 lemon
   salt
   freshly ground black pepper
6 boneless, skinless chicken breasts
1 medium onion, chopped
1 (16-ounce) can plum tomatoes,
   drained and chopped

18 green olives, pitted and coarsely
   chopped
1 tablespoon fresh parsley, chopped,
   divided
1 teaspoon fresh thyme or ½
   teaspoon dried thyme, divided

Preheat oven to 375 degrees. In a medium bowl, add 2 tablespoons oil, half the minced garlic, the lemon juice, salt, and pepper. Mix well.

Coat the chicken on both sides with the garlic mixture. Lay chicken in a pan in a single layer. Marinate at room temperature for 30 minutes.

In a large skillet, heat the remaining 2 tablespoons of oil over medium heat. Add the onion and remaining garlic. Sauté until onions are translucent, but not brown. Add tomatoes and olives and cook for 15 minutes or until thickened. Stir in ½ the parsley and ½ of the thyme. Remove from heat and spread mixture over chicken. Bake 25-30 minutes or until cooked through. Baste; remove to platter and sprinkle with the rest of the parsley and thyme.

Yield: 6 servings

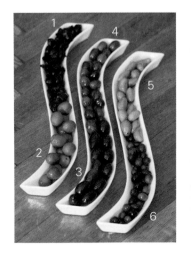

Olives

1 MEDITERRANEAN CURED - *Wrinkly, dried, cured and are sometimes enhanced with spices and aromatics; can be bitter*

2 BELLA DI CERIGNOLA - *Bright, green, and plump, mildly sweet flavored*

3 KALAMATA - *dark purplish Greek olives with a tangy flavor.*

4 BRINE-PACKED BLACK - *these are a bit firmer than kalamata but have the same color and tang*

5 CATALAINE - *Spanish, a muted green color, mild and crisp*

6 NICOISES - *black French olives with a rich but mild taste.*

roast turkey with caramelized onion-balsamic gravy

I love this turkey recipe. The key is the gravy, which rewards all your efforts with a creamy, rich taste. For ease, it can be started the day before or when you put the turkey up to roast. You won't want to wait for the holidays to use this recipe.

Roast Turkey:

- 4 tablespoons olive oil
- 1 teaspoon salt
- 1 teaspoon freshly ground black pepper
- 1 tablespoon paprika
- 1 tablespoon garlic powder

- 3 tablespoons apricot rib sauce or duck sauce
- 1 (10- to 14-pound) turkey, fresh or defrosted
- 8-10 ounces apricot nectar or pineapple juice

Gravy:

- 6 cups chicken stock
- turkey neck and giblets (optional)
- 1 onion, quartered
- 1 bay leaf
- 6 tablespoons margarine

- 2 large onions, halved and thinly sliced
- 1 teaspoon dried rosemary
- 1 teaspoon dried sage
- ⅓ cup all-purpose flour
- ½ cup balsamic vinegar

Roasted Turkey:

Preheat oven to 400 degrees. Make a paste out of the olive oil, salt, pepper, paprika, garlic powder, and apricot rib sauce.

Rub the spice mixture all over the turkey. Place turkey, breast side down, in a large roasting pan. You can sprinkle on more of the pepper, paprika, and garlic powder, if desired. Let turkey come to room temperature for 20 minutes. Bake 2 hours, covered.

Lower the temperature to 350 degrees and uncover. Turn turkey, breast side up, being careful not to prick skin. Bake 1 hour.

Flip turkey over again and baste with apricot nectar or pineapple juice every 15 minutes for ½-1 hour. Turkey is done when juices run clear when pierced with a fork. Place turkey on serving platter; reserve liquid in pan for gravy.

Gravy:

Combine the chicken stock, turkey giblets if desired, quartered onion, and bay leaf in a pot. Simmer about 1 hour or until reduced to 3 cups of liquid, skimming the surface if necessary.

In a large skillet, melt margarine over medium-high heat. Add sliced onions, rosemary, and sage and sauté about 15 minutes or until onions are golden. Add flour; stir 1 minute. Gradually whisk in chicken stock mixture, discarding bay leaf and quartered onion. Boil about 3 minutes or until the gravy thickens, stirring often.

After transferring the turkey to the platter, pour the juices from the pan into a measuring cup. Skim off the fat. Add the juices to the gravy. Add vinegar to the roasting pan. Scrape up the browned bits. Pour the vinegar with the browned bits into small saucepan. Boil about 3-4 minutes or until reduced to ¼ cup. Add to the gravy. Rewarm the gravy and thin with more chicken stock if necessary. Pour over sliced turkey or serve on the side.

Yield: 12-15 servings

tarragon chicken

½ cup flour	1 cup dry white wine	
½ teaspoon black pepper	1 pound sliced mushrooms	
1 teaspoon dried tarragon	1 (14-ounce) can diced tomatoes	
2 chickens, cut in ⅛ths	1 (8-ounce) can tomato sauce	
¼ cup vegetable or canola oil	1 clove garlic, chopped	
¼ cup margarine	fresh parsley, chopped	

Preheat oven to 350 degrees. Place flour, pepper, and tarragon in a large zip-lock bag. Add chicken pieces, in batches, to the bag; shake to coat. Remove chicken, reserving flour mixture.

In a large skillet, heat the oil and margarine over medium-high heat. Add chicken in a single layer to skillet; brown on all sides. Once the chicken browns, remove to a baking pan, reserving the skillet drippings and oil.

Add the reserved flour mixture to the skillet. Whisk in the wine over medium heat until the mixture is thick and smooth.

Pour mixture over chicken. Add mushrooms, tomatoes, tomato sauce, and garlic. Cover and bake 1 hour and 15 minutes or until chicken is done. Garnish with fresh parsley.

Yield: 8 servings

tangy citrus chicken

¾ cup lemonade concentrate, defrosted
¼ cup ketchup
3 tablespoons brown sugar
3 tablespoons white vinegar
1 teaspoon soy sauce
¼ teaspoon ground ginger
¼ teaspoon paprika
¼ teaspoon chili powder
¼ teaspoon garlic powder
¼ teaspoon onion powder
¼ teaspoon dried thyme
¼ teaspoon dried oregano
¼ teaspoon dried basil
¼ teaspoon salt
¼ teaspoon freshly ground black pepper
1 chicken, cut into ⅛ths
½ cup flour
¼ cup canola oil

Preheat oven to 350 degrees. In a medium bowl, mix the lemonade concentrate, ketchup, brown sugar, vinegar, soy sauce, ginger, paprika, chili powder, garlic powder, onion powder, thyme, oregano, basil, salt, and pepper. Set aside.

Dredge the chicken in the flour. In a large pot, heat the oil over medium-high heat. Brown the chicken until the skin is crisp on all sides. Remove the chicken pieces to a baking pan in a single layer.

Pour the spice mixture over the chicken. Bake covered for 1 hour 15 minutes. Uncover and run under the broiler for 2-3 minutes. Watch to make sure the skin doesn't burn.

Yield: 4 servings

pomegranate chicken

This recipe was given to me by Foremost caterers. I was not surprised that the chicken turned out beautifully, with crisp mahogany-colored skin. But I was shocked to find that it was so easy to prepare. The only slight difficulty was in finding the pomegranate syrup and juice. Try a health food store or one that specializes in Mediterranean, Indian, or Persian food items. Alternatively, you can ask your supermarket to special order it. Foremost recommends having your butcher French the breast. However, when I tried using a regular breast with bones, the result was terrific.

6 chicken breasts, with skin (can also use a whole chicken, cut in ⅛ths, with skin)

3 cups pomegranate juice

2 cups pomegranate syrup

8 garlic cloves, roughly chopped

¼ cup chopped fresh mint, extra for garnish

⅛ cup freshly ground black pepper

2 tablespoons margarine

Place the chicken in a zip-lock bag or a shallow plastic container that has a cover. Completely cover with the pomegranate juice, syrup, garlic, mint, and pepper.

Marinade at least overnight or up to 2 nights. Shake the bag or turn the container every so often.

Preheat oven to 350 degrees. Remove chicken from marinade, placing the marinade into a pot. Set aside.

In a separate pan, heat the margarine over high heat. Add the chicken, skin side down, taking care not to splatter the hot margarine. Sear the chicken about 4-6 minutes or until the skin is nice and crisp. As long as your heat is right, the skin may seem like it is sticking a little but it will release once it's perfectly seared.

Place the pot of marinade over a medium flame and boil it about 30 minutes or until it reduces by at least half and is syrupy. Make sure it doesn't burn. Skim continuously to remove the chicken impurities that will rise to the surface.

Remove the chicken to a baking pan. Bake chicken, skin side up, for 40 minutes or until cooked through. Serve with sauce dribbled over it.

Yield: 6 servings

poached chicken in leek broth

This is a very beautiful and healthy dish. The leek ribbons make each cutlet look like a perfectly wrapped present. Complement the colors of the white chicken and green leeks by serving them atop a one or two tone vegetable puree. You can find these in the side dish section on page 211.

4 leeks, divided
6 boneless, skinless chicken breasts
2 bay leaves
   Kosher salt
8 whole black peppercorns

juice of 2 lemons
3 sprigs fresh parsley
1 cup white wine
   chicken broth or chicken bouillon
   diluted with water

Cut the very bottom off 2 of the leeks. Separate each leek into individual long leaves. Clean the leaves. Using a sharp knife, cut each leaf in half so you have long ½-inch ribbon-like strips.

Pour water to depth of 1 inch in a large pot; bring to a boil. Drop the leek ribbons into the boiling water and blanch for 30 seconds or until leek is softened; quickly remove from the water.

Lay 2 leek ribbons to form a plus sign. Place a chicken cutlet in the center. Tie each ribbon around the cutlet, knotting in the middle. Use scissors to trim any long pieces.

Repeat process for all six cutlets. Place the chicken in a single layer in a large pot or heavy skillet. Slice the other two leeks into ½-inch strips. Scatter them over the chicken. Add the bay leaves, salt, peppercorns, lemon juice, parsley sprigs, and wine. Add enough chicken broth to cover the chicken.

Bring the liquid, uncovered, to a boil over high heat. Reduce heat to medium and poach for 15 minutes or until chicken has lost its pink color. If the tops of any of the packets are exposed, spoon some of the poaching liquid over them as they cook.

Yield: 6 servings

chicken oreganata

This is a gorgeous all-in-one meal. I like to use a pretty oven-to-table baking dish to avoid transferring the chicken to a serving platter. Be sure to use fresh oregano leaves and fresh garlic. If you can't find the grape tomatoes, use 2 extra plum tomatoes.

2 plum tomatoes, diced	½ teaspoon Kosher salt
1 cup grape tomatoes, halved	½ teaspoon freshly ground black pepper
4 Yukon gold potatoes, unpeeled and diced	½ teaspoon garlic powder
1 onion, quartered	¼ cup fresh oregano leaves
1 chicken, cut in ⅛ths, with skin	¼ cup olive oil
3 garlic cloves, chopped	

Preheat oven to 450 degrees. In the bottom of a heavy baking dish, place the tomatoes, potatoes, and onions. Place the chicken pieces on top of the vegetables. Sprinkle on the chopped garlic, salt, pepper, garlic powder, and oregano. Drizzle with the oil. Bake uncovered for 45 minutes-1 hour.

Yield: 4 servings

☞ *Creative Flower Vases*
While perusing the aisles of your supermarket, look for interesting cans. Sometimes an eye-popping label can make a witty container for flowers. Look for large cans such as whole tomatoes. Also try pitchers or mugs for a charming touch.

honey mustard cornish hens

I like to use David Elliot 1-pound Cornish hens because each hen amounts to a single serving. A larger 1½- to 2-pound hen will serve 2 people. You can easily cut the hens in half after cooking. I butterfly the hens to cut the cooking time and to make it easier to carve on each person's plate.

4 (1-pound) Cornish hens	black pepper
4 large garlic cloves, thinly sliced	Kosher salt
2 lemons, halved	dried thyme
olive oil	honey mustard, store bought

Preheat oven to 400 degrees. To butterfly the hens, use poultry shears to cut along each side of the backbone; remove the backbone. Use the palm of your hand to flatten each hen. Lay the hens in a flat roasting pan.

With your fingers, gently loosen the skin on the hens. Slide a few pieces of garlic under the skin, around the breast of the hen. Squeeze juice from ½ of lemon under the skin of each hen.

Brush each hen with olive oil. Season with pepper, salt, and thyme. Bake for 30-35 minutes. Remove hens from the oven and set it to broil. Brush each hen with a thin layer of honey mustard.

Return the hens to the oven and broil for 5 minutes. If your honey mustard is the dark variety, broil hens far from the heat or the honey in the mustard will burn. Otherwise, broil 6-8 inches away from heat, watching to make sure it doesn't burn. Less broiling time may be necessary either way.

Yield: 4 servings

artichoke chicken

This chicken gets a thumbs up from friends and relatives for its taste and aroma. I give it two thumbs up for ease. If you want to double the recipe, don't double the ingredients. You won't be able to fit 12 cutlets into a skillet in one batch anyway, so just make the recipe twice. You don't have to clean the pan in between, but this will ensure that all of the chicken will have the amazing flavor of the garlic. Also, if you prepare the dish in advance and reheat it, cook the chicken just until it's no longer pink. Don't overcook the chicken or else it will be dry when reheated the next day.

3 tablespoons margarine	8 ounces sliced mushrooms
8 garlic cloves, minced, divided	1 (14-ounce) can artichoke hearts,
6 boneless, skinless chicken breasts,	packed in water, drained
pounded to an even thicknesss	2 tablespoons white wine
1 tablespoon olive oil	1 tablespoon fresh lemon juice

In a large skillet, melt the margarine. Add ½ the garlic and cook for 1 minute over medium heat. Add the chicken and cook 4-6 minutes per side or until cooked through. Remove to serving platter.

Place the oil into the same skillet. Add the remaining garlic and cook 1 minute. Add the mushrooms and cook for 3 minutes. Use a spatula to scrape up the browned bits. Add the artichokes; cook for 1 minute. Add the wine and lemon juice. There won't be a lot of liquid, but bring it to a boil. Lower the heat and simmer for 5 minutes. Use the spatula to gently break the artichoke hearts apart into chunks. Pour the mushrooms and artichokes over the chicken. Serve immediately.

Yield: 6 servings

hush puppy chicken

I remember Sunday night family dinners at the deli. Hush puppies, knish encrusted hot dogs on a stick, a kid's soul food, was always on my crave list. This chicken dish reminds me of that delicacy with an adult twist.

2 tablespoon canola or vegetable oil	6 puff pastry squares, or puff pastry
1 small onion, chopped	sheets, cut into 6 (5- by 5-inch)
1 cup water	squares
¼ teaspoon salt	deli mustard
1½ tablespoon margarine	6-8 ounces pastrami
⅓ cup nondairy creamer	6 boneless, skinless chicken breasts,
1 cup instant mashed potato flakes	pounded to an even thickness

Preheat oven to 350 degrees. Lightly grease a baking sheet. In a medium saucepan, heat the oil. Add the chopped onion and sauté for 8-10 minutes or until onions are golden. Add the water, salt, and margarine to the saucepan. When margarine is melted, remove the pan from the heat; stir in the nondairy creamer and instant mashed potato flakes. Mix with a fork. Set aside.

Roll out each of the 6 puff pastry squares. Drizzle each with mustard. Lay 3-4 pieces of pastrami in a single layer over the mustard on each square.

Place 1 heaping tablespoon of the mashed potatoes into the center of a chicken cutlet. Roll up both ends of the cutlet towards the center. Place seam side up in the center of the puff pastry. Pull the four corners of the puff pastry square towards the middle to enclose the packet. Place the packet seam side down on the prepared baking sheet. Repeat process with all six cutlets. Bake for 45-50 minutes.

Yield: 6 servings

apricot-almond stuffed chicken

1 tablespoon margarine
2 large onions, chopped
1 (16-ounce) jar apricot jam
1 cup red wine
2 whole chickens or 1 large pullet
2 (6.3-ounce) boxes rice pilaf mix,
  cooked according to package

4 garlic cloves, minced
  paprika
½ cup raisins, optional
½-¾ cup sliced almonds

Preheat oven to 350 degrees. In a large skillet, melt the margarine over medium heat. Add the onions and sauté about 10 minutes or until onions are brown. Add the apricot jam and the wine to the pan; simmer 3-4 minutes or until jam is melted. Remove from heat; set aside.

Stuff the cooked rice pilaf into the cavity of the chickens or pullet. Don't overstuff; you may have some left over. Rub the garlic all over the skin of the poultry. Sprinkle with paprika and rub in.

Pour the onion mixture over the poultry and massage it all over the skin. Sprinkle with more paprika. Toss on the raisins, if desired, and the almonds. Bake uncovered for 1½ hours, basting occasionally.

Yield: 6-8 servings

chicken with brandy and mushrooms Meat

It's very easy to double this recipe. You need a skillet large enough to hold 2 cut-up chickens and sauce. If you don't have a large skillet, you can brown the chicken in batches and then place the pieces in a large roasting pan. Double the sauce, following the directions below, but instead of placing the chicken back into the pan, pour the sauce over the chicken pieces in the roasting pan. Then bake in a 350 degree preheated oven uncovered for 1½ hours, basting every 15 minutes.

	vegetable oil	¼	cup brandy
	flour	⅓	cup red wine
	salt	½	cup chicken stock
	freshly ground black pepper	4	ounces sliced mushrooms
1	chicken, cut in ⅛ths, skin removed	⅓	pound or 6 ounces cooked
3	garlic cloves, 2 chopped and 1		smoked turkey, cubed
	minced	1½	teaspoons tomato paste
2	sprigs fresh thyme, stems removed		

In a very large skillet, heat vegetable oil to depth of ½ inch over medium heat. Season the flour with salt and pepper. Dredge the chicken pieces in the flour.

When oil is hot enough (dip a wooden toothpick or skewer into it and it should bubble), brown the chicken on both sides; remove from pan. Set aside.

Discard most of the oil. Add the garlic and sauté 3 minutes. Add the thyme leaves, brandy, wine, chicken stock, mushrooms, turkey, and tomato paste; bring to a boil.

Return the chicken to the pan. Lower the heat. Cover and simmer for 1 hour.

Yield: 4 servings

chicken provence
with cider-roasted vegetables

This bountiful dinner of perfectly roasted chicken and root vegetables is so simple to prepare. For the peppercorn medley, mix together black, white, green, and pink peppercorns found in the spice section. You can crush them yourself with a pepper grinder or the back of a spoon, or choose the kind that comes with a grinder built right into the spice bottle.

3 beets, peeled and cut into wedges
3 Idaho potatoes, peeled and cut into chunks
3 parsnips, peeled and cut into 2-inch chunks
1½ cups baby carrots
2 large Vidalia onions, cut into chunks
4 tablespoons dark brown sugar
4 tablespoons olive oil
2 tablespoons apple-cider vinegar
1 whole chicken
3 tablespoons margarine, softened at room temperature

¾ teaspoon dried tarragon leaves
¾ teaspoon dried rosemary leaves, slightly crushed
¼ teaspoon dried oregano
½ teaspoon ground peppercorn medley
½ teaspoon ground marjoram
½ teaspoon dried thyme leaves
2 teaspoons chopped flat leaf parsley paprika

Preheat oven to 450 degrees. Place the beets, potatoes, parsnips, carrots, and onions in a large roasting pan.

In a medium bowl, whisk together the brown sugar, oil, and vinegar. Pour mixture over the vegetables and toss to coat well. Place the chicken, breast side down, in the center of the roasting pan (it can be on top of some of the vegetables).

Place the softened margarine into a small bowl. Sprinkle in the tarragon, rosemary, oregano, peppercorns, marjoram, thyme, and parsley. Using a spoon, stir the herbs into the margarine so they are evenly distributed into a paste.

Using your fingers, gently lift the skin of the chicken and rub some of the herbed margarine under the skin. Rub the rest of the margarine evenly over the outside of the chicken.

Generously sprinkle with a lot of paprika, rubbing into the skin of the chicken. Place in the oven uncovered and roast for 1 hour.

Lower the heat to 350 degrees. Stir the vegetables. Flip the chicken over and sprinkle the top of the chicken generously with paprika. Roast for another 15 minutes. Remove from oven and let stand 10 minutes before serving.

Yield: 4 servings

sun-dried tomato and garlic-crusted chicken Meat

5 slices of firm white bread, crusts
  removed
½ cup oil-packed sun-dried tomatoes,
  drained; 4 tablespoons oil
  reserved, divided
2 fresh basil leaves

2-3 garlic cloves
  salt
  freshly ground black pepper
6 boneless, skinless chicken breasts,
  pounded to an even thickness

Preheat oven to 375 degrees. In the bowl of a food processor fitted with a metal blade, pulse the bread until it forms thick bread crumbs. Add the tomatoes, 2 tablespoons of the reserved oil, basil, and the garlic. Pulse until coarsely chopped and well combined. Season with salt and pepper.

Heat 2 tablespoons reserved oil in a large skillet. Add the chicken and cook for 2 minutes on each side.

Transfer the chicken to a baking sheet. Spoon the bread crumb mixture over each cutlet, pressing to adhere. Bake for 10 minutes or until heated through.

Yield: 6 servings

The Scoop on Skillets
When a recipe calls for a medium skillet, use one with an 8-inch diameter.
When a recipe calls for a large skillet, use one with a 10-inch diameter.
When a recipe calls for a very large skillet, use one with a 12- to 14-inch diameter.
My favorite skillet is a nonstick 14-inch one. It easily holds two cut chickens. It's a real time saver when I cook for a crowd, because I can double a recipe and not have to make it in batches.

maple-glazed turkey roast

Your guests are sure to gobble up this tasty dish. I am always looking for ways to serve a boneless turkey roast. This very healthy meal is a nice change from chicken. Using a boneless turkey roast is a lot simpler than preparing a whole turkey. My supermarket carries whole turkey breasts on the bone, which also work well. Turkey dries out easily, so keep an eye on the time. Cut into the roast if necessary to make sure it is no longer pink. But make sure not to overcook it.

1 (5-pound) boneless turkey roast with skin, tied
3 tablespoons olive oil
2 cloves garlic, minced
1 teaspoon dried marjoram, crushed
1 teaspoon finely grated fresh orange zest (optional)

¼ teaspoon salt
¼ teaspoon freshly ground black pepper
½ cup plus 2 tablespoons maple syrup (not pancake syrup)
¼ cup orange juice
½ cup dry white wine

Heat oven to 450 degrees. In a small bowl, combine the oil, garlic, marjoram, orange zest, salt, and pepper. Rub this spice mixture all over the turkey.

Place the turkey in a pan and roast for ½ hour. In a small bowl, combine the maple syrup and orange juice. Pour the maple syrup glaze over the turkey. Cover loosely with foil. Reduce the temperature to 350 degrees and continue to roast for another 1½ hours or until it reaches an internal temperature of 165 degrees, basting occasionally.

Let turkey stand covered with foil for 15 minutes. (It will rise 5 degrees during standing time.) Meanwhile, pour the glaze from the turkey into a small pot. Add the wine; cook over medium heat on the stovetop about 3-4 minutes or until the liquid is reduced by half. Pour the glaze over the turkey.

Yield: 8-10 servings

seared duck breasts

Duck is perfect for special fall and winter nights. This simple recipe is no more difficult to prepare than a chicken cutlet. I couldn't decide which of these excellent sauces to include in the book, so I am giving you both. The duck preparation remains the same for either. Follow the cooking directions for duck that is medium-rare, the way it should be served.

Duck:

4 large boneless duck breasts (they may come as 1 butterflied breast; if so slice down the middle to separate them)
2 garlic cloves, minced

zest of 1 orange
juice of 1 orange
1 teaspoon dried thyme
salt
freshly ground black pepper

Blueberry Port Sauce:

6 ounces fresh blueberries
1¼ cups port wine

1 tablespoon red currant jelly
1 teaspoon Dijon mustard

Balsamic, Rosemary, and Shallot Sauce:

1 tablespoon olive oil
6 shallots, finely sliced
leaves from 4 sprigs fresh rosemary (about 2 tablespoons)
½ cup red wine

½ cup balsamic vinegar
¾ cup chicken stock
1 tablespoon red currant jelly
4 tablespoons margarine, diced

Duck:

Score the duck breasts with a tight pattern of Xs in the skin with a sharp knife. This will allow the copious amount of fat to render evenly and promote even browning.

In a small bowl, combine the minced garlic, orange zest, orange juice, and thyme. Place the duck breasts into a zip-lock bag. Pour the marinade over them. Place in refrigerator and marinate for 1-3 hours, turning occasionally.

Preheat oven to 375 degrees. Preheat a large, ungreased flat-bottomed sauté pan on medium-high heat for 5 minutes. Remove the duck from the marinade. Generously season the duck with salt and pepper, rubbing the seasonings into the scored fat. Sear the breasts, skin side down, for 8 minutes or until browned. Turn the breasts over and cook for another 4-5 minutes, making sure all of the skin is browned. If necessary, use tongs to hold the breasts on their side to brown skin all sides. Carefully pour off the fat as it accumulates, if necessary. Place in the preheated oven for 10 minutes. Remove and set aside to rest for at least 10 minutes.

Blueberry Port Sauce:

In a medium saucepan, cook 3 ounces blueberries, port, and jelly over a high heat for 8-10 minutes or until it reduces to a thin consistency. Remove from heat and add the mustard and remaining 3 ounces fresh blueberries.

Balsamic, Rosemary, and Shallot Sauce:

In a medium saucepan, heat the oil over medium heat. Add the shallots and rosemary; cook for about 10 minutes or until caramelized. Add the wine and balsamic vinegar. Keep the heat high and boil about 3-4 minutes or until reduced to a thick syrup. Add the stock and boil until it reduces by half. Add the jelly and cook for 5 minutes. Add the margarine and stir to thicken the sauce.

To serve, cut the duck across the grain (not lengthwise) into ¼-inch-thick slices and fan on a plate. Cover with sauce.

Yield: 4 servings

orange chicken

Meat

4 tablespoons orange juice	¾ cup whole almonds, shelled but
4 tablespoons orange marmalade	with the skins left on (unblanched)
6 teaspoons Dijon mustard	¼ cup fresh parsley
1 chicken, cut into ⅛ths or ¼ths	¼ teaspoon salt
2 slices white bread	

In a small bowl, mix the orange juice, marmalade, and mustard. Dip each chicken piece in the marinade mixture, placing them in a pan in a single layer. Pour the extra marinade over the chicken. Set aside.

In the bowl of a food processor fitted with a metal blade, place the bread, almonds, parsley, and salt. Pulse until coarse crumbs are formed. Don't over-process or the mixture will get pasty.

Pour the crumbs into a plate. Dip each chicken piece into the crumb mixture, heavily coating all sides. Return the chicken to the baking pan in a single layer. Place in the refrigerator for 1 hour or up to 8 hours.

Preheat oven to 350 degrees. Bake for 1 hour and 15 minutes, uncovered. If the crumb coating starts to burn, cover the pan with foil.

Yield: 4 servings

honey & pecan-crusted chicken
with apricot chutney

Apricot Chutney:

- 1 (16 ounce) jar duck sauce
- 1 cup dried apricots, chopped

Honey & Pecan-Crusted Chicken:

- ½ cup honey
- ¼ teaspoon salt
- ¼ teaspoon freshly ground black pepper
- ½ teaspoon paprika
- 2 teaspoons garlic powder
- 1½ cups corn flake crumbs
- ¾ cup chopped pecans
- 6 boneless, skinless chicken breasts, pounded flat to an even thickness

Combine the duck sauce with the chopped apricots. Let the chutney sit for at least an hour.

Preheat oven to 400 degrees. Lightly spray a cookie sheet with nonstick cooking spray.

In a medium bowl, combine the honey, salt, pepper, paprika, and garlic powder. Whisk to combine. In a shallow dish, combine the corn flake crumbs with pecans.

Brush the chicken cutlets with the honey mixture and then dredge in the pecan mixture. Place in a single layer in the prepared pan; spray the tops with cooking spray. Bake for 20 minutes.

Serve the chicken with the apricot chutney.

Yield: 6 servings

 Cutting Dried Fruit

When cutting dried fruit spray your knife blade with nonstick cooking spray. This will prevent the fruit from sticking to the knife.

n Israel, the holidays of Shmini Atzeret and Simchat Torah are on the same day, following Sukkot. Outside of Israel, we celebrate them as separate days in succession. As such, they take on different characters. Shmini Atzeret is the quiet aftermath of Sukkot. Traditionally, it is viewed as an intimate moment between God and the Jewish people, as though He were saying, "Now that Sukkot is over and the guests have gone home, let's just spend one more day together, without ceremony or fanfare."

The mood of Simchat Torah, however, evolved through Jewish history as one of exultant celebration over our prize possession — the Torah. The source of Jewish belief and practice, the Torah is the ultimate guidebook. The Torah text is divided into sections that are read publicly on a weekly basis. This cycle is completed on Simchat Torah, and the new reading begins again, immediately after its completion. Though Shavuot is the anniversary of the giving of the Torah to the Jews at Mount Sinai, Simchat Torah is the time for celebrating our never-ending dedication to its study.

In the synagogue on Simchat Torah, every Torah scroll is removed from the ark and taken in grand procession around the synagogue seven times. (Each circling is called a *hakafah*, collectively *hakafot*.) The children are elated — merrily lining up behind the Torahs with their

colorful flags and mini Torah scrolls. At each *hakafah*, the intensity of joy builds; the singing becomes louder, the dancing more ecstatic.

The jubilation of a community is always greater than that of a private *simchah*. The sounds you hear are the sounds of the people of Israel, celebrating for generations the precious gift entrusted to them. They are celebrating their Jewish heritage together. In the process, their children absorb the idea that the Torah — which is the central focus of so much fun and exaltation on Simchat Torah — is both the source of happiness and the national treasure of the Jewish people.

simchat torah menu

APPETIZER:
Chicken Negamaki
page 22

SALAD:
Endive Salad with Shallot Vinaigrette
page 84

ENTREE:
Roasted Shoulder of Veal in Mushrooms
pages 136

SIDE DISHES:
Scalloped Potatoes
page 206
Caramelized Carrots
page 212

DESSERT:
Chocolate Cookies and Cream Trifle
page 275
Marble Fudge Cookies
page 269

Bursting with joy, our lively Simchat Torah table combines minimum fuss with maximum aesthetic impact. Begin with a floor-length orange tablecloth; then layer it with colored place mats and napkins (which are actually inexpensive dish towels and dish cloths). Place drinking glasses on rubber hot pad holders. Put wine and liquor glasses at each setting for the inevitable "*L'Chaim!*" Use orange organza to tie up each chair with a bolero for festive personality and charm. Perky dishes and modern silverware finish off the table with a vivacious air. Their haphazard placement adds to the appeal. Multicolored candy strewn across the table will delight both children and adults.

At the center of this enchanting table is a large cantaloupe. Cut a hole into the top where the stem grows. Shake out the seeds and pour water into the melon. Fill this unique vase with gorgeous, orange gerbera daisies. (Set a cup in the hole to hold the water and the cantaloupe will still be edible later on.) Our arrangement was set on a pewter candleholder, but it could be supported in any number of ways.

A charming touch is to serve foods resembling rolled Torah scrolls. In that spirit, we chose Chicken Negimaki to begin the meal. This rolled chicken dish, with its colorful pepper and scallion strips, offers an innovative angle on traditional fare. Fun and color pop up again with a multicolored, multi-textured salad. The rolled and tied veal roast is a delicious star of this meal. Scalloped Potatoes and Caramelized Carrots also excel in their supporting roles. We finish off this meal with luscious Chocolate Cookies and Cream Trifle and Marble Fudge Cookies. You'll have a hard time pulling yourself away from the table!

wine list

CLOS DU NOUYS, VOUVRAY

The Asian-flavored Chicken Negemaki calls for an off-dry or very fruity wine
and this French wine would be a lovely choice.

ROBERTO COHEN/ABARBANEL CLOS DE VOUGEOT
ROBERTO COHEN/ABARBANEL GRAND CRU
ROBERTO COHEN/ABARBANEL POMMARD
ROBERTO COHEN/ABARBANEL ALOXE CORTON
HAGAFEN PINOT NOIR
HERZOG BROUILLY

There are many excellent choices for Roasted Shoulder of Veal.
Burgundy is a classic pairing with veal and mushrooms.

The burgundies we recommend range in different prices,
the most expensive, Grand Cru, retails for about $400 a bottle.
The velvety Hagafen Pinot Noir is elegant and graceful
with hints of berries and earth integrated with notes of vanilla,
is another wonderful choice for this classic dish.

A Crus beaujolais, such as the Herzog Brouilly, offers an everyday value.

SABRA LIQUEUR

Cookies and Cream Trifle and Marble Fudge Cookies
go well with this liqueur, alone, or poured into coffee.

Rack of Lamb with
fig-port-shallot sauce

meat

braised lamb shanks
with root vegetables and barley

3   tablespoons olive oil
8   lamb shanks, tied with kitchen twine
    salt
    coarsely ground black pepper
½   cup pearl barley, uncooked
1   tablespoon olive oil
2   stalks celery, coarsely chopped
2   carrots, peeled and coarsely
    chopped
1   large potato, peeled and cut into
    chunks
2   small turnips, peeled and cut into
    small chunks

2   parsnips, peeled and cut into chunks
1   large leek, cleaned very well and
    sliced into into 8 pieces
2   onions, peeled and quartered
5   cloves garlic, peeled and cut into
    quarters
2   cups port wine
1   cup red wine
10 ounces chicken stock (fresh or
    canned)

Preheat oven to 350 degrees. Heat 3 tablespoons olive oil in a large soup pot over medium-high heat until very hot and almost smoking.

Season the shanks on both sides with salt and pepper. In 2 or 3 batches as not to crowd the pot, sear the shanks in the oil about 4-5 minutes per side or until golden brown on all sides. As the shanks are done, remove them and place in a large baking dish or tin in a single layer. Sprinkle with the pearl barley, set aside.

To the pot, add 1 tablespoon of olive oil, celery, carrot, potato, turnip, parsnip, leek, onion, and garlic. Cook until shiny, about 10 minutes, stirring occasionally to make sure no vegetables stick to the bottom of the pot. Add the port and the red wine. Let it simmer over the heat, at a low boil, about 10 minutes or until the liquid reduces by half. Add the chicken stock.

Pour the vegetables and wine stock over the lamb shanks. Cover tightly with foil and bake for 1½ hours or until tender. Can be made 2 days in advance.

Yields: 4 servings

rack of lamb with fig-port-shallot sauce

This is my all time favorite way to prepare lamb. I save it for special occasions and always receive accolades from my family and friends. This recipe was inspired by one in Food & Wine magazine. Its dramatic presentation makes for an incredible dinner that is sure to impress. The fig sauce turns a gorgeous amber color. The flavors come together in a way that makes you feel like you've just dined in the most expensive restaurant, without ever leaving your driveway.

4 tablespoons olive oil, divided
2 teaspoons dried rosemary
2 teaspoons dried minced thyme
2 shallots
2 racks of baby lamb chops, 8-9 chops per rack; have butcher French the bones

1 cup port wine, divided
8 fresh Mission figs or 6 dried figs, cut into quarters
½ cup chicken stock

Preheat oven to 450 degrees. In a food processor fitted with a metal blade, process 2 tablespoons olive oil, rosemary, thyme, and shallots 30-45 seconds or until a thick paste forms.

Rub the herb paste into the lamb. Heat 2 tablespoons olive oil in a medium oven-proof skillet. Add the lamb, fat side down, and cook over a high heat for 5 minutes. Turn the lamb and cook for an additional minute so that both sides are brown.

Add ½ cup port to the skillet. Place the skillet in the oven and roast for 18 minutes. If your skillet is not oven-proof cover the handles with foil.

Remove the skillet from the oven. Place the lamb on a platter; cover with foil to keep warm. Add the remaining ½ cup of port and the figs to the skillet. Bring to a simmer. Use a spatula to loosen the brown bits from the pan. Add the stock and simmer for 3-4 minutes. The sauce will thicken and be a nice amber color. Pour sauce over the lamb and serve.

Yield: 4 servings

Table Setting Ideas

Every aspect of a table setting adds to its appeal and ambiance. Scatter rose petals, real or silk, for a gorgeous touch to any table. Or completely cover a table with autumn leaves, then top with a clear plastic cloth. Try using an old-fashioned quilt or silk scarf as a tablecloth. Pieces of trailing ivy draped across the table or cut into napkin rings also work beautifully.

The Well-Dressed Table

1 Bread and butter plate with butter knife	11 Fish knife
2 Coffee cup and saucer	12 Soup spoon
3-4 Dessert spoon and cake fork	13 Soup bowl
5 Red wine	14 Appetizer plate
6 White wine	15 Dinner plate
7 Water glass	16 Charger
8 Champagne and sparkling wine flute	17 Fish fork
9 Brandy snifter	18 Salad fork
10 Dinner knife	19 Dinner fork

herb-crusted silver tip roast

1 shallot, peeled and quartered	2 teaspoons dried sage
4 cloves garlic, peeled	3 teaspoons Kosher or coarse salt
4 teaspoons olive oil	1½ teaspoons ground black pepper
2 teaspoons dried thyme leaves	1 (4- to 5-pound) silver tip roast, tied

Preheat oven to 400 degrees. In the bowl of a food processor fitted with a metal blade, chop the shallot and garlic. Add the oil. Pulse 1-2 times. Remove the garlic mixture to a small bowl. Add the thyme, sage, salt, and pepper. Stir to combine.

Pat the meat dry with paper towels. Place it in a roasting pan. Rub the meat all over with the herb paste.

Cover and chill 2-3 hours. (If you skip this step, reduce the cooking time. During the last 15-20 minutes, cut into the meat to make sure it is not getting well done.)

Bake uncovered for 30 minutes. Lower heat to 350 degrees. Bake for 1½ hours or until desired degree of doneness. Don't cook longer than 2½ hours or the meat will toughen. Also, keep in mind that the meat will continue to cook for about 15 minutes after you take it out of the oven. (see beef roasting guide on page 133)

Let meat stand for 15-20 minutes before slicing. The juices will return to the center of the roast, making it moist and easier to carve.

Yield: 8 servings

sweet-and-sour brisket

So simple yet so delicious, this dish is perfect when you have no time to fuss in the kitchen.

1 (32-ounce) jar sauerkraut, partly drained
5 pounds beef brisket
1 (28-ounce) can whole, peeled tomatoes
1 (16-ounce) box dark brown sugar

Preheat oven to 350 degrees. Pour the sauerkraut over the brisket. Add the tomatoes with their liquid. Sprinkle with the brown sugar. Cover with foil and bake for 3 hours.

Yield: 8-10 servings

barbecue brisket

This is a wonderfully flavored brisket that gets away from the sweet-and-sour type. The beer tenderizes the meat so if you are using a larger brisket, you can double the other ingredients; but use only 1½ times the amount of beer or the meat will get too soft.

1 (5-pound) brisket	4 cloves garlic, minced
1 teaspoon salt	1 cup chili sauce
½ teaspoon black pepper	1 cup water
½ teaspoon paprika	¼ cup fresh parsley, chopped
1 onion, chopped	1 (10-ounce) bottle of beer
2 stalks celery, chopped	fresh parsley

Preheat oven to 325 degrees. Wash and dry the brisket, cutting away most of visible fat. Sprinkle the brisket with salt, pepper, and paprika.

Place the brisket, fat side up, in a heavy baking pan. Surround with the onions, celery, and garlic. Pour chili sauce on top of the brisket. Slowly pour the water into the pan, around the brisket. Sprinkle with the parsley.

Bake, uncovered, for 1 hour. Remove from oven and pour the beer over the brisket. Do this slowly so it doesn't wash off the chili sauce. Cover the brisket and cook 3 hours longer or until tender.

Cool to room temperature. Place in refrigerator. Remove any accumulated fat from the top. Slice and reheat in the sauce.

Garnish with a sprinkling of fresh minced parsley.

Yield: 10 servings

marinated silver tip roast beef

An inexpensive thermometer is a must for expensive roasts like this one. Timing is crucial. Since all ovens are different, use the 1 hour cooking time as a guide but check the thermometer for perfect results. It will have the measures for rare, medium, and well done marked.

Marinated Roast:

1 cup red wine	2 cloves garlic, minced
grated zest and juice of 1 large orange	1½ teaspoons dried rosemary
⅓ cup soy sauce	1 teaspoon dried thyme
⅓ cup olive oil	½ teaspoon whole black peppercorns
¼ cup balsamic vinegar	1 (5-pound) silver tip roast

Spice Rub:

1 tablespoon olive oil	½ teaspoon black pepper
½ teaspoon salt	½ teaspoon paprika

Marinated Roast:

In a cruet or large bowl, whisk or mix the wine, orange zest, orange juice, soy sauce, oil, balsamic vinegar, garlic, rosemary, thyme, and peppercorns.

Place the roast in a baking pan. Pour the marinade over the roast. Cover and refrigerate for at least 1 hour or up to 4 hours. Drain the roast and let it come to room temperature, about 1 hour. Preheat oven to 425 degrees.

Spice Rub:

Make a paste of the olive oil, salt, black pepper, and paprika. Rub it into the silver tip. Roast in the oven for 1 hour, for medium-rare.

Let stand 10-15 minutes before carving to give the juices time to come to the center of the roast.

Yield: 8-10 servings

Beef Roasting Guide
Thermometer reading of the meat's internal temperature:
Rare = 135-140 degrees
Medium = 155-160 degrees
Well done = 165-170 degrees

challah-stuffed veal roulade

I've tried this recipe with a stuffed breast of veal, but it is fatty and a bit unwieldy to eat with "Flintstone" like proportions. This cut of meat is prettier and easier to manage. You'll need 10 pieces of kitchen twine to close the brisket up with. Have them cut and prepared in advance. Wooden toothpicks are good to have on hand as well.

Challah Stuffing:

- 2 teaspoons olive oil
- 1 onion, finely chopped
- 3 cloves garlic, minced and divided
- ¾ pound chopped veal
- 6 medium cremini mushrooms, sliced, or 4 ounces sliced mushrooms

- ¼ cup red wine
- ¼ cup fresh parsley, chopped
- 2 cups cubed challah (roughly 2 challah rolls or ½ medium challah remove most of crust)
- salt
- black pepper

Veal Brisket:

- 1 (5-pound) veal brisket
  paprika
- 2 cups beer

- 2 cups chicken stock
  parsley

Challah Stuffing:

Preheat oven to 500 degrees. In a large skillet, heat the oil and the onion over medium-high heat for 6-7 minutes. Add 1 minced garlic clove. Add the chopped veal and brown. Mix in the mushrooms; saute 3-4 minutes. Remove from heat. Add wine, remaining garlic, chopped parsley, challah cubes, salt, and pepper.

Prepare the Veal:

Lay the stuffing in a long mound down the length of the veal brisket. Using the prepared kitchen twine, wrap the two sides of the brisket to form a roll covering the stuffing. Tie at 2-inch intervals; use toothpicks as needed to seal the ends.

Place veal in a baking pan; sprinkle with paprika. Place in hot oven and roast for 20 minutes. Lower to 350 degrees; pour chicken stock and beer over the veal. Tightly cover the pan with foil and bake for 1½ hours longer, basting every so often.

Remove to a platter and cover loosely with foil to keep warm. Pour remaining liquid into a small pot and cook over medium-high heat until reduced by a third.

Remove and discard string from veal roll; slice. Serve with sauce; sprinkle the top with fresh parsley for garnish.

Yield: 8-10 servings

---

grilled marinated london broil

In our house, my husband is king of the grill. However, his castle is not well equipped. Instead of basting the steak gingerly with a brush and marinade, he removes the steak from the grill and, by hand, plunges it back into the bag that it had been marinating in. I must admit the results are fabulous. The "plunging" occurs 3-4 times during the cooking process. The marinade may seem very sweet, but all of the sugars burn off while the meat grills.

2½ pounds London broil	¼ cup honey
½ cup soy sauce	1 teaspoon ground ginger
½ cup teriyaki sauce	1 teaspoon ground black pepper
⅓ cup mild-flavored molasses	1 tablespoon sugar
⅓ cup lemon juice	2 teaspoons garlic powder
½ cup vegetable or peanut oil	

Score the meat on both sides by making shallow, diagonal cuts ¼ inch deep at 1-inch intervals forming a diamond pattern. Place the meat in a large zip-lock bag.

Combine the soy sauce, teriyaki, molasses, lemon juice, oil, honey, ginger, pepper, sugar, and garlic powder.

Pour the marinade into the bag over the meat, tossing to coat. Refrigerate 4 hours or overnight.

Spray the grill with nonstick cooking spray. Preheat grill to medium-hot heat.

Remove meat from marinade, reserving marinade in the bag. Grill, basting occasionally, for 10 minutes on each side for medium-rare or until desired degree of doneness.

Transfer steak to carving board; let stand 5 minutes. Cut across the grain into thin strips. Arrange on a platter and serve.

Yield: 8 servings

🖝 *Marinade Tips*

For marinades to permeate deeply into your meat, score or prick steaks all over. Discard meat marinade once it has been used. If you plan to reuse it with the grilled food, boil the sauce to remove any contamination from the uncooked meat.

roasted shoulder of veal in mushrooms Meat

I got this recipe from my friend's mother-in-law. The night that I prepared it for a taste-testing party I listed it on the evaluation form as Mrs. Ratzker's Veal Roast. This dish was the hit of the evening. One taster commented, "I know Mr. Ratzker and now I know why he's always smiling."

1 (4- to 5-pound) boneless shoulder veal roast, rolled and tied in butcher string
  Kosher or regular salt
  black pepper
4 cloves garlic, peeled and roughly chopped, divided
15 dried porcini or other dried mushrooms (about ½-1 ounce)
½ cup white wine

5 tablespoons vegetable or canola oil, divided
3 bay leaves
3 onions, 1 chopped, 2 cut into rings
1 ounce dried cremini mushrooms or other dried mushrooms
4 tablespoons margarine
4 tablespoons all-purpose flour
3 tablespoons deli mustard

Rub the veal with salt and pepper. Make 15 small cuts along the top and sides of the roast. Stick a garlic piece and a dry mushroom into each hole.

Place the rest of the chopped garlic, wine, 2 tablespoons oil, bay leaves, and the chopped onion into a zip-lock bag. Place the veal into the bag and massage the mixture into the roast. Seal the bag and let marinate in the refrigerator, at least 4 hours or preferably overnight.

Remove the veal from the refrigerator and bring to room temperature. Meanwhile, place the 1-ounce of dry mushrooms in a small bowl and cover with ½ cup warm water. Let it reconstitute for 20 minutes. Set aside.

In a large pot, melt the margarine and add the remaining 3 tablespoons of oil. Fry the onion rings over medium heat for 15 minutes or until soft and golden, stirring occasionally to keep from sticking to the pot.

Remove the veal from the bag, reserving the liquid and contents; pat the roast dry with paper towels. Rub the flour all over the veal.

Turn the heat up slightly. Place the veal into the pot, pushing the onions to the sides. Make sure the veal sizzles when it hits the pot; if it doesn't your oil is not yet hot enough. Brown the veal on all sides, about 4-5 minutes per side. If the roast sticks a little, it will release itself when the moisture is gone and the meat is properly sealed. If it is really sticking, then your heat is too high; turn the heat down just slightly.

Add the reserved liquid and contents from the zip-lock bag. Add the reconstituted mushrooms and the liquid they were soaking in.

Turn the heat to low and cook covered for 2 hours. Turn the veal over a few times during cooking.

When the roast is done, remove it from the pot. Add the mustard to the gravy and onions in the pot and mix well.

Place the veal back into the pot or transfer the gravy and the veal to a disposable tin. Let the roast cool completely. Refrigerate and cut when cold. If you cut the veal while it's warm it will fall apart. Rewarm the sliced veal with the gravy and serve.

Yield: 7-8 servings

tangy country-style ribs   Meat

	salt	¼	cup Worcestershire sauce
	black pepper		(see note page 98)
4	pounds very meaty beef spareribs	½	cup chili sauce
5	cloves garlic, each cut in half	2	cloves garlic, minced
1	cup dark or light brown sugar	1	teaspoon dry mustard
¼	cup ketchup	½	teaspoon ground black pepper
¼	cup soy sauce		

Preheat oven to 350 degrees. Salt and pepper the ribs. Place the ribs in a baking tin. Sprinkle with the garlic halves. Wrap the dish very tightly in aluminum foil. Bake 1½ hours. Unwrap the baking pan and drain all of the drippings; set aside.

In a medium bowl, combine the brown sugar, ketchup, soy sauce, Worcestershire sauce, chili sauce, minced garlic, dry mustard, and black pepper. Stir to combine.

Pour over the ribs. Marinate at room temperature for an hour or refrigerate overnight, just bring back to room temperature for 20 minutes before cooking.

Preheat the oven to 350 degrees. Bake the ribs for 30-40 minutes, basting with the rib sauce. The ribs can also be grilled.

Yields: 8 servings

italian meatballs and spaghetti

I know many excellent Kosher cooks, yet as a group we just haven't got meatballs down pat. Most that I have eaten are either bathed in cranberry sauce or dumped into a watery sauce. No judgments here, but for more of an authentic Italian dinner, try this version. It is a combination of recipes from two little old Italian ladies that I know. Meatballs are like children to them; their sauce provides real Italian nachas. Grab some garlic bread and Mangia!

Meatballs:

2 pounds very fresh ground beef
4 slices white bread, crusts removed
¼ cup seasoned dry bread crumbs
1 large egg
½ teaspoon freshly ground black pepper
½ teaspoon dried basil, crumbled by hand

½ teaspoon dried oregano, crumbled by hand
½ teaspoon garlic powder
½ teaspoon onion powder
¾ cup warm water
olive oil
vegetable or canola oil

Sauce:

3 cloves garlic, chopped
1 medium onion, finely chopped
1 (28-ounce) can crushed tomatoes
1 (28-ounce) can whole peeled tomatoes in puree, roughly chopped
1 (6-ounce) can tomato paste
1 teaspoon kosher salt
½ teaspoon freshly ground black pepper

2 teaspoons sugar
½ teaspoon dried red pepper flakes
3 teaspoons fresh basil leaves, or ½ teaspoon dried
½ teaspoon dried oregano, crumbled by hand

1 pound spaghetti

Meatballs:

Place the ground beef into a large mixing bowl. In the bowl of a food processor fitted with a metal blade, process the bread to make thick bread crumbs. Add this bread to the beef. Toss in the dry bread crumbs, egg, pepper, basil, oregano, garlic powder, onion powder, and water. Using your hands, gingerly toss to lightly combine so the ingredients are evenly distributed.

In a large pot, over medium heat, pour equal amounts of olive and vegetable oil to a depth of ½ inch.

Lightly form the meat into golf ball-size balls. (Packing the meat mixture too tightly will result in tough meatballs.) When oil is hot enough, add the meatballs and fry for 6-8 minutes or until brown on all sides. You may need to do this in batches. Set aside meatballs.

When all of the meatballs are done, spill out most of the oil, leaving some of it and the brown bits from the meat in the pot.

Sauce:

Add the chopped garlic to the pot and let it soak up the oil for a few minutes. Heat the oil and garlic over medium-low heat for 2 minutes. Add the onion and sauté for 5-6 minutes or until onion becomes tender and garlic is fragrant. Use a wooden spoon to loosen the brown bits. Add the crushed tomatoes, whole tomatoes, and tomato paste. Simmer, don't boil, for 10-15 minutes.

Add the salt, pepper, sugar, red pepper flakes, basil, and oregano. Simmer for 10 minutes. Add the meatballs to the pot. Cover and simmer on low for ½ hour.

Prepare pasta, cooked al dente according to package directions. Serve the meatballs and sauce over the spaghetti.

Yield: 8 servings

ა⁊

dijon veal chops with shallot sauce Meat

1⅓ cups dry white wine		freshly ground black pepper
2 cups beef broth (can be made with beef bouillon cubes and water)	6	tablespoons Dijon mustard
1 shallot, minced	1½	cups dry bread crumbs
1 teaspoon crumbled dried rosemary	¼	cup (½ stick) margarine, cut into 4 pieces
4 (1-inch-thick) veal chops		

In a medium stockpot, combine wine, beef broth, shallot, and rosemary. Bring to a boil and reduce heat. Cook about 15-20 minutes or until the sauce reduces to ⅓ cup. Set aside, keeping warm.

Sprinkle the veal chops with black pepper. Spread with the mustard and coat with the bread crumbs. Shake off excess bread crumbs; loose bread crumbs in the pan will burn under the broiler. Place the veal chops in a broiling pan.

Broil the veal chops 6 inches from the heat source for 10 minutes each side. Remove to a platter. Add the margarine to the shallot sauce a piece at a time and swirl to combine. Spoon over the veal chops.

Yields: 4 servings

ა⁊

beef short ribs with horseradish

Beef short ribs are a kind of flanken, just longer and a little meatier. If you can't get them, regular flanken will do, just use strips that are as thick as possible and cut them into 3- to 4-inch pieces. This dish can be made in advance; it gets even better when reheated.

5 pounds beef short ribs
4 tablespoons flour, divided
1 tablespoon margarine
1 tablespoon vegetable oil
1 onion, sliced into thick rings
2 carrots, thickly sliced
1 rib celery, sliced
2 cups beef stock or broth (can be made from bouillon)
1 (28 ounce) can chopped tomatoes; if using whole canned tomatoes, drain, seed, and chop them

1 cup red wine
1 bouquet garni of 6 parsley stems, 3 sprigs fresh thyme, and 1 bay leaf (see page 155)
2 cloves garlic, 1 chopped and 1 minced
1 tablespoon tomato paste
6 teaspoons bottled white horseradish, divided
freshly ground black pepper
chopped fresh parsley

Preheat the oven to 350 degrees. Dredge the short ribs in 3 tablespoons of flour.

In a large pot, melt the margarine with the oil over medium-high heat. Get the oil mixture hot enough so that the meat sizzles when added. If your oil is heated to the right temperature it will sear it on contact, not burn it. Add meat in a single layer; you will need to do this in 2-3 batches. Brown the meat well on both sides, about 6-8 minutes.

Remove the meat from the pot. Reduce the heat to medium. Add the onion, carrot, and celery. Cook about 7-9 minutes, scraping up the brown bits as the onions caramelize.

Return the short ribs to the pot. Sprinkle with the remaining tablespoon of flour, stirring to coat.

Add the beef stock, tomatoes, wine, bouquet garni, chopped and minced garlic, and tomato paste.

Raise the heat and bring to a simmer. Add 2 teaspoons of the horseradish and mix in. Cover the pot and place it in the oven.

Simmer, stirring occasionally until the meat is tender, about 1¾ -2 hours. Just before serving, add the remaining horseradish and season with pepper. Sprinkle with parsley for garnish.

Yield: 6 servings

rosemary-pesto baby lamb chops
with olive-wine sauce

2 cups curly parsley		freshly ground black pepper
6 tablespoons fresh rosemary, stems removed		16 baby lamb chops, fat trimmed
2 cloves garlic		½ cup pitted black olives
4½ tablespoons olive oil		1 cup dry red wine
salt		3 tablespoons margarine

Preheat broiler to high. Place parsley, rosemary, and garlic in the bowl of a food processor fitted with a metal blade. Process to a coarse paste. With machine running, gradually add olive oil. Season pesto with salt and pepper.

Press the pesto around the outside rim of each lamb chop. Place on a broiling pan. Broil 10 minutes per side. Arrange the lamb chops on a serving platter; set aside.

Meanwhile, place the olives in the food processor and process to a coarse paste.

Pour the wine into a small saucepan and cook over medium heat about 5 minutes or until the liquid is reduced by half. Add in the olives. Swirl in the margarine one tablespoon at a time until the sauce has thickened slightly, about 1 minute.

Pour the sauce over the lamb chops and serve immediately.

Yield: 4 servings

sausage with peppers and onions

When you walk down the streets of Manhattan, the aroma from the sausage and peppers vendors fills the air. I started seeing sausages sold by a number of Kosher butchers, who told me that they've become quite popular. My butcher sells a few varieties. I like the flavor of the veal, but you can try the turkey, beef, or other flavors as well. This dish is a little different, easy, and quite delicious.

1 tablespoon olive oil	1 large Vidalia or sweet onion, sliced
1 pound Italian veal sausage	into thin rings
½ cup beer	1 tablespoon fresh oregano or 1
1 red bell pepper, sliced into long,	teaspoon dried oregano
very thin strips	salt
1 yellow bell pepper, sliced into long,	freshly ground black pepper
very thin strips	

Heat olive oil in a large skillet over medium heat. Cook sausage until browned on all sides. Remove sausage from pan. You can leave them whole or cut them into pieces. Set aside.

Pour in the beer to deglaze the pan, scraping up browned bits from the pan. Add the red pepper, yellow pepper, and onion. Sprinkle with the oregano.

Cook about 20-25 minutes or until the peppers and onions are very soft and caramelized. Stir occasionally to make sure they are not burning; if they are, turn the heat down. You want the onions really golden, sweet, and sticky. Season with salt and pepper. Add the sausages back into the pan and cook for another 5-10 minutes.

Serve in hoagie rolls or over pasta.

Yield: 4 servings

pot roast

When you exit the elevator in my mother-in-law's building, you are led by the nose to her doorway. The aroma of something great always wafts down her hallway. Her impromptu feasts don't require a special occasion, just a butcher order and knowing friends or family might be stopping by. This pot roast is one of my favorite dishes that she prepares. It's so tender that you can cut it with a fork. If unexpected guests arrive, you can always toss in a few extra carrots and potatoes to stretch the meal.

Pot roast involves browning beef and then braising it on the stove covered in liquid for several hours. This moist cooking process tenderizes the meat. Inexpensive cuts of meat work best. I am not sure why pot roast has dropped off the radar screen of younger cooks, but when you try this recipe you'll rediscover why our mothers and grandmothers prepared it so often.

2 tablespoons olive oil	3 carrots, peeled and sliced, or 2 cups baby carrots
1 tablespoon margarine	
flour	3 Idaho potatoes, peeled and cut into chunks
1 (5-pound) boneless roast	
1 onion, sliced	2 parsnips, peeled and cut into chunks
1½ packages dry onion soup mix (from a 2¾-ounce box)	prepared horseradish or store-bought barbecue sauce

In a large pot or Dutch oven, heat the olive oil and margarine. Sprinkle flour over the meat. When the oil is hot but not smoking, sear the roast on all sides until golden brown. Remove from pot; set aside.

Add the sliced onion to the pot. Sauté about 5-6 minutes or until translucent, scraping up the brown bits from the pot as you sauté the onion.

Return the roast to the pot. Add water to cover ⅔rds of the way up the roast. Sprinkle with the dry onion soup mix. Bring to a boil. Reduce to a simmer; cook, covered, for 2 hours. After 2 hours, turn the pot roast over. Add the carrots, potatoes, and parsnips. Re-cover and cook for another 1-1½ hours. Transfer meat to cutting board and let rest for 5 minutes. Slice meat. Place on platter with the vegetables. Serve with either jarred prepared horseradish or bottled barbecue sauce.

Yield: 8 servings

filet split with shallot soy sauce

Are you in the mood for a quality steakhouse dinner, but unable to get into the city? Prepare this dish for a truly memorable dinner. Simply pour some glasses of red wine and prepare a side dish of your favorite potatoes.

The sauce is even better when made a day ahead. Swirl the margarine in just before serving. If you make the steak in advance, store it unsliced and separate from the sauce or it will absorb too much of the soy sauce. Don't confuse filet split or minute steak split with small minute steaks. The minute steak split is from the same cut of meat as minute steaks. But the whole cut is sliced horizontally and the vein is removed, making this a first quality, tender, large piece of meat. The filet gets sliced on the diagonal after cooking.

Filet:

- 6 shiitake mushrooms, stems removed
- 6 ounces sliced portobello mushroom caps, stems removed
- 1 bunch or ⅔ ounces chives

- 2 tablespoons unsalted margarine
- 1 (1-inch-thick) filet split, also known as minute steak split, cut in half; or 4 (1-inch-thick) beef filet mignon

Shallot Soy Sauce:

- 1 (10-ounce) bottle low-sodium soy sauce
- 4 garlic cloves, sliced
- 3 large shallots, thinly sliced
- ½ cup seasoned rice vinegar

- 2 teaspoons whole black peppercorns
- 2 tablespoons honey
- 4 tablespoons unsalted margarine, sliced

Filet:

In the bowl of a food processor fitted with a metal blade, process the shiitake mushrooms until finely chopped. Remove to a bowl. Process the portobello mushrooms and chives until finely chopped; mix with the shiitake mushrooms.

In a large skillet, melt the margarine over medium heat. Add the mushroom mixture and sauté for 5 minutes. Add the steaks and cook for 15 minutes until medium rare, turning once during the cooking process. The mushrooms will get crusted to the steaks as they cook.

Shallot Soy Sauce:

In a medium saucepan over high heat, heat the soy sauce, garlic, shallots, vinegar, peppercorns, and honey. Bring to a boil. Reduce the heat to medium and cook about 20 minutes. Remove from heat; whisk in the margarine 1 tablespoon at a time, until well blended.

To serve, place each filet mignon steak or a few slices of the filet split in the center. Spoon 3-4 tablespoons of the shallot-soy sauce over each plate, making sure to get the shallots and garlic in the sauce.

Yield: 4 servings

meat loaf

The only addition this easy, inexpensive, and satisfying recipe needs is mashed potatoes and green beans. With more zip than old-fashioned meat loaf, it's sure to be a crowd-pleaser.

2 teaspoons dry mustard powder	2 pounds ground meat or combination of beef and veal
2 teaspoons water	1 large egg
¾ cup regular or quick-cooking rolled oats (not instant)	2 tablespoons ketchup
1 tablespoon oil	¾ teaspoon salt
1 red bell pepper, seeded and diced	¼ teaspoon dried thyme
3 scallions, sliced	¼ cup ketchup
2 garlic cloves, finely chopped	1 tablespoon dark brown sugar
	1 teaspoon spicy brown mustard

Preheat oven to 350 degrees. Lightly spray a loaf pan with nonstick cooking spray. In a large bowl, stir together the dry mustard and water. Set aside.

Place the oats in the bowl of a food processor fitted with a metal blade and process until crumbly. Set aside.

In a medium skillet, heat the oil at medium heat. Add the red pepper and cook about 5 minutes or until softened, stirring occasionally. Add scallions and garlic. Cook for 1 minute longer. Add the skillet contents to the bowl with mustard.

Add oats, ground meat, egg, 2 tablespoons ketchup, salt, and thyme. Mix gently with a wooden spoon or wet hands until blended. Transfer the meat into the prepared loaf pan and bake for 30 minutes.

In a small bowl prepare the glaze. Mix the ¼ cup ketchup, brown sugar, and spicy mustard. Spoon evenly over the center of the loaf. Bake an additional 30 minutes or until brown on top and the meat loaf pulls away from the sides. Let stand 10 minutes before serving.

Yield: 8 servings

cholent

Cholent is a traditional stew eaten on Shabbat day. Every culture, actually every family has their own special version of cholent. A crockpot is the perfect vessel to cook the cholent in and don't forget the crock pot disposable liners for a quick easy cleanup.

3-4 beef bones	salt
6 medium potatoes, peeled and cut into chunks	pepper
	paprika
1 pound beef stew or flanken	minced onion
½ cup pearl barley	garlic powder
¼ cup dried red kidney beans	1 roll kishka
¼ cup dried white navy beans	½ cup ketchup
¼ cup dried lima beans	1 (12 ounce) can regular Coca Cola
1 large onion, quartered	

Place the beef bones, potatoes, beef, barley, beans, and onion into the crock pot in the order listed. Season with salt, pepper, paprika, minced onion, and garlic powder. Place the unwrapped kishka roll on top. Add in the ketchup and can of soda. Add water to come to the top of the pot.

Cover and cook on HIGH for 6 hours, then before Shabbat, turn the heat setting to LOW and cook overnight or until ready to serve.

vegetarian cholent

My friend was famous for this dish on the Upper West Side singles scene. He had Shabbat regulars who would show up with their friends week after week for a plate of this hot delicacy. When he got married and left for the suburbs there was a huge outcry in the neighborhood. But I don't know if it was because one of the good ones was off the market or because his Vegetarian Cholent recipe was going with him.

½ cup dried red kidney beans	3 cloves garlic, chopped
½ cup dried white navy beans	3 carrots, peeled and cut into chunks
1 cup dried brown lentils	1 cup old fashioned oats (not the quick cook or 1 minute type)
4 Idaho potatoes, peeled and cut into chunks	
	½ cup pearl barley
1 large onion, chopped	3 tablespoons Kosher or coarse salt

Place the kidney beans, navy beans, and lentils in a large pot. Cover with water. Bring to a boil, covered and cook for 5 minutes. Turn the heat off and let the mixture sit covered for 1 hour. Rinse thoroughly and drain.

Place the bean mixture into the crock pot. Add the potatoes, onion, garlic, and carrots. Add water to come to the top of the pot.

Cover and cook on HIGH for an hour. Uncover and add the oats, mix in. Pour in the barley, pushing it just below the surface, but not pushed all the way to the bottom. If necessary add more water to come to the top. Sprinkle with coarse salt. Cover and turn the heat down to LOW and cook overnight until ready to serve.

Chanukah

Chanukah provides just the warm glow we need in the dead of winter. Its illuminating message is that miracles do happen, often when least expected.

The story of Chanukah occurred in the year 165 CE during the time of the Second Holy Temple of Jerusalem. When King Antiochus, the Syrian-Greek ruler of Judea, was assured by Hellenistic Jews that most of the Jewish population would welcome Greek culture (or could be coerced to accept it), he imposed outrageous anti-religious laws. Shabbat, circumcision, and the proclamation of the Jewish months were forbidden. Next, idol worship was mandated throughout Judea, and particularly in the Holy Temple itself.

Infuriated, a small group of Jews — inspired by Matityahu, patriarch of the Hasmonean family known as the Maccabees – banded together to battle the Greek empire. At the time, it was considered a suicide mission. They knew they couldn't overpower the Greek army and its Hellenist allies. But they felt there was no choice: better to go down fighting for the Torah than to abandon it.

And yet they were victorious: inexplicably, unbelievably, totally victorious. Tales of valor abound, from the bravery of Judah Maccabee to Judith, a courageous Jewish widow who enticed a Greek general to consume rich, creamy cuisine until he fell asleep, and then promptly beheaded him. (She must have been some cook!) Her story has given us the custom of serving dairy foods on Chanukah.

It was clear to the victors that they had won only

through a series of miracles, yet the most striking miracle still awaited them. Finding just enough sanctified oil to last for one day in the Temple Menorah, they were resigned to the fact that it would soon burn out. But the oil burned for eight full days, long enough for new oil to be processed. This overt miracle prompted the sages to declare the eight-day holiday of Chanukah to thank the Almighty for both the military triumph and the miracle of the oil.

The custom of frying Chanukah foods in oil is a tasty reminder of this event.

Today, the eternal light of the Menorah burns in our hearts. The warm *Chanukiah* lights in our windows joyfully transmit the message that the spiritual light of Torah can be dimmed temporarily, but never extinguished.

chanukah menu

Potato Latkes
page 36

APPETIZER:
Portobello Pesto Stacks
page 38

ENTREES:
Greek Tomato-Spinach Pizza
page 182
Rigatoni a lá Norma
page 174
Parmesan Crusted Grouper
page 162

DESSERT:
Beignéts / Banana Beignéts
page 279

There's no better way to start off Chanukah than to set your table aglow with candles. The incredible variety of candles available can be tailored to fit any color scheme or mood. They are most effective, as pictured on our table, when set in large groupings of assorted shapes and heights. Our choice of all blue complements this table and creates an inviting ambience.

Elevate each place setting on a rectangular pedestal place mat. This is simpler than it looks! Use large styrofoam rectangles covered with blue fabric. Straight pins secure the fabric to the underside of each rectangle. Tie ribbon around each corner to simulate a wrapped present. On the corner of each "place mat" is another small styrofoam box. Wrap these with mylar foil to resemble a mini present. Place a collection of dreidels, some modern and some antique, atop each of these presents and across the table. Any kind of dreidel can be used; feel free to combine silver with wood, plastic, or glass.

We went all out to bring in varying shades and textures of blue. It's okay if the colors don't match exactly. We even found wine and water bottles in our featured hue. Strips of mylar foil and glittery ribbons are sparingly placed across the table in a lattice design.

To commemorate the Chanukah miracle of oil, our menu opens and closes with a sizzle. It runs the gamut from a wonderful rendition of traditional Potato Latkes to modern Beignets (fried dough balls rolled in powdered sugar). In between, we feature dairy foods such as Parmesan-Crusted Grouper. We also include a pasta dish that highlights fried eggplant. Greek Tomato-Spinach Pizza is sure to delight both young and old.

wine list

BARTENURA PINOT GRIGIO
RASHI PINOT GRIGIO

These wines are made from Pinot Grigio select grapes grown in Italy. Either is a great choice for the Portobello Pesto Stacks. They are well-balanced, dry, with fruity flavors.

BARTENURA CHIANTI

Both the Rigatoni ala Norma and the Parmesan Crusted Grouper
pair well with this Tuscan wine.

BARTENURA MOSCATO DI ASTI (BLUE BOTTLE)
CARMEL DI MOSCATO

For the Beignets we selected wine that goes well with fruit or light desserts. The Moscato grape is aromatic with a fresh peachy perfume.

Parmesan Crusted Grouper

fish

pan-seared tuna with middle eastern parsley dip

4 (6-ounce) ahi tuna steaks
olive oil
salt
black pepper
2 tablespoons olive oil
¾ cup techina
2 cloves garlic, minced
zest from 1 lemon
juice from 3 lemons
⅔ cup (about ½ bunch) flat leaf Italian parsley leaves, chopped

10 red cherry tomatoes
10 yellow cherry tomatoes
½ small red onion, minced very finely by hand or in food processor
salt
black pepper
olive oil
apple-cider vinegar

Brush the fish with olive oil and season with salt and pepper. Heat 2 tablespoons olive oil in a skillet. Sear the tuna 2 minutes per side for rare. You can also grill the fish on the barbecue. Set aside.

Place the techina, garlic, lemon zest, and lemon juice in a blender or food processor and blend for 15 seconds. Fold in the parsley; set aside. Sauce can be made 1 or 2 days ahead and kept in the refrigerator.

On your platter, cut each tomato in half and scatter the 2 colors of tomatoes, cut side down, around the plate. Sprinkle with the minced onion. Season with salt and pepper.

With your finger over the mouth of the olive oil bottle, lightly drizzle oil over the platter.

With your finger over the mouth of the apple-cider vinegar bottle, drizzle a few splashes of the vinegar.

Chill the platter. This can be done early in the day or the night before serving. Place the fish over the tomatoes, spoon parsley sauce over the fish.

Yield: 4 servings

Heavenly Herbs

With fresh herbs readily available in supermarkets year-round, there's no need to rely on dried. Fresh herbs wake up the palate and add pizzazz to any dish.

To store herbs, wrap them loosely in a barely damp paper towel and seal in a zip-lock bag for up to 5 days.

Stems of basil, parsley, and cilantro can be kept like a bunch of flowers with their stems in a glass of water. Cover with a plastic bag and refrigerate for up to a week.

With the exception of rosemary, which can withstand long cooking times, fresh herbs are usually added to a dish towards the end of cooking to preserve maximum flavor. Dried herbs are usually added at the beginning of cooking so their flavor can develop.

Snip fresh herbs like dill and parsley off their stems with a pair of scissors.

Dust plates with finely chopped herbs for an elegant garnish.

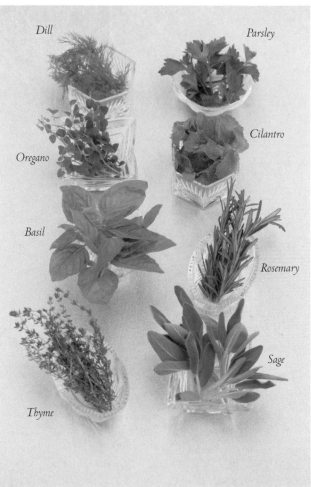

Dill

Parsley

Oregano

Cilantro

Basil

Rosemary

Thyme

Sage

1 teaspoon dried herb
is equal to
1 tablespoon fresh herb

If using dried herbs, after measuring, crush them between your fingers to release the flavor.

Bouquet Garni

To flavor soups and stews, combine various herbs and spices. Tie in a small square of muslin or cheesecloth and drop into your pot. Remove the package prior to serving.

Placecards

Placecards are a creative way to avoid seating confusion and to bring flair to your place setting. Placecards can be tailored to your decor, holiday, or theme and are limited only by your imagination. See above for some of our ideas.

walnut-coated flounder
with lemon butter sauce

Everyone loves fried flounder. However, it's nice to find an alternative to deep frying this popular fish. I also like this recipe because it offers a more upscale way to serve seafood that I know my family will eat. The recipe combines a lot of nice flavors, which blend together well. This recipe can also be done with sea bass; just increase the cooking time to 15 minutes. The sauce is wonderful over any fish as well.

Walnut-Coated Flounder:

6 (6-ounce) flounder fillets	2 tablespoons prepared white
salt and pepper	horseradish
1 cup unflavored bread crumbs	1½ tablespoons whole-grain Dijon
¾ cup chopped walnuts	mustard
2 tablespoons shelled sunflower	¼ cup finely grated Parmesan cheese
seeds	2 tablespoons fresh minced parsley
3 tablespoons unsalted butter, melted	

Lemon Butter Sauce:

¾ cup Vermouth or sherry wine	8 tablespoons (1 stick) butter cut
3 tablespoons chopped shallots	into quarters
juice from 1 lemon	1½ tablespoons chopped fresh dill

Walnut-Coated Flounder:

Preheat the oven to 350 degrees. Spray a large baking pan with nonstick cooking spray. Arrange the fish in the prepared pan. Sprinkle each fillet with salt and pepper. Set aside.

In the bowl of a food processor fitted with a metal blade, mix the bread crumbs, walnuts, and sunflower seeds. Pulse until the nuts are finely ground but not pasty. Transfer to a bowl and mix in the melted butter, horseradish, mustard, Parmesan, and parsley. Set aside.

As you pick up each fillet, spray it on both sides with nonstick cooking spray. This will help the coating adhere to the fish.

Gently press the crumb mixture on to each fillet, top and bottom. Bake for 10 minutes or until the fish is cooked through. Turn the oven to broil. Broil fish until the crust is golden, but watch it the entire time because it can burn very easily.

Lemon Butter Sauce:

Over a high heat, bring the Vermouth, shallots, and lemon juice to a boil. Turn the heat down a little and allow the mixture to reduce to ¼ cup, about 6 minutes. Turn the heat down to low and add the butter, whisking until melted. Remove from heat. Stir in dill.

Transfer the fish to plate or a platter and drizzle sauce over the fish. Serve any extra sauce in a bowl on the side.

Yield: 6 servings

pistachio-crusted salmon with vanilla rum butter over smashed sweet potatoes Dairy

Hats off to my friend John Stilley for this masterpiece.

Vanilla Rum Butter:

- 1 cup heavy cream
- 4 tablespoons (½ stick) butter
- 2 ounces dark rum
- 1 teaspoon vanilla extract

- 2 tablespoons sugar
- 1½ teaspoons cornstarch
- ¼ cup cold water

Pistachio-Crusted Salmon:

- ½ cup shelled pistachio nuts
- ½ cup unflavored homestyle bread crumbs, or Japanese panko bread crumbs

- 4 (6- to 8-ounce) salmon fillets, all pin bones removed
- 1½ tablespoons butter, melted

Smashed Sweet Potatoes:

- 4 medium sweet potatoes, peeled and cut into chunks
- 4 tablespoons (½ stick) butter

- salt
- ¼ cup dark brown sugar

Vanilla Rum Butter:

Heat the cream, butter, rum, vanilla, and sugar over low heat, allowing it to just barely simmer for 5-6 minutes or the cream will bubble over.

In a small bowl mix the cornstarch into the water, stirring quickly. This makes a slurry that will thicken the sauce. Whisk the slurry into the sauce; remove it from heat. Set aside. Can be served warm or chilled, and the sauce can be made up to a week in advance.

Pistachio-Crusted Salmon:

Preheat the oven to 375 degrees. In a food processor fitted with a metal blade, process the pistachio nuts until chopped. Don't over process or it will be pasty. Add the bread crumbs and pulse a few times to combine.

Place the salmon in a baking or broiling pan. Brush with the melted butter. Press the pistachio mixture into the fillets, a handful at a time, making sure to cover all surfaces of the fish.

Bake for 15 minutes or until done.

Smashed Sweet Potatoes:

Place the potatoes in a pot and cover with water. Bring to a boil and cook about 20 minutes or until soft. Reserve 2 tablespoons of the cooking water and set it aside. Drain the potatoes. While they are still steaming hot, use a mixer to whip the potatoes. Add in the butter, salt, brown sugar, and reserved water. The potatoes can be made in advance and reheated.

To serve, place the sweet potatoes in the center of the plate; drizzle the vanilla rum butter over the sweet potatoes. Place a salmon fillet in the middle; drizzle with more sauce.

Yield: 4 servings

tuna in scallion peppercorn cream sauce Dairy

4 (6- to 8-ounce) tuna steaks
  salt
  freshly ground black pepper
1 tablespoon olive oil
1 clove garlic, chopped
2 shallots, sliced
½ cup scallions, chopped

1 tablespoon whole green
  peppercorns
  pinch flour
¼ cup brandy
½ cup vegetable stock
¼ cup heavy cream

Season the tuna steaks with salt and pepper. Place the olive oil into a large skillet. Heat over medium-high heat. Add the garlic and sauté 30 seconds. Add the tuna steaks and sear 3-4 minutes per side. Remove to a platter.

Add the shallots, scallions, and peppercorns to the pan. Sauté 4-6 minutes. Season with salt and pepper. Sprinkle the pan with flour. Add the brandy, reduce heat and simmer for 4-5 minutes. Add the vegetable stock, stirring until thickened. Add the cream. Pour the sauce over the tuna.

Yield: 4 servings

Citrus Potpourri

A citrus potpourri will get a fishy odor, or any foul smell, out of your kitchen. Roughly cut a lemon, a lime, and an orange. Place them in a pot of water. Add a cinnamon stick and a few whole cloves. Bring to a boil, then turn down to a low simmer. A pleasant aroma will permeate the room.

champagne-poached salmon
with a champagne cream sauce

Poaching involves partially or completely submerging the fish in a gently simmering liquid. This makes it almost impossible to dry out even the most delicate fish. When poaching, try to maintain a bare simmer; a more vigorous boil may cause the food to fall apart or cook unevenly. Poaching is done on a stovetop. If you have a long narrow fish poacher, as I do, you will need to use a front and back burner at the same time.

You can serve this salmon fresh, but it is even better if you cover and refrigerate the poached salmon for at least 3 hours or up to a day. Let stand at room temperature for ½ hour before serving.

Kosher champagnes have greatly improved over the past few years. You will need a full 750 ml bottle. If you can, splurge for a better bottle. The 15-20 dollar range is fine; you don't need to go for the 40 dollar bottles, but the lowest level champagne tastes acidic in this recipe.

Inspiration for this delicacy goes to Emeril Lagasse and the TV Food Network.

Poached Salmon:

1 tablespoon butter	1 teaspoon freshly ground black pepper
4 cups champagne	
1 shallot, chopped	5 (6-ounce) salmon fillets, skin removed
6 sprigs fresh dill	
3 tablespoons salt	2 tablespoons minced fresh dill

Champagne Cream Sauce:

½ cup chopped shallots	½ teaspoon salt
1 cup champagne	¼ teaspoon freshly ground black pepper
1½ cups heavy cream	
4 tablespoons (½ stick) butter, cut into pieces	

Poached Salmon:

Grease a fish poacher or a large straight-sided sauté pan with 1 tablespoon butter. Add the champagne, shallot, dill, salt, and pepper. Bring to a boil over high heat. Reduce the heat to medium and gently simmer for 5 minutes.

Add the salmon fillets to the poacher or pan. Sprinkle minced dill on top of the salmon. Spoon the liquid over the fillets. Cook uncovered about 10-15 minutes or until the salmon is firm and cooked through; may need longer if the fillets are thicker in the middle. Spoon the liquid over the fillets as they gently simmer in the poaching liquid. You will see the fillets become a lighter color as they become fully poached. Using a slotted spatula, remove the fillets from the pan.

Champagne Cream Sauce:

Combine the shallots and champagne in a saucepan. Bring to a boil and cook about 6 minutes or until almost of the liquid is evaporated. Add the heavy cream, bring to a boil, lower the flame and simmer about 3-4 minutes or until cream thickens and is reduced by almost half.

Whisk in the 4 tablespoons butter. Pass the sauce through a strainer, pressing on the solids to extract as much liquid as possible. Season with salt and pepper. Serve sauce over salmon.

Yield: 5 servings

parmesan-crusted grouper

½ cup grated Parmesan cheese
⅓ cup butter, softened, not melted
2 tablespoons mayonnaise
2 scallions, thinly sliced

2 large or 4 small (1-inch-thick) grouper fillets
1 lemon
freshly ground black pepper

Preheat broiler to high. In a small bowl, combine the Parmesan, butter, mayonnaise, and scallions. Set aside.

Place the grouper fillets on a lightly greased broiler pan. Squeeze the juice from 1 lemon over the fillets and sprinkle with black pepper.

Broil 6 inches from heat for 10 minutes. Remove from oven. Spread the tops of the fillets with cheese mixture.

Return to oven and broil for 2 minutes longer or until the topping is lightly browned and bubbly. Remove fillets to platter.

Yield: 4 servings

teriyaki salmon

My sister and brother-in-law are famous for their barbecues. People wait all year for them. This is one of their popular specialties; it is a snap to prepare and absolutely delicious.

1 large (6-ounce) or 4 small salmon fillets, skin removed
Dijon mustard
¾ cup teriyaki sauce
¾ cup soy sauce
½ cup dark brown sugar

Brush both sides of the fillet with a thin coating of the mustard. Lay the salmon in a large pan.

In a mixing bowl, mix the teriyaki, soy sauce, and brown sugar. Stir until the sugar is dissolved. Pour half of the marinade over the salmon, reserving the other half. Marinate 1-4 hours.

Preheat grill. Grill the salmon for 6-8 minutes per side, depending on thickness. Baste the salmon often during cooking with the reserved marinade.

Yield: 4 servings

pecan-crusted lemon sole
with mango sauce

Dairy

This unusual combination really works. The finished dish's various colors and textures are gorgeous. Lemon sole is easy to work with and is not "fishy" tasting at all. I like to buy large fillets and cut them into two servings after cooking.

1 shallot, chopped	¼ cup orange juice
¾ cup dry sherry	2 teaspoons rice vinegar
¼ teaspoon salt	8 ounces pecans, chopped
¼ teaspoon white pepper	3 tablespoons butter
2 large ripe mangoes, peeled and pitted	2 (16-ounce) lemon sole fillets, skin removed

In a small pot, heat the chopped shallot, sherry, salt, and white pepper over medium heat. Cook until almost all of the liquid is evaporated.

While the sherry is reducing, puree the mango, orange juice, and rice vinegar in a blender or a food processor fitted with a metal blade. Add the puree to the pot. Remove from heat and set aside.

Preheat oven to 400 degrees. Place the butter in a large oven-proof skillet or a skillet with the handle double-wrapped in foil. Press the nuts into each side of the fish. They won't adhere very well, just make sure some of them stick. Melt the butter over medium-low heat. Place the fish into the pan and sauté for 2-3 minutes. Flip the fish over and finish in the oven, cooking for 8-12 minutes or until fish is done.

Yield: 4 servings

☞ *Cutting a Mango*

To indicate the direction of the large seed inside, look for the flat side of the mango. Slice through the mango as close to this pit as possible. Repeat on the other side of the pit. Score the flesh (but not through to the skin) in a criss-cross patterns. Pop the fruit up by turning the skin inside out.

Carefully cut the cubes of fruit off of the skin. Eat fresh or use in your recipe.

blackened tilapia or red snapper

This dish is an authentic Cajun, mouth-on-fire delicacy. Blackened refers to the spices, not the lack of cooking prowess. If you are worried about the heat, only coat one side of the fish with the spice mixture, although it will still be hot. I like to make up a big batch of the spices and keep them in a baby food jar so that dinner preparation on this dish (it's also great on thinly pounded chicken breasts), is a snap. If you have a cast-iron skillet, it is the way to go. If not, use a nonstick frying pan and get it very hot as well. Warn your guests, pour a big pitcher of ice water, and enjoy!

2 teaspoons onion powder	1 teaspoon dried basil leaves
2 teaspoons garlic powder	1 cup butter, melted
1½ teaspoons cayenne pepper	4 (6-ounce) tilapia or red snapper fillets
1 teaspoon ground white pepper	
1 teaspoon ground black pepper	4 medium fresh tomatoes, each cut in half, tops trimmed so they sit flat
1 teaspoon paprika	oregano
1 teaspoon dried thyme leaves	sour cream
1 teaspoon dried oregano leaves	

Spray a large frying pan or well-seasoned cast-iron skillet with nonstick cooking spray. In a flat plate combine the onion powder, garlic powder, cayenne, white pepper, black pepper, paprika, thyme, oregano, and basil. Mix well.

Dredge each fillet in the melted butter, then coat with the spice mixture on one or both sides. Reserve the melted butter.

If using a cast-iron skillet, get it white hot. If not, heat the frying pan over medium-high heat until very hot but not smoking.

Carefully place the fillets in the skillet and sear about 3-5 minutes or until blackened. Pour 1 tablespoon of reserved melted butter on each fillet. Flip the fish over and pour 1 tablespoon of melted butter over each fillet and blacken the other side, about 2-3 minutes. If you only spiced one side then the second side won't get black, just cook the fish through until it is done. Remove fish to dinner plates.

Brush the tomato halves with the melted butter and sprinkle with oregano. Sear the tomatoes in the frying pan about 3 minutes or until soft. Flip to the other side and cook 1-2 minutes longer.

Serve each fillet with a big dollop of sour cream and two tomato halves.

Yield: 4 servings

glazed yellowfin tuna
with arugula and shiitake salad

1 cup balsamic vinegar	3 shallots, minced
¼ cup mild molasses	1 clove garlic, minced
4 (6-ounce) yellowfin tuna steaks, ahi grade	6 ounces shiitake mushrooms, stems removed, roughly chopped
Kosher salt	¼ cup balsamic vinegar
freshly ground black pepper	salt
2 cloves garlic, minced	freshly ground black pepper
½ teaspoon dried thyme	½ teaspoon dried thyme
4-6 fresh basil leaves, minced	4 handfuls baby arugula leaves
6 tablespoons olive oil, divided	1 tablespoon balsamic vinegar

Blend 1 cup of balsamic vinegar with the molasses in a small saucepan. Place over medium heat. Cook until reduced by ⅔rds, about 10 minutes; it will be syrupy. Remove from heat. If it is too thick, add ¼ cup of water and place over medium heat until it gets syrupy again. Remove from heat and set aside in a bowl or squeeze bottle.

Season the tuna steaks with the salt, pepper, garlic, thyme, basil, and 1 tablespoon olive oil. Rub it into both sides.

Heat 2 tablespoons olive oil in a medium or large skillet over medium-high heat. Sear the tuna on all sides, just enough to seal and color the tuna, about 1 minute per side. Keep the center medium-rare. Remove and let rest.

Heat 2 tablespoons of olive oil in the skillet over medium to high heat. Add the shallots and garlic. Sauté until slightly softened, 30-45 seconds, add the shiitake caps and sauté until they are browned, about 7-9 minutes. Stir to keep from sticking to the pan. Pour in the ¼ cup balsamic vinegar and loosen the browned bits from the pan. Remove from heat. Season with the salt, pepper, and thyme.

Toss the arugula with 1 tablespoon of olive oil and 1 tablespoon balsamic vinegar. Lay the tuna steaks on a plate or platter. On top of each steak put a handful of the arugula leaves. In the center of the leaves place a mound of the warm shiitake mixture. Drizzle with the molasses glaze.

Yield: 4 servings

chilean sea bass
with roasted tomato vinaigrette

Dairy

This gorgeous orange-colored vinaigrette is lovely when paired with simple-to-prepare fish. You can pour it over the fish or decorate the plate with it.

Due to its high-oil content, Chilean sea bass doesn't dry out like leaner fish. It yields a delicious and moist flavor. Chilean sea bass is almost identical to the sablefish or black cod in its texture and characteristics, so feel free to substitute these as well.

4 ripe plum tomatoes	salt
1 garlic clove, sliced	freshly ground black pepper
1 teaspoon Dijon mustard	½ cup plain dry bread crumbs
1 teaspoon balsamic vinegar	4 (7-ounce) Chilean sea bass fillets,
2 teaspoons red wine vinegar	skin removed
¼ cup olive oil	2 tablespoons butter

Preheat oven to 500 degrees. Cut the tomatoes in half lengthwise. Lay them cut side down on a baking sheet. Roast the tomatoes for 15 minutes. The skin will blister and may even blacken. That is okay, it just adds to the smoky flavor.

Remove tomatoes from oven and lower the temperature to 400 degrees. Place the roasted tomatoes in the bowl of a food processor fitted with a metal blade. Add the garlic, mustard, balsamic vinegar, and red wine vinegar. Pulse until it is all pureed. Slowly add the olive oil and continue to puree until it is incorporated. The mixture will be smooth and creamy. Season with salt and pepper. Set aside. You can make the vinaigrette in advance; just bring to room temperature before serving.

Place the bread crumbs in a shallow bowl or plate. Roll each fillet in the bread crumbs, pressing them into the fillet so they will adhere.

In an oven-proof skillet, heat the butter over a medium flame. When butter melts, add the fillets to the skillet and sauté about 6-8 minutes or until golden brown. Turn them over and sauté another 6 minutes or until golden.

Place the skillet in the preheated oven 4-6 minutes ot until the fillets are cooked through. The fish should appear white when flaked with a fork.

Drizzle each fillet or plate with the vinaigrette.

Yield: 4 servings

tu b'shvat

hough it is winter, the fifteenth day in the Hebrew month of Shvat is the "New Year" of the trees, a time when we stop to reflect on the many blessings that rise from the land. Our Torah laws convey the important lesson that every blessing carries with it a responsibility: for the Jewish farmer in the Land of Israel, no harvest is complete until he shares his abundance with the poor and landless. The basis for this is his awareness that no matter how hard he toils, his seedlings will not grow unless God allows the right amounts of rain, sun and soil to combine harmoniously for his benefit.

It is more than likely that the strong Jewish "instinct" to give charity began in this agricultural setting. Like the farmer, we know that when God gives us sustenance –whether in great or small measure – it is our duty to share our blessings with others.

The Land of Israel, which refused to yield wealth to its conquerors for almost 2,000 years, is once again thriving. Israeli produce and wines are superb: you can almost taste the bright sun, water and special soil of the Land of Israel in them. Wheat, barley, grapes, figs, pomegranates, olives and dates are known collectively as *Shivat HaMinnim*, "The Seven Species," and they express the spiritual and physical richness of the Land. We emphasize these foods on Tu B'Shvat. If we have not had occasion to taste them in the past year, it is an opportunity to thank God for giving us life and the health to enjoy the moment by saying the blessing "*Shehechiyanu.*"

It's particularly fitting to eat fruits imported from Israel. Though it is a festive day, Tu B'Shvat does not require observances other than the custom of eating of nuts and fruits, particularly those of the Seven Species. But somehow, that is enough. For when we taste

these luscious gifts from Israeli trees, we are reminded of the Land itself. In our minds, we can be transported to its orchards and farms; view the magnificent mountains, the rushing streams and fertile valleys — and celebrate the splendor of this spiritual Land, blessed by God to blossom for His people.

tu b'shvat menu

APPETIZER:
Pistachio Chicken Skewers
with Blackberry Sauce
page 31

SALAD:
Strawberry Fields Salad
page 81

ENTREE:
Rack of Lamb
with Fig-Port-Shallot Sauce
pages 129

SIDE DISHES:
Slow-Roasted Tomatoes
page 199
Squash Risotto
page 216

DESSERT:
Castaway Cake
page 266

H ost a Tu B'Shvat celebration that appeals to all the senses! Wonderful Israeli or Hebrew music, beautiful decor, tantalizing aromas, and — of course — delicious and meaningful foods will make it a memorable occasion.

We set this table with an opulent gold silk sharkskin taffeta cloth. At each place setting, wheat stalks are tucked into damask napkins and tied with gold tassels. Scatter fresh dates and nuts upon the table. Wrap tall brass candlesticks in grape vine. (Wheat stalks and grape vine are both

available at crafts-supply stores or at most florists.) Fresh fruits, flowers, wheat, and barley stalks are skewered into floral oasis foam and set into the tops of the candlesticks.

On a side table, a beautiful ceramic tray depicts the Seven Fruits of Israel. Next to the tray are as many of the seven species we could find. We also set out an assortment of wines, most of them from Israel.

The first course sets the tone of this holiday dinner. Begin the meal with Pistachio Chicken Skewers placed, stick side down, in fluted bud vases. Each vase rests in a triangular plate holding the blackberry dipping sauce. The salad is comprised of many fruit and nut ingredients such as strawberries and almonds. The Rack of Lamb and its Fig-Port-Shallot Sauce also fit right into our theme. To cap off the evening, serve a vanilla Castaway Cake with a crown of perfectly caramelized coconut.

wine list

HERZOG CALIFORNIA MERLOT
BINYAMINA MERLOT RESERVE

The blackberry flavors in these reds echo the blackberry sauce that surrounds the
Pistachio Crusted Chicken Skewers.

GAMLA MOSCATO

This Israeli wine is a semi-sweet white and is ideal for the Strawberry Fields Salad.

HAGAFEN SYRAH
TEAL LAKE SHIRAZ

The Hagafen full-bodied Syrah from California has the elegance of Merlot and the
structure of Cabernet Sauvignon. This Shiraz is an Australian wine with a medium body.
It is distinctive for its spicy and fruity flavors. Both go well with the Rack of Lamb.

RASHI MOSCATO DI ASTI

With its sweet muscat flavor this light effervescent white is a perfect pairing
for the Castaway Cake or any fruit dessert.

baby blintzes

pasta
&dairy

rigatoni ala norma

Asian eggplants are light purple, narrow, and slightly sweet. They can be found in Asian markets or at upscale supermarkets. They are not as bitter as their American counterparts, which makes them perfect for this recipe. It is important to salt the eggplants; this drains them of water and keeps the eggplant slices from soaking up the olive oil or becoming soggy. As a point of interest, most people think eggplants are a vegetable. However, they are a fruit, in particular, a berry.

6 medium Asian eggplants, unpeeled and cut into ½-inch-thick slices	2 (28- to 32-ounce) cans whole plum tomatoes, drained and chopped
salt	1 tablespoon sugar
1¼ cups or more olive oil, divided	3-4 fresh basil leaves, chopped
freshly ground black pepper	1 pound rigatoni, uncooked
4 large cloves garlic, roughly chopped	fresh basil leaves

Lay the eggplant slices in a single layer. Lightly salt both sides. Cover with paper towel and let sit for 20 minutes. Press on the paper towel occasionally to soak up the water.

In a large pan, heat 1 cup (or more) of olive oil over medium-high heat. Make sure you have at least an inch of oil so it will cover the slices of eggplant and eliminate the need for flipping each piece over. When oil is very hot, carefully add the eggplant in batches and fry until golden on both sides. Transfer to a paper towel and drain. Season generously with salt and black pepper.

Place the ¼ cup olive oil in a large pot. Add the garlic and sauté until golden. Add the

tomatoes and any accumulated juices. Add the sugar and simmer about 15 minutes; the sauce will thicken. Add the basil and simmer 3-4 minutes longer.

While sauce is simmering, prepare the pasta according to directions until al dente. Drain, reserving 1 cup of the pasta water in case the sauce needs a little thinning.

Toss the pasta with the eggplant and sauce. Garnish with fresh basil leaves.

Yield: 6-8 servings

angel hair primavera in rosé sauce

Although I usually prefer using fresh herbs, the dried spice version works better in this recipe.

6 tablespoons olive oil
½ teaspoon dried basil
½ teaspoon dried thyme
½ teaspoon dried oregano
½ teaspoon dried parsley
¼ teaspoon crushed red pepper flakes
2 tablespoons dried minced onion
1 clove fresh garlic, minced
8 ounces tomato sauce
½ teaspoon parve chicken bouillon powder
1 tablespoon sugar

6 ounces heavy cream
½ cup white wine
3 tablespoons olive oil
¼ cup water
½ carrot, thinly sliced
½ cup sliced mushrooms
¾ cup broccoli florets, chopped into small pieces
¾ cup cauliflower florets, chopped into small pieces
8 ounces angel hair pasta, uncooked

In a large skillet, heat the 6 tablespoons olive oil over medium heat. Add the basil, thyme, oregano, parsley, and red pepper. Stir.

Add the minced onion and the minced garlic. Cook 2 minutes. Don't let the onion get too brown. Add the tomato sauce and bring to a boil. Add the parve chicken bouillon powder and sugar; stir. Reduce the heat; add the cream and white wine. Remove from heat and set aside.

In another pan, heat the 3 tablespoons olive oil and water over medium heat. Add the carrots, mushrooms, broccoli, and cauliflower. Sauté for 8-10 minutes or until soft.

In a large pot of boiling water, cook the angel hair pasta for two minutes. Drain. Toss the pasta with the sauce and vegetables.

Yield: 8 servings

penne arrabbiata

1 pound penne pasta, uncooked
3 tablespoons olive oil, divided
3 medium garlic cloves, 1 chopped
  and 2 thinly sliced
2 tablespoons tomato paste
1 (28-ounce) can diced tomatoes, in
  juice
1 tablespoon dark brown sugar

1 tablespoon fresh parsley, chopped
1 tablespoon fresh basil, chopped
½ teaspoon red pepper flakes
¼ cup white wine
1 teaspoon salt
  chopped fresh parsley and basil
  freshly grated Parmesan cheese,
  optional for dairy meals

Cook pasta according to package directions until al dente. Keep warm.

In a large saucepan, heat 1 tablespoon olive oil over medium heat. Add the chopped garlic and cook 30 seconds. Add tomato paste and cook 2 minutes. Add the tomatoes in juice and brown sugar; simmer 30 minutes. Set aside.

In a small saucepan, heat 1 tablespoon olive oil over medium heat. Add the thinly sliced garlic and cook 30 seconds. Add parsley, basil, and red pepper flakes. Cook 30 seconds longer. Add wine and bring to a boil; boil for 30 seconds.

Stir the wine mixture into the tomato sauce. Add salt and simmer 4-5 minutes. Toss the sauce with hot pasta in large bowl with remaining 1 tablespoon of olive oil. Garnish with chopped parsley and basil. For dairy meals, grate a little fresh Parmesan on top, if desired.

Yield: 8-10 servings

pasta pesto with fresh mozzarella, tomatoes, and avocado

If necessary, you can dice the vegetables and make the pesto for this recipe in advance. Just toss the ingredients together before serving or else the pesto will dry out a little. To keep your pesto fresh, pour it into a jar and top it off with olive oil. When ready to use, pour off the extra oil and stir the pesto. This dish is delicious at room temperature and looks great on a buffet. If you serve the dish hot, don't rinse the pasta after you drain it. By retaining the heat, the fresh mozzarella will melt just a little when tossed together for a delicious touch in texture and taste.

½ pound large (not jumbo) pasta shells or rigatoni, uncooked
2 cups loosely packed fresh basil, rinsed and dried
¼ cup olive oil, plus 1 tablespoon olive oil
1 clove garlic, peeled
1½ tablespoons pine nuts, plus extra for garnish
½ cup finely grated Parmesan cheese, extra for garnish

salt
freshly ground black pepper
2 medium red tomatoes
2 medium yellow tomatoes
1 avocado, peeled, pitted, and diced
¾ cup fresh hand-rolled mozzarella, diced
1 teaspoon red wine vinegar

Cook pasta according to package directions until al dente. Set aside.

In the bowl of a food processor fitted with a metal blade, process the basil leaves with the ¼ cup olive oil, garlic, and pine nuts, and Parmesan. Pulse to a smooth puree. Add salt and pepper to taste. Set aside.

Cut the red and yellow tomatoes in half. Scoop out the seeds and discard. Using a very sharp knife, dice the tomatoes.

In a large bowl toss the tomatoes, avocado, mozzarella, and pasta. Add the remaining tablespoon of olive oil and vinegar. Season with salt and pepper. Stir in the basil mixture and toss until combined.

Garnish with pine nuts, freshly shaved Parmesan, and a sprig of basil, if desired.

Yield: 8-10 servings

spinach cheese lasagne

1 (10-ounce) package frozen chopped spinach, defrosted and squeezed dry of liquid
1 pound cottage cheese
1 large egg
½ teaspoon oregano

freshly ground black pepper
3 (7-ounce) bags shredded mozzarella, divided
1 (26-ounce) jar marinara sauce
9-12 lasagne noodles, uncooked
1 cup water

Preheat oven to 350 degrees. In a large mixing bowl, combine the spinach, cottage cheese, egg, oregano, pepper, and ½ of the mozzarella.

Grease a 9- by 13-inch shallow pan. Ladle a thin layer of sauce on the bottom of the pan. Lay down 3-4 noodles, ½ of the cheese mixture, and a layer of sauce. Top with 3-4 more noodles, the rest of the cheese mixture, and a layer of sauce. Add 3-4 more noodles, a layer of marinara sauce, and top with the remaining mozzarella. Pour water around the sides. Cover and bake for 45 minutes; uncover and bake 30-40 minutes longer. Cheese will be melted and bubbly.

Yield: 10-12 servings

Perking up Jarred Pasta Sauce
There are some great pasta sauces on the market today. When you've got no time to prepare just toss them over your cooked pasta. If you are cooking with a jarred pasta sauce, "rinse" the jar with a small amount of good red wine and add it to the sauce while it's heating. The wine helps get the last bit of sauce out of the jar and adds a flavor boost.

mosaic onion tart

This wonderful tart of tomatoes, peppers, onions, Cheddar cheese, and olives is a feast for the eyes and taste buds. Use long plum tomatoes, rather than round plump ones, so the tomato strips will be the same length as the pepper strips.

Crust:

- 1½ cups unbleached all-purpose flour
- 1 teaspoon salt
- ½ cup (1 stick) unsalted butter, chilled and cut into pieces
- 3-4 tablespoons cold water

Filling:

- 1 tablespoon olive oil
- 2 very large Vidalia or other sweet onions, sliced
- 1½ cups grated Cheddar cheese
- 1 yellow bell pepper, cut lengthwise into ¼-inch strips and ends trimmed so strips lay flat
- 1 green bell pepper, cut lengthwise into ¼-inch strips and ends trimmed so strips lay flat
- 3 medium plum tomatoes, cut lengthwise into ¼-inch strips and seeded
- ½ cup sliced black pitted olives
- ½ teaspoon dried oregano freshly ground black pepper

In the bowl of a food processor fitted with a dough blade, combine the flour, salt, and butter. Process until the mixture resembles coarse crumbs. Add the water a tablespoon at a time and pulse until a ball of dough forms. Wrap the dough in plastic wrap and chill in the refrigerator.

Preheat the oven to 375 degrees. Heat the olive oil in a large skillet and add the onions. Cook about 10-15 minutes or until the onions are soft.

Remove the dough from the refrigerator. On a lightly floured surface, roll out the dough into a 12- by 12-inch square. Lightly grease a 9- by 9-inch square baking pan. Ease the dough into the pan. Roll the dough down so that it comes an inch below the top of the pan. Use your thumb and forefinger to crimp the edges decoratively.

Prick the crust all over with a fork. Pre-bake for 8-10 minutes. Remove from oven and let cool for 10 minutes.

Cover the bottom of the tart with the onions. Sprinkle on the Cheddar cheese. Arrange the yellow pepper, green pepper, and tomato strips in alternating stripes atop the cheese. You should have two vertical rows of alternating stripes. Or feel free to improvise a design. Scatter the olives over the tart and sprinkle with oregano and pepper.

Bake for 30 minutes or until the crust is golden and the cheese is melted.

Yield: 9-12 servings

tomato, black olive, and mozzarella orzo gratin

Dairy

This is a great accompaniment to fish or a nice salad.

1 pound orzo
8 tablespoons olive oil
2 onions, finely chopped
5 cloves garlic, chopped
3 ribs celery, chopped
4 tablespoons all-purpose flour
2 cups vegetable stock
1 (28-ounce) can plum tomatoes, well drained

4 tablespoons parsley, chopped
3 tablespoons fresh basil, julienned
½ cup black olives, pitted and sliced
2 cups mozzarella, divided
2 cups Parmesan cheese, divided
salt
freshly ground black pepper

Preheat oven to 400 degrees. Spray a large baking dish with nonstick cooking spray. Set aside.

Bring a large pot of salted water to a boil. Add the orzo and cook for half of the recommended cooking time. (The orzo will finish cooking when you bake it.) Drain well and transfer to a large bowl; set aside.

In a large skillet, heat the olive oil over medium-high heat. Add the onion and garlic and cook until softened, stirring. Add the celery and cook for 5 minutes longer. Stir in the flour and cook for 3 minutes, stirring. Add the vegetable broth, tomatoes, parsley, and basil. Simmer the mixture for 5 minutes; use the back of the spoon to break up the tomatoes.

Remove skillet from heat and add the vegetables into the orzo. Add the olives, 1 cup of the mozzarella, and 1½ cups of the Parmesan. Season with salt and pepper.

Transfer the mixture into the prepared baking dish. Top with remaining mozzarella and Parmesan. (The dish can be prepared up to this point, one day in advance. Keep covered and in the refrigerator.)

Bake for 40-50 minutes or until heated through and the cheese is melted.

Yield: 8-10 servings

caramelized onion and walnut tart Dairy

The beauty of this recipe is that you can use dough purchased from your local pizza store or supermarket. It's a great shortcut when preparing this brunch food.

2 tablespoons butter
4 medium onions, peeled and thinly sliced
2 teaspoons sugar
1-2 tablespoons yellow cornmeal

1 pound pizza dough
1 (6.5-ounce) container garlic and herb soft cheese spread, like Aloutte
½ cup walnut pieces

Preheat the oven to 425 degrees. In a medium pot, melt the butter. Add the onions and sugar. Cover and cook over medium heat for 25-30 minutes or until the onions are golden brown, stirring occasionally to make sure the onions do not stick or burn. Remove onions from heat; set aside.

Lightly grease an 11- or 12-inch tart pan with a removable bottom. Sprinkle with the cornmeal.

On a lightly floured surface, roll out the dough into a large circle. Place the dough into the pan. Press the dough into and up the sides. Use scissors or a knife to trim any overhang. Prick all over with a fork.

Bake for 10-12 minutes or until lightly browned. Remove from oven and spread the cheese spread over the hot crust. Top with the onions. Sprinkle the walnut pieces. Bake for 10 more minutes or until heated through.

Yield: 8-10 servings

greek tomato-spinach pizza

¼ cup olive oil

2 cups chopped onion

3 garlic cloves, minced

3 (10-ounce) boxes frozen chopped spinach, thawed and squeezed dry

2 teaspoons dry oregano

½ cup chopped fresh basil

½ teaspoon freshly ground black pepper

15 ounces ricotta cheese

10 sheets phyllo dough, thawed

¼ cup (½ stick) butter, melted

4-6 fresh tomatoes, evenly sliced

1½ cups grated mozzarella cheese

Preheat the oven to 400 degrees. In a skillet, heat the olive oil over medium heat. Add the onion and garlic; sauté about 5 minutes or until onions are translucent.

Add the spinach and sauté until all excess moisture has evaporated. Add oregano, basil, and black pepper. Mix well; remove from heat. Mix in the ricotta cheese; set aside.

Grease a large jelly roll pan (the kind with a small rim). Lay one sheet of phyllo in it; the phyllo may be just a little bigger than the pan. Brush the sheet of phyllo with melted butter. Top with the second sheet of phyllo and brush with melted butter. Repeat the process until all ten sheets are buttered. Roll the ends of overlapping phyllo onto itself to form the "pizza crust".

Using a spatula, spread the spinach ricotta mixture in an even layer over the phyllo.

Arrange the tomatoes over this layer. Sprinkle with the mozzarella. Bake 25-30 minutes or until golden brown.

Yield: 12 servings

peach muffins

1 large egg
1 cup milk
¼ cup (½ stick) butter, melted
⅔ cup sugar
½ teaspoon salt
¼ teaspoon cinnamon
1 teaspoon fresh lemon juice

¼ teaspoon vanilla
2 cups all-purpose flour
3 teaspoons baking powder
2 ripe peaches, unpeeled and
  chopped (about 1½ cups)

Preheat the oven to 350 degrees. Grease 12 muffin tins.

In a large mixing bowl, beat the egg. By hand, stir in the milk, melted butter, sugar, salt, cinnamon, lemon juice, and vanilla.

In a separate bowl, sift the flour and baking powder together. Mix into the wet ingredients until just blended; do not over-mix or the batter will toughen. Fold in the peaches very gently.

Fill the muffin tins ¾ full, using an ice-cream scooper. Bake 20 minutes.

Yield: 12 muffins

morning glory muffins

2 cups all-purpose flour
2 teaspoons baking soda
2 teaspoons cinnamon
¼ teaspoon salt
1¼ cups sugar
2 cups finely shredded carrot
½ cup pecan pieces
½ cup raisins

¼ cup sweetened flaked coconut
3 large eggs
½ cup corn oil
1 cup applesauce
2 teaspoons vanilla
1 Granny Smith apple, peeled, cored, and coarsely shredded

Preheat oven to 350 degrees. In a large bowl, sift together the flour, baking soda, cinnamon, and salt. Stir in the sugar. Set aside.

Fold in the shredded carrot, pecans, raisins, and coconut. Toss well.

In a separate bowl, whisk together the eggs, oil, applesauce, and vanilla. Add the apple into the egg mixture. Add this to the flour mixture, stirring constantly until batter is well combined.

Divide the batter among the 18 muffin cups, filling them ¾ full. Bake 15 minutes in the middle of the oven. Turn the oven to broil and broil the muffins for 2 minutes. This will make the tops puffed and golden.

Yield: 18 muffins

Butter Molds
Experimenting with butter molds can personalize various occasions. Purchase plastic candy molds at an arts-and-crafts or party-supply store. They come in dozens of shapes: shells, teddy bears, stars, hearts, sunflowers etc. Spray the mold with nonstick cooking spray. Pat softened butter or margarine into each mold, then freeze until ready to use.

onion cheddar bread

2 tablespoons butter, divided
½ cup chopped onion
½ cup milk
1 large egg, slightly beaten
1½ cups packaged biscuit mix, such as Bisquick
1 cup Cheddar cheese, shredded, divided

1 tablespoon poppy seeds, divided
2 teaspoons butter
1 onion, thinly sliced into rings (try to keep the rings intact), cut in half lengthwise

Preheat oven to 400 degrees. Grease an 8-inch round baking pan. In a medium skillet, melt 1 tablespoon of the butter. Add the chopped onion and sauté about 5-6 minutes or until tender.

In a mixing bowl, combine the milk and egg. Add the biscuit mix and stir until just moistened. Add the onion mixture, half the Cheddar cheese, and half of the poppy seeds.

Spread the batter into the prepared pan. Sprinkle the remaining cheese and poppy seeds on top.

In the skillet, melt the 2 teaspoons butter over medium heat. Add the onion and sauté until wilted.

Arrange the cooked onion slices on top of the bread. Melt the remaining tablespoon of butter and drizzle over the top of the bread. Bake for 20 minutes. Cut into wedges. Serve warm.

Yield: 8 servings

Onion Primer

CHIVES *are thin, long green onions. They make a nice garnish when left whole or chopped.*

SCALLIONS *are also known as green onions. They have a pungent flavor.*

YELLOW ONIONS *are sweet onions that are great for caramelizing. Some varieties include Vidalia and Walla Walla.*

WHITE ONIONS *have a sharp flavor. The small variety of white onions are known as pearl onions.*

RED ONIONS *are valued for their color and look great in salads.*

SHALLOTS *have a mild, delicate flavor and are wonderful in sautés and sauces.*

LEEKS *are mellower than onions.*

strawberry bread

Parve

This bread is a lovely addition to any brunch table. Serve it with assorted jams or butter molds. Since the strawberry bread is parve, it also serves nicely as an accompaniment to a salad or soup course.

3 large eggs	3 cups all-purpose flour
1 cup oil	1 teaspoon salt
2 cups sugar	1 teaspoon baking soda
1 tablespoon vanilla	¼ teaspoon baking powder
2 pints strawberries, hulled and mashed	1 tablespoon cinnamon

Preheat oven to 350 degrees. Spray 2 loaf pans with nonstick cooking spray. Set aside.

In a large mixing bowl, beat the eggs at a medium speed. Add the oil, sugar, vanilla, and strawberries.

In a separate bowl, mix the flour, salt, baking soda, baking powder, and cinnamon. Add it into the strawberry mixture; fold to combine.

Pour into prepared loaf pans. Bake for 1 hour or until tester inserted in center comes out clean.

Yield: 12-14 servings

☞ *Hulling Strawberries*
To hull a strawberry, push a sturdy plastic drinking straw up through the bottom of the berry and out the top. The diameter of most straws is perfect to dislodge the stem without taking out too much of the flesh. This trick is fast and neat.

zucchini bread

Parve

This recipe is fabulous at a brunch or when served with a hot bowl of zucchini soup.

1½ cups all-purpose flour	1 cup sugar
1 teaspoon ground cinnamon	2 medium zucchini, unpeeled and grated
½ teaspoon baking soda	
¼ teaspoon salt	¼ cup canola oil
¼ teaspoon baking powder	1 large egg

Preheat oven to 350 degrees. Using margarine, lightly grease the bottom and halfway up the sides of a 8- by 4- by 2-inch loaf pan. Set aside. In a medium bowl, combine the flour, cinnamon, baking soda, salt, and baking powder. Set aside.

In a separate bowl, combine the sugar, grated zucchini, oil, and egg. Stir.

Add in the flour mixture. Stir until just combined.

Pour mixture into prepared loaf pan and bake for 55-60 minutes. Cool in pan for 10 minutes. Turn the zucchini bread out of the pan and cool completely on a rack.

Yield: 16 servings

cinnamon buns

Children from all over my neighborhood call to request a batch of these amazingly gooey cinnamon buns. I use a separate bread machine for dairy recipes. If you don't, you can use nondairy creamer in place of the milk in the dough. Obviously the rest of the recipe will remain dairy, but your bread machine will stay parve. You can also make the dough by hand if you don't own a bread machine. Credit for this recipe goes to the allrecipes.com Web site.

Cinnamon buns:

1 cup warm milk
2 large eggs, room temperature
⅓ cup margarine, melted
4½ cups bread flour
1 teaspoon salt
½ cup sugar
2½ teaspoons bread machine yeast
  or rapid-rise yeast

1 cup dark brown sugar, firmly packed
2½ tablespoons ground cinnamon
⅓ cup butter, softened, not melted
  (can be microwaved for 30 seconds)

Glaze:

1 (3-ounce) package cream cheese,
  softened
¼ cup butter, softened (not melted)

1½ cups confectioner's sugar
½ teaspoon vanilla extract
⅛ teaspoon salt

Cinnamon buns:

Place the milk, eggs, melted margarine, flour, salt, sugar, and yeast in the pan of the bread machine in the order recommended by the manufacturer. Select dough cycle. Press start.

After the dough has doubled or the cycle is complete, turn it out onto a lightly floured surface; cover and let rest for 10 minutes.

In a small bowl, combine the brown sugar and cinnamon.

Roll the dough into a 16- by 21-inch rectangle. Spread the dough with the ⅓ cup butter and sprinkle with the brown sugar/cinnamon mixture.

Starting with the long side of the rectangle, roll up the dough. Cut into 12-14 slices.

Place the rolls in a lightly greased 9- by 13-inch baking pan. It's okay if it doesn't fill the pan, the rolls will expand. Cover and let rise until nearly doubled, about 30 minutes.

Preheat oven to 400 degrees. Bake the rolls about 15 minutes or until golden brown.

Glaze:

In a mixing bowl, beat the cream cheese, ¼ cup butter, confectioner's sugar, vanilla, and salt. While the rolls are still warm and in the pan, frost them with the glaze.

Yield: 12-14 servings

baby blintzes

These can be served hot, warm, or at room temperature.

8 ounces farmer cheese (regular, not unsalted)
8 ounces cottage cheese (2% or 4% milkfat)
3 tablespoons sour cream
⅓ cup sugar
½ cup all-purpose baking mix, such as Bisquick

1 teaspoon vanilla
3 tablespoons melted butter
3 large eggs
12 raspberries
24 blueberries
  cinnamon/sugar
  sour cream

Preheat oven to 350 degrees. Heavily grease a muffin tin with butter or nonstick cooking spray. In a large bowl, mix the farmer cheese, cottage cheese, sour cream, sugar, baking mix, vanilla, melted butter, and eggs with an electric mixer at medium speed.

Fill each of the muffin compartments halfway with the mixture. Place 1 raspberry and 2 blueberries on top of each muffin tin. Bake 20-25 minutes.

Remove from oven. Before serving sprinkle each baby blintze with cinnamon/sugar mixture and a small dollop of sour cream.

Yield: 12 servings

challah souffle

This rich, decadent souffle has the classic flavors of French toast. It is wonderful when served at a brunch and easy to assemble the night before.

1 medium challah, 4 challah rolls, or 4 large croissants
1 (8-ounce) package cream cheese, softened
½ cup (1 stick) butter, softened at room temperature for 15 minutes, plus extra for serving on the side

¾ cup maple syrup (not pancake syrup), divided, plus extra for serving on the side
10 large eggs
3 cups light cream
1 teaspoon cinnamon
2 tablespoon confectioner's sugar

In the bowl of a food processor fitted with a metal blade, coarsely chop the challah or croissants.

Distribute chopped bread evenly over the bottom of a 9- by 13-inch casserole or baking dish.

Combine the cream cheese, butter, and ¼ cup maple syrup in the food processor; pulse until smooth. Spread over the chopped bread.

In a separate medium bowl, beat the eggs, remaining ½ cup maple syrup, and cream. Pour over the mixture. Sprinkle with cinnamon. Cover and refrigerate overnight.

Preheat oven to 350 degrees. Uncover the souffle and bake for 45-50 minutes or until puffed and golden. Sprinkle with confectioner's sugar. Serve with warmed maple syrup and softened butter.

Yield: 12-14 servings

A Floral Cake
This makes a wonderful centerpiece. It's gorgeous, has flair, and contains no calories! Soak a 9-inch-round, 6-inch-tall piece of floral Styrofoam in water for 1-2 minutes. Cut the flowers of your choice to a height of 1 inch. Place blossoms around the sides of the mold, tightly overlapping so that no Styrofoam shows. Repeat this process for the top. Place this flower cake on a cake plate. You can stick a knife in it for effect.

spinach cheese frittata

This Italian-style omelet bursts with flavor. It's delicious at any temperature, so there is no need to serve it right out of the oven. Try serving at a dairy lunch or late breakfast.

2 teaspoons olive oil
1 bunch scallions, thinly sliced
10 ounces frozen chopped spinach, thawed and squeezed dry
8 large eggs
1 cup shredded Swiss or Muenster cheese
½ cup fresh basil leaves, chopped

1 garlic clove, minced
½ teaspoon dried thyme
¼ teaspoon salt
¼ teaspoon freshly ground black pepper
2 tablespoons grated Parmesan cheese, divided
1 tablespoon butter

Preheat oven to 400 degrees. In a nonstick 10-inch skillet with oven-safe handle (or with handle wrapped in double thickness of foil for baking in the oven later), heat oil over medium heat until hot. Add the scallions and cook about 2 minutes or until wilted. Add the spinach and cook about 10 minutes, stirring until moisture has evaporated.

In a large bowl, whisk together the eggs, Swiss or Muenster cheese, basil, garlic, thyme, salt, pepper, and 1 tablespoon Parmesan. Stir the spinach mixture into the egg mixture.

In the skillet, melt the butter over medium heat. Add the spinach/egg mixture back into the skillet and cook for 1 minute, stirring once. Reduce heat to low and cook 5 minutes longer. Mixture will begin to set around the edges. Sprinkle with remaining 1 tablespoon Parmesan. Place skillet in the preheated oven and bake for 10 minutes or until fritatta sets. Loosen edges of fritatta and slide onto a platter.

Yield: 6 servings

purim

Purim is the one festival that encourages behavior that is normally restrained in Jewish life: synagogues become boisterous; adults freely imbibe wine and spirits; zany costumes, masks and giddy celebration are the order of the day. Why does traditional, stately Judaism tolerate these hi-jinks?

It's all a front. In rabbinic lore, Purim has the gravity and holiness of Yom Kippur, but these are masked by revelry. The essence of Purim is that life is filled with illusions.

We learn this subtle message from the *Megillah* itself. The story it tells seems to be one of typical court intrigue and human valor: A paranoid king, a scheming villain, a pious Jewish queen and her wise uncle each play a role in this tale of schemes and counter-schemes. The story is full of wild coincidences and ironic twists as seemingly unrelated events come together in a rapid, bizarre finale.

But it's not that simple. In writing the *Megillah*, Queen Esther and her uncle Mordechai wove in allusions to the spiritual forces at work under what appear to be mundane politics and pure luck. They understood clearly that the threatened

Jews (all the Jews in the world, at that time) were saved from extinction because they united in brotherhood and repentance. Throughout the *Megillah*, they hint that the Hand of God moved the entire process through a series of covert miracles.

Jewish custom merrily goes along with this theme of illusion. We masquerade to hide reality. We conceal luscious fillings beneath the dough in hamantaschen. We strengthen Jewish brotherhood by giving gifts and charity to the poor and by sending mishloach manot — wonderful packages of food — to our friends and neighbors.

And we feast. Just as the *Megillah* opens with the opulent feast of the Persian monarch, it ends with the Jews feasting in celebration of their miraculous victory. Good cooks have been concocting their versions of a royal Persian banquet ever since.

So pull out your finest wines and your most creative ideas, and share the moment with fellow Jews all over the world who know that life — especially life as a Jew — is never what it seems.

purim menu

The boisterous, joyous mood of Purim appears on our table, which screams with color. Begin by setting down a bold multicolored tablecloth. We used a patchwork of raw silk in vibrant colors. Glue regal purple trim down to hide the seams where the fabrics meet. In honor of Queen Esther, cut large crown-shaped place mats out of gorgeous beaded fabric. Glue on large plastic gems for a finished effect. Real flowers, used sparingly, can be set in small patterned bud vases down the center of the table and scattered around the place settings. Tall purple and orange tapers set the table aglow. Whimsical accents balance the importance of the occasion with a bit of humor. The finishing touches — silver groggers (noisemakers) and masks — adorn each guest's place setting.

In one corner, we placed a spectacular Shalach Manot basket surrounded by charity boxes, groggers, and a stunning silver *Megillah* case. Large crepe paper flowers on a bare sideboard fill the empty corners of the room.

It is customary to have a challah on the table. The Talmud records that to avoid eating non-kosher food, Esther ate only seeds while living in the king's palace. Our challah is richly covered with poppy, sesame and sunflower seeds as a tribute to her commitment. We selected a menu that picks up on the themes and nuances of the holiday. The meal starts with Won ton Wrapped Chicken. The hidden chicken filling represents the hidden layers of the Purim miracles. Another take on this dish stems from the fact that Haman superstitiously drew "lots" to determine the "auspicious" date for the Jews to be annihilated. Our small, envelope-shaped appetizers represent those lots.

The entree is a roast turkey. We chose to feature turkey as a play on the *Megillah's* description of King Achashverosh's vast empire that stretched from India (in Hebrew, *Hodu*) to Ethiopia. The Hebrew term for turkey is *tarnegol Hodu* – "Indian chicken." As it is a *mitzvah* to drink on Purim, the sweet potatoes are glazed with Jack Daniels.

All three desserts reflect a tradition of the holiday: the Hamantasch, a traditional cookie, represents Haman's three-cornered hat; the Chocolate and Vanilla Rope Cookies remind us of the rope used to hang Haman and his ten sons; and in keeping with the theme of hidden miracles, the elegant Warm Apple and Pear Beggar's Purses, contain a hidden center.

The food, the décor and the mirthful ambience create an unmistakable aura of merriment. You guests will never forget this Purim banquet!

wine list

HAGAFEN JOHANNISBERG RIESLING

This versatile wine shows a beautiful tropical bouquet with aromas of apricot.
It pairs perfectly with our Won Ton Wrapped Chicken.
In general it goes well with Asian, Indian, or Middle Eastern food.

GIGONDAS RHONE
HAGAFEN PINOT NIOR

We recommend this wine for the Roast Turkey.
The acidity and flavors of the Gigondas will stand up to the Balsamic Onion Gravy.

The Pinot Nior is another terrific choice.

KEDEM 50TH ANNIVERSARY PORT
HAFNER ICEWINE (EISWEIN)

This port is a full-bodied wine that is best served with pastry and fruit
which makes it ideal for our Warm Apple and Pear Beggar's Purses.

Flavorful Eiswein is produced from frozen grapes that are quickly pressed to capture the
concentrated sugar. High acidity balances the sugar so the wine is not cloyingly sweet.
Therefore it will go well with Hamantashen and the Black and White Rope Cookies.

Slow-Roasted Tomatos

side dishes

glazed sweet potatoes

Once you start eating these sticky sweet potatoes, you won't be able to stop.

4-5 pounds sweet potatoes, peeled
    (about 5 large)
  4 tablespoons (½ stick) margarine
  1 cup dark brown sugar

1 tablespoon vanilla extract
¼ teaspoon salt
¼ cup whiskey or bourbon, such as
    Jack Daniels

Preheat oven to 375 degrees. Cut the sweet potatoes into ½-inch slices. Steam the sweet potatoes for 10 minutes or until soft but not mushy. Remove potatoes from the steamer and set aside.

In a small saucepan, melt the margarine over medium heat. Add the brown sugar, vanilla, and salt, stirring until the sugar is dissolved. Stir in the whiskey or bourbon and cook for 5-10 minutes or until slightly thickened, stirring occasionally.

Spray a large 9- by 13-inch glass baking dish with nonstick cooking spray. Place the sweet potatoes in the pan and drizzle the sauce over the top.

> 🐟 Another way to present this dish is to cut each potato in half lengthwise. Cut each half into 4 wedges. After the dish is cooked, set the slices of sweet potato in a star burst or flower petal design on your serving platter. Fill the center with cranberry sauce.

Bake uncovered for 1 hour. Baste with the sauce every 10 minutes to keep the potatoes from drying out.

Yield: 8-10 Servings

slow-roasted tomatoes

Parve

This beautiful and simple side dish is accented by fresh oregano. Use any combination of cherry and grape tomatoes. Feel free to improvise with the color; orange tomatoes work just as well.

4-5 garlic cloves, chopped
¼ cup fresh oregano leaves
½ cup olive oil
    salt

    freshly ground black pepper
2 pints red cherry or grape tomatoes
2 pints yellow cherry or grape tomatoes

Preheat oven to 350 degrees. In a medium bowl, combine the garlic, oregano, olive oil, salt, and pepper. Add the tomatoes and toss. Pour into a baking dish. Roast uncovered for 40 minutes. Serve warm.

Yield: 8-10 servings

butternut squash muffins

Parve

As much as I love serving fresh vegetables as side dishes, my family enjoys kugels and the like. These muffins are a favorite. More upscale than carrot muffins, they still hold the same homey appeal. Serve warm or at room temperature. These are a great accompaniment to squash soup.

2 cups all-purpose flour
1 cup whole wheat flour
1 cup sugar
4½ teaspoons baking powder
1½ teaspoons ground cinnamon
¾ teaspoon salt
3 large eggs, lightly beaten

1 tablespoon vanilla
1 cup apple cider or apple juice
½ cup vegetable oil
2 (20-ounce) packages frozen butternut squash cubes, thawed, divided
    cinnamon-sugar

Preheat oven to 350 degrees. Heavily grease and flour 2-3 muffin trays.

In a large bowl, combine the flours, sugar, baking powder, cinnamon, and salt. In a medium bowl, combine the eggs, vanilla, apple cider, and oil. Add the egg mixture to the flour mixture, stirring until moistened. Set aside 30 of the prettiest butternut squash cubes and fold remaining cubes into the batter. Spoon batter into greased muffin tins, filling ⅔s full. Top each muffin with a reserved squash cube. Sprinkle with cinnamon-sugar. Bake for 25-30 minutes. Remove from pans and cool on wire racks. If you make the muffins in batches, regrease and flour the tins before refilling. Do not use paper cup liners.

Yield: 2½ dozen muffins

mushroom tart

In a pinch you can use a package of 2 deep-dish frozen pie shells instead of the puff pastry. After the pie shell is filled, as a decorative touch take the fluted edges from the second crust and place it around the inside of the first crust for a double ruffled effect. Use the remainder to cut into strips for the lattice.

2 sheets puff pastry or 1 (17.3-ounce) package puff pastry	½ teaspoon freshly ground black pepper
⅓ cup margarine	1 tablespoon flour
1-2 medium onions, finely chopped	⅓ cup nondairy creamer
1½ pounds sliced mushrooms, any combination of cremini, shiitake, or portobello	1 tablespoon dry white wine
	1 egg, beaten
⅛ teaspoon salt	sesame seeds

Preheat oven to 350 degrees. Roll out the puff pastry dough into a large square. Ease it into a deep-dish pie pan. Let excess dough hang over the sides; use a knife to trim edges. Bake for 10 minutes. It is okay if it's puffy; the mushrooms will weigh the dough back down. Set aside.

Increase oven temperature to 400 degrees. In a large pan, melt the margarine over medium heat. Add the onions and sauté about 5 minutes or until onions are translucent. Add the mushrooms and sauté for 5 minutes longer.

Add the salt, pepper, and flour. Pour in the nondairy creamer. Stir about 2-3 minutes or until thickened. Stir in the wine. Pour the mixture into the prepared crust.

Using the second puff pastry sheet, cut long ½-inch strips and form a lattice design over the top of the tart. Brush with beaten egg. Sprinkle with sesame seeds.

Bake, uncovered, on the lowest shelf for 20-30 minutes.

Yield: 8-10 servings

✎ If lattice making is not your thing, you can use cookie cutters to cut out uniform shapes, like leaves or stars and scatter them across the top of the tart. Brush with egg and sprinkle sesame seeds on top.

green beans with crispy shallots

⅓ cup vegetable oil
4-5 shallots, thinly sliced into rings or strips
2 tablespoons margarine

2 tablespoons olive oil
2 pounds fresh green beans
salt
freshly ground black pepper

In a small pan, heat the vegetable oil over medium heat until hot but not smoky. Fry the shallots about 5-7 minutes or until shallots are brown and crispy. Make sure they don't burn. Remove from heat, discarding the oil.

In a large pan, heat the margarine and olive oil over medium heat. Add the green beans and sauté about 5 minutes or until the beans are bright green. Season with salt and pepper. Remove from heat. Toss the shallots over the green beans.

Yield: 8-10 servings

roasted garlic string beans with mango

Parve

This recipe's crunch, color, and incredible flavor make it my absolute favorite way to serve green beans.

- 2 pounds green beans, trimmed
- 5-6 scallions, halved and ends trimmed
- 7-8 garlic cloves
- ¼ cup balsamic vinegar
- 3 tablespoons water
- ½ cup olive oil
- 1 (0.92-ounce) packet roasted garlic dry salad dressing mix
- 2 tablespoons Dijon mustard
- 3 tablespoons honey
- 1-2 fresh mango, peeled and diced; or ⅓ pound dried mango, soaked in warm water for 5 minutes then cut into very small pieces
- 2 handfuls sunflower seeds
- 2 handfuls chopped walnuts

In a large pot of salted boiling water, cook green beans about 6 minutes or until crisp-tender. Drain; run beans under cold water and drain again.

In the container of a food processor fitted with a metal blade, process the scallions, garlic, balsamic vinegar, water, oil, dressing packet, mustard, and honey. Pulse until emulsified and smooth. May be done in advance. Can keep in refrigerator for 4-5 days. Remove from refrigerator at least ½ hour before using and shake very well.

Pour the dressing over the green beans. Right before serving, add the mango, sunflower seeds, and walnuts. Mix well.

Yield: 12 servings

toasted israeli couscous with summer vegetables

Meat

¼ cup balsamic vinegar
½ teaspoon grainy Dijon mustard
2 garlic cloves, coarsely chopped
½ cup olive oil
⅛ teaspoon salt
⅛ teaspoon freshly ground black pepper
1 green zucchini, peeled and cut into small pieces
1 yellow squash, unpeeled and cut into small pieces

12 cherry or grape tomatoes
½ cup red onion, finely chopped
20 ounces chicken stock
1 teaspoon powdered chicken bouillon (preferably the meat kind; its more flavorful than the parve kind)
1 tablespoon margarine
1 tablespoon olive oil
1 (8.8-ounce) package Israeli couscous

In a cruet or jar, pour the vinegar, mustard, garlic, olive oil, salt, and pepper. Whisk or shake vigorously so the mixture emulsifies and is well combined.

In a bowl, combine the zucchini, squash, tomatoes, and onion. Pour half of the marinade over the vegetables and let stand at room temperature for 15 minutes.

In a pot, heat the chicken stock. Add the powdered bouillon. Keep warm.

In a large pan, melt the margarine over medium heat. Add the olive oil. Add the vegetables and their marinade into the pan and sauté for 6-8 minutes. Using a slotted spoon, remove the vegetables from the pan, leaving some of the marinade behind.

Add the couscous to the pan. Toast about 3-4 minutes or until lightly golden brown over medium heat. Cover the couscous with the hot chicken stock and bring to a boil. Lower to a simmer and cook, covered, about 8-10 minutes or until the couscous is tender and the liquid is mostly absorbed.

Stir in the vegetables. Toss with remaining marinade. Serve at room temperature.

Yield: 6-8 servings

sun-dried tomato & portobello risotto Meat or Parve

Mushrooms:

4 tablespoons balsamic vinegar
1 cup red wine
2 garlic cloves, minced
 salt

 freshly ground black pepper
8 (3- to 4-inch) portobello
 mushrooms, stems removed

Risotto:

½ cup (1 stick) margarine
1 large onion, finely chopped
2 cups Arborio rice, uncooked

1 cup white wine
6 cups chicken or vegetable broth
6 sun-dried tomatoes, julienned

Mushrooms:

In a large glass bowl, combine the balsamic vinegar, wine, garlic, salt, and pepper. Add the mushrooms and marinate for 1 hour. Remove the mushrooms from marinade and grill or broil for about 5 minutes or until tender. Remove from heat and set aside.

Risotto:

In a large saucepan, melt the margarine over medium-high heat. Add the chopped onion and sauté about 4-6 minutes or until translucent. Add the rice, stirring often, for about 3-4 minutes. Stir in the white wine. Gradually add the broth, stirring in 1 cup at a time, allowing the rice to absorb the broth before adding more. Additions will take between 20-30 minutes.

After all of the liquid is absorbed, add the sun-dried tomatoes. Season with salt and pepper.

Place a mushroom on each plate. Using an ice-cream scoop, top with a mound of risotto. Alternatively, chop up the mushrooms and toss in with the risotto.

Yield: 8 servings

spinach leek tart

This elegant square tart boasts wonderful flavors.

- 1 (17½-ounce) package frozen puff pastry, thawed, divided
- 2 large eggs, divided
- 4 tablespoons margarine, divided
- 3 garlic cloves, minced
- 2 shallots, minced
- 4 ounces or 1½ cups cremini mushrooms, stems removed, sliced
- 1 tablespoon Port, Madeira, sherry or other red wine
- 2 leeks, thinly sliced; use white and pale green part only
- 1 (10 ounce) box frozen chopped spinach, thawed and squeezed dry
- ½ cup chicken broth
- 1 teaspoon rosemary
- 1 teaspoon grated lemon zest juice from ½ lemon pinch Kosher salt pinch freshly ground black pepper
- 3-4 tablespoons bread crumbs

Preheat oven to 400 degrees. Roll out each of the puff pastry sheets into a 10- by 10-inch square. Place 1 puff pastry sheet on an ungreased baking sheet. (I like to have it covered with parchment paper for easy cleanup.) Cut the other pastry sheet into 8 (1-inch-wide) strips. Brush the edges of the flat sheet with cold water. Lay 4 of the strips around the edges to form a flat rim like a picture frame. Brush this rim with cold water. Lay the other 4 strips on top of these to form a higher rim. Trim the corners as necessary so it is a neat square. Press the strips to adhere.

Beat 1 egg lightly and brush on the pastry frame. Prick the tart all over the bottom with a fork. Place in oven and bake about 7-10 minutes or until puffed and golden. Remove from oven, set aside.

Melt 2 tablespoons of margarine in a large skillet over medium heat. Add the garlic and shallots and sauté 3-4 minutes or until shallots are soft. Add the mushrooms and sauté 7-8 minutes or until they are soft. Add the wine and scrape up the brown bits from the bottom of the pan.

Add the remaining 2 tablespoons margarine. When it is melted, add the leeks and spinach and sauté about 10 minutes or until leeks are soft and shiny. Add the chicken broth and simmer until the liquid is mostly evaporated. Stir in the rosemary, lemon zest, lemon juice, salt, and pepper. Remove from heat.

Lightly beat the remaining egg and add it to the spinach-leek mixture, mixing well. Carefully spoon the mixture into the prebaked tart, keeping the rim clean. Sprinkle with the bread crumbs. Bake for 15 minutes. Serve warm.

Yield: 8 servings

☞ *Cleaning Leeks:*
Remove any wilted outer leaves. Cut off the roots. Slice the leek in half lengthwise.
Hold the leek under the faucet, lifting and separating the leaves with your fingers to loosen any dirt. Continue rinsing until all grit is removed.

scalloped potatoes

I love to make these potatoes in an oven-to-table dish. The brown crust around the rim of the dish adds a rustic look. Plus, serving it in its baking dish means one less platter for me to wash.

6 tablespoons margarine
½ cup flour
2 large onions, chopped
½ cup mayonnaise
½ teaspoon salt

28 ounces chicken stock
9-10 large Idaho potatoes, peeled and
   sliced into ¼-inch-slices
   freshly ground black pepper
   paprika

Preheat oven to 350 degrees. Spray a 9- by 13-inch glass or ceramic baking dish with nonstick cooking spray.

In a large pot, melt the margarine over medium-high heat. Add the flour, stirring constantly. Add the onions, mayonnaise, salt, and chicken stock. Stir until smooth. Cook until the sauce thickens.

With a ladle, place a layer of the sauce into the bottom of the prepared pan. Spread a layer of overlapping potatoes. Top with a layer of sauce. Repeat, alternating with layers of potatoes and sauce. There should be a total of three sauce layers and two potato layers, with sauce on top.

Sprinkle the top layer with pepper and paprika. Bake uncovered for 1½ hours or until golden.

Yield: 10-12 servings

shallot butter mashed potatoes

These mashed potatoes are creamy and whipped. Sour cream, potatoes, butter, milk, shallots—need I say more?

1 teaspoon butter, softened
1 shallot, diced
4 tablespoons butter, softened
1 tablespoon fresh parsley, minced
2½ pounds Yukon gold or baking potatoes, peeled and cubed

2 garlic cloves, halved
½ cup milk
3 tablespoons sour cream
¾ teaspoon salt
⅛ teaspoon black pepper

In a small skillet, melt 1 teaspoon butter over medium heat. Add the shallots and cook 3-4 minutes. Remove from heat; let cool for 5 minutes.

Combine sautéed shallot, 4 tablespoons butter, and parsley. Stir until well blended; cover and refrigerate.

In a large pot, bring potatoes and garlic, covered with water, to a boil. Reduce heat and simmer for 25-30 minutes. Drain. Place the potatoes back into the empty pot. Add the milk, sour cream, salt, and pepper. Beat with a mixer until smooth and creamy. Add the shallot butter and mix until smooth.

> ☞ You can prepare the potatoes and shallot butter in advance. Store each in separate covered containers in the refrigerator. Add the butter to the potatoes right before heating. Mix the butter into the hot potatoes

Yield: 8 servings

❧

roasted garlic mashed potato galette

Parve

This free-form torte is filled with such creamy mashed potatoes you would bet that they were dairy. Though there are a lot of steps in this recipe, you can do most of them simultaneously to shorten the process. The potatoes don't need to be peeled, so they are a breeze to make. After baking, transfer the heavy torte onto your serving platter. Instead of lifting it, try sliding the torte from the baking sheet directly onto your platter. You can also make these as individual mini free-form tortes. As a time saver you can purchase pie dough (not pie shells) that can be rolled out and used in place of the homemade dough.

Dough:

- 3 ¼ cups flour
- ¼ teaspoon Kosher salt
- 1 tablespoon sugar
- 6 tablespoons pure vegetable shortening
- ¾ cup (1½ sticks) margarine, cut into small chunks
- ½ cup plus 2 tablespoons ice water

Potato Filling:

- 2 large garlic heads
- 3 pounds small red potatoes
- 3 tablespoons margarine
- 3 tablespoons olive oil
- 1 cup nondairy sour cream (optional)
- ½ cup reserved cooking water from potatoes
- 2 tablespoons chopped fresh chives
- salt
- freshly ground black pepper

Egg Wash:

- 1 egg yolk
- 2 tablespoons water
- 1 fresh chive, chopped

Preheat oven to 400 degrees. Cut a ½-inch slice off the top of each garlic head to expose the cloves. Wrap the remaining heads in foil. Bake for 50-60 minutes or until very soft. When done, remove from oven. Set aside.

Dough:

In the bowl of a food processor fitted with a metal or dough blade, or a stand mixer fitted with a dough blade, combine flour, salt, and sugar. Add the shortening and margarine. Pulse about 30 seconds or until mixture resembles coarse crumbs. Add the ice water and pulse until mixture just comes together. Remove the dough, wrap in plastic, and refrigerate for 45 minutes or overnight if you want to make dough in advance.

Potato Filling:

In a large pot, bring potatoes and water to cover to a boil. Reduce heat and simmer for 30 minutes or until potatoes are tender. Drain, reserving ½ cup of the water. Transfer to a large mixing bowl.

Add the margarine, olive oil, nondairy sour cream, reserved cooking water, chives, salt, and pepper. Beat until light and fluffy.

With zip lock bags on your hands to protect them from the odor, squeeze the roasted garlic from the heads into the potatoes, discarding the skins. Beat until fluffy.

Assemble the galette:

On a piece of parchment paper, roll out the dough into a large thin circle 14 inches in diameter. Slip the parchment with the dough onto a cookie sheet, preferably one that has no sides. If you don't have a flat cookie sheet, you can invert a regular cookie sheet.

Place the potatoes in a large mound in the center of the dough, leaving 5-6 inches of dough on the sides empty. Gently lift the dough from the outside edges of the circle and fold it over the potatoes. There will be potatoes in the center that are not covered by the dough. You might need to overlap the dough in a few places; the free-form style allows for an appealing rustic look.

Egg Wash:

Whisk the egg yolk and water together. Brush the exposed dough with the egg wash. The wash will give it a nice golden color so be generous. Bake 40-50 minutes. Sprinkle the exposed potatoes with fresh chopped chives.

Yield: 10 servings

asparagus tivoli

This recipe was given to me by a friend while we waited in the carpool line. I'm glad it was my day to pick up the kids, because this is a great way to serve asparagus. Use a vegetable peeler to shave some of the "thorns" off the asparagus stalks for a prettier presentation. You can also substitute green beans with the same dressing.

1 pound asparagus, bottoms trimmed, cut on an angle
¼ cup fresh scallions, minced
1 tablespoon apple-cider vinegar
2 tablespoons lemon juice
2 tablespoons Dijon mustard
2 teaspoons sugar

⅓ cup olive oil
1 tablespoon fresh parsley, chopped
3 tablespoons fresh dill, chopped
salt
¼ teaspoon freshly ground black pepper
⅓ cup pecans, coarsely chopped

In a pot of boiling water, cook the asparagus for 5-7 minutes. To keep the color bright, do not overcook. Drain; run under cold water to stop the cooking process and drain again.

In a medium jar or cruet, combine the scallions, vinegar, lemon juice, mustard, sugar, oil, parsley, dill, salt, and pepper. Shake well until combined.

Pour dressing over asparagus and top with pecans right before serving.

Yield: 6 servings

hot-and-spicy barbecue potatoes

Parve

As the name implies, these roasted potatoes are hot and spicy. If you prefer milder flavors, only use half the amount of the cayenne pepper and chili powder. Feel free to tinker with the amounts of spices, but don't leave out the sweet paprika. This spice gives the potatoes their gorgeous russet color. This dish goes great with roasted chicken or anything that is made on the grill.

8-10	large red-skinned potatoes, unpeeled and quartered	1	teaspoon sweet paprika
¼	cup vegetable oil	2	teaspoons garlic salt
1	teaspoon cayenne pepper	1	teaspoon garlic powder
1	teaspoon chili powder	1	teaspoon onion powder
		2	teaspoons sugar

Preheat oven to 400 degrees. Place the potatoes in a baking pan. In a small bowl, add the oil, cayenne, chili powder, sweet paprika, garlic salt, garlic powder, onion powder, and sugar. Mix well. Pour spice mixture over the potatoes. Toss to coat. Bake potatoes uncovered for 55-60 minutes or until brown and tender. Shake the pan occasionally.

Yield: 6-8 servings

vegetable puree

Meat

You will get rave reviews on this healthy low-carb substitute for whipped potatoes. It turns a simple vegetable into a delicious and visually appealing treat. The recipe is written for cauliflower, but can be prepared with carrots as well. Just use 8 peeled and sliced carrots and let simmer longer.

2½	pounds fresh cauliflower florets, chopped	2½	teaspoons Kosher salt
5	garlic cloves, sliced	8	tablespoons soy milk
1⅔	cups chicken broth	5	teaspoons margarine
			freshly ground black pepper

In a large pot, place the cauliflower, garlic, chicken broth, and salt. Bring to a boil. Cover and reduce to medium heat. Simmer about 10 minutes or until cauliflower is very tender.

Transfer the pot contents to the bowl of a food processor fitted with a metal blade. Add the soy milk and margarine. Process until smooth. Season with black pepper.

Yield: 6 servings

roasted caramelized carrots

For ease of preparation you can purchase bags of pre-sliced carrots. They are sold in bias cuts and coins, either are fine and a real timesaver.

3 pounds carrots, peeled and sliced
    into ¼-inch discs

½ cup sugar
3-4 tablespoons vegetable oil

Preheat oven to 400 degrees. In a large bowl, combine the carrots, sugar, and oil. Toss to coat. Spread the carrots into disposable tins in a single layer.

Roast about 45 minutes-1 hour on the middle and top racks of the oven until carrots are caramelized and begin to shrivel. Shake occasionally to prevent the carrots from burning.

Yield: 8-10 servings

yerushalmi kugel

This kugel is a great version of the Israeli specialty. It contrasts caramelized noodles with a tantalizing kick from the pepper.

4½ cups water
½ cup (1 stick) margarine
1 cup sugar
1 heaping teaspoon freshly ground black pepper

2 teaspoons salt
12 ounces fine noodles, uncooked
2 eggs
4 tablespoons dark brown sugar
3 tablespoons vegetable oil

Heavily grease a bundt pan with nonstick cooking spray or margarine. Set aside. Preheat oven to 350 degrees.

In a pot, bring the water, margarine, sugar, pepper, and salt to a boil. Turn off the heat. Add the noodles. Stir. Cover the pot and let stand 12-15 minutes.

In a small bowl, mix the eggs, brown sugar, and vegetable oil. Add egg mixture to the noodle mixture. Re-cover the pot. Let stand 10-15 minutes.

Pour into the prepared bundt pan. Bake 1¼ hours-1½ hours. Remove from pan immediately when done.

Yield: 10 servings

corn kugel

This kid-friendly recipe is a cross between corn pudding and kugel. I have tried to eliminate nondairy creamer from my cooking because of all the chemicals. Soy milk is a wonderful replacement and is used here.

2 (15-ounce) cans creamed-style corn
¼ cup sugar
½ cup (1 stick) margarine, melted
3 large eggs
½ cup flour

1 teaspoon baking powder
¾ cup soy milk, regular or vanilla
   flavored
¼ cup water
1 teaspoon vanilla

Preheat oven to 350 degrees. In a large bowl, mix the corn, sugar, margarine, eggs, flour, baking powder, soy milk, water, and vanilla. Pour into a lightly greased 9- by 13-inch rectangular baking dish. Bake uncovered 1½ hours.

Yield: 12-14 servings

spinach rice

This recipe demonstrates one of the many easy ways you can dress up plain rice.

2 tablespoons margarine
2 onions, minced in a food processor
1 cup enriched long-grain white rice
22 ounces chicken stock
1 (10-ounce) box frozen chopped
   spinach, thawed and squeezed dry

salt
freshly ground black pepper
garlic powder

In a large frying pan, melt the margarine over medium-high heat. Add the onion and rice. Sauté until lightly brown, stirring to keep from sticking.

Add the chicken stock, spinach, pepper, and garlic powder. Reduce heat to a simmer; cover and cook about 20 minutes or until all the liquid is absorbed.

Yield: 10-12 servings

cranberry-apple torte

Crust:

2 cups all-purpose flour, sifted
2 cups dark brown sugar
1½ cups oatmeal (quick-cooking or 1-minute type)

1 cup (2 sticks) margarine, melted
2 teaspoons cinnamon

Filling:

4 Cortland apples, peeled and cut into small chunks
1 (16-ounce) can whole berry cranberry sauce

2 tablespoons all-purpose flour, sifted

Preheat oven to 375 degrees. Heavily coat a 9-inch springform pan with nonstick spray; set aside.

In a large bowl, mix the 2 cups flour, brown sugar, oats, margarine, and cinnamon. Reserve 1½ cups of this mixture. Press the remainder into the prepared pan and halfway up the sides with the palm of your hand.

In a medium bowl, combine the apples, cranberry sauce, and 2 tablespoons flour. Mix with a spoon. Pour the apple mixture into

the crust. Sprinkle the reserved oat mixture over the top. Use the back of a spoon to gently press the oats so that they evenly cover the top and meet the crust that is coming up the sides, this is what will enclose the filling. Bake for 40 minutes.

Yield: 10-12 servings

squash risotto

This recipe works well as written, but typically when preparing risotto you should bring the stock to a simmer in a separate pot. Add ½ cup of the simmering broth to the rice and stir until the rice absorbs the liquid. When the rice dries out, add another ½ cup and continue to stir and cook. Keep adding liquid, but don't drown the rice. Risotto is not boiled rice. For this technique and the recipe below, be sure to cook at the right temperature. If the liquid evaporates too quickly the rice won't cook evenly. Proper risotto should be creamily bound together, not dry or runny.

1 onion, diced	2 cups risotto (Arborio rice), uncooked
3 tablespoons canola oil	6 cups chicken or vegetable stock,
2 yellow squash, unpeeled and cut	do not use bouillon cubes
into small pieces	
1 (20-ounce) bag frozen butternut	
squash cubes, do not defrost	

Sauté the onion in oil 6-8 minutes or until soft. Add the yellow squash and the butternut squash; sauté 7-10 minutes. The squash will separate as it cooks.

Add the risotto and broth; bring to a simmer. Reduce heat and barely simmer 30-40 minutes or until liquid is absorbed.

Yield: 8 servings

✎ A Ribbon & Sticker Garland

For a whimsical touch to decoratively fill space on your table create a sticker garland. Start with a few yards of thin ribbon. Purchase large, same shaped adhesive stickers. Place 1 sticker centered on the ribbon, back it with a matching sticker. Repeat with remaining stickers, spaced across the length of ribbon. Weave the garland gently around your table.

traditional potato kugel

My Mom makes the best potato kugel. She lovingly grates each potato by hand. She does this with a full heart, like everything she does for my family. However, hand grating makes me nervous. Luckily, this recipe captures the taste and flavor of hand grated potatoes with the ease of a food processor.

½ cup vegetable or canola oil	1 teaspoon freshly ground black pepper
8 medium potatoes	
2 medium onions, quartered	2½ tablespoons sugar
1 tablespoon salt	5 large eggs, beaten with a whisk

Preheat oven to 425 degrees. Place the oil into a large 9- by 13-inch rectangular baking pan; set aside.

Fill a large bowl with cold water and add some ice cubes. Peel the potatoes and place them into the bowl of cold water. This will prevent them from turning brown.

Finely chop the onions in the container of a food processor fitted with a metal blade. Remove them to a large bowl. Cut the potatoes into chunks and place them into the food processor; process until almost smooth. Add the potatoes to the onions.

Add the salt, pepper, and sugar to the potato mixture. Add the eggs and stir until thoroughly combined.

Place the baking pan with oil into the oven. When the oil sizzles, carefully remove from oven and spoon some of it into the potato mixture. This will help make the kugel fluffy. Mix well. Pour the potatoes into the oiled pan. Bake uncovered for 1 hour.

Yield: 12-14 servings

zucchini-tomato gratin

4 tablespoons (½ stick) margarine, divided
3 tablespoons olive oil, divided
1½ pounds zucchini (about 3 medium), peeled and thinly sliced
1 medium onion, finely chopped
1 garlic clove, chopped
4 medium round tomatoes, coarsely chopped
salt
freshly ground black pepper
½ cup unflavored bread crumbs

Preheat oven to 400 degrees. Lightly grease a shallow oven-proof dish. Set aside.

In a large skillet or saucepan, heat 2 tablespoons of the margarine and 1 tablespoon of the oil over medium heat. Add the zucchini. Cover and cook 5-6 minutes or until tender; set aside.

In a medium skillet, warm the remaining 2 tablespoons of olive oil over moderate heat. Add the onion and cook for 5 minutes. Add the garlic and continue cooking for 1 minute longer. Reduce the heat and add the tomatoes. Cover and cook for 15 minutes. Season well with salt and pepper. Pour off some of the liquid.

Stir the zucchini into the tomatoes. Pour evenly into the prepared dish. Sprinkle with bread crumbs and dot with remaining 2 tablespoons of margarine. Bake uncovered for 25-30 minutes or until top is golden and crisp.

Yield: 8-10 servings

rosemary potatoes with caramelized shallots & mushrooms

Parve

2 tablespoons margarine
5-7 shallots, sliced into rings
7-10 cremini mushrooms, sliced
1 tablespoon red wine
2 pounds baby red potatoes, as small as possible, can also be mixed with same size white skinned potatoes, unpeeled

3 tablespoons olive oil, plus extra for brushing
1 teaspoon dried rosemary
2 teaspoons garlic powder
Kosher salt
freshly ground black pepper

Preheat oven to 400 degrees. In a skillet, melt the margarine over medium-high heat. Add the shallots and mushrooms; sauté for 5 minutes. Add the wine and sauté for 5 minutes longer or until the shallots and mushrooms are soft and golden. Remove from heat.

Scrub the potatoes and place them in a baking pan. Brush with olive oil. Sprinkle with the rosemary, garlic powder, salt, and pepper. Toss the shallots and mushrooms into the potatoes and mix. Drizzle with the 3 tablespoons olive oil.

Roast uncovered, stirring occasionally, for 1-1½ hours or until potatoes are soft when tested with a knife. If potatoes are larger they will take longer to cook.

Yield: 8-10 servings

herbed brown rice

I like long-grain brown rice because the grains remain separate and fluffy. One of my friends omits the mushrooms from this recipe and adds a handful of currants when the pot is initially removed from heat.

4 cups chicken stock
4 tablespoons margarine
1 small onion, finely chopped
8 ounces sliced mushrooms, finely chopped
1 shallot, finely chopped
2 garlic cloves, minced
2 cups long-grain brown rice, rinsed and drained

½ teaspoon dried basil
½ teaspoon dried oregano
½ teaspoon dried thyme
½ teaspoon freshly ground black pepper
½ teaspoon Kosher salt

In a small saucepan, bring the chicken stock to a boil. In large skillet that has a tight fitting lid, melt the margarine over medium heat. Add the onion, mushrooms, shallot, and garlic. Sauté 6-8minutes. Add the rice and cook for 3-4 minutes, stirring occasionally.

Add the basil, oregano, thyme, pepper, and salt. Add the boiling stock. Stir. Cover and reduce heat to a simmer for 45-50 minutes or until all the stock is absorbed. Remove from heat; do not remove lid. Let stand for 10 minutes. Fluff with a fork.

Yield: 8-10 servings

acorn squash with frosted cranberries

Parve

Acorn squash, like all winter squash, can be dangerous to cut. I have the produce department at the supermarket cut them in half and wrap them in plastic wrap. If you can only find large acorn squash, just cut the squash in half. After they are softened by cooking, you can cut each half in half again for more manageable servings. Cranberries have a short season. So buy a few extra bags in the autumn when they are available and store them in the freezer.

Acorn Squash:

- 4 small acorn squash, cut in half around the "waist," seeds removed
- 4 tablespoons dark brown sugar
- 4 tablespoon honey
  pinch ground ginger
- ¼ teaspoon cinnamon
- 4 tablespoons margarine, room temperature
  salt
  freshly ground black pepper

Frosted Cranberries:

- 1 cup water
- 1 cup sugar, plus extra for frosting
- 2 cups fresh or frozen cranberries, unthawed

Acorn Squash:

Preheat oven to 375 degrees. Place the acorn squash cut side down in a baking pan. Pour ½ inch of water around the squash. Bake 45 minutes.

Frosted Cranberries:

In a saucepan, bring the water and sugar to a boil over medium-high heat. When sugar dissolves, reduce heat and add the cranberries. Simmer for 15 minutes. Drain off liquid. Remove the berries to a sheet of waxed paper; use a fork to keep them separated. Set aside.

Remove squash from oven and pour off the water from the pan. Turn the squash cut side up. In a small bowl, mix the brown sugar, honey, ginger, cinnamon, margarine, salt, and pepper. Divide mixture evenly among each of the squash halves. Return to the oven for another 30-35 minutes, basting with sauce until squash is soft.

Toss the cranberries with a little sugar to coat them. Remove the squash to a platter and fill each cavity with frosted cranberries.

Yield: 8 servings

An Array of Apples

Pictured on our tray:

- ∿**McINTOSH** are excellent for eating and are great for apple sauce. They don't hold up well when baked whole, but are fine for kugels.
- ∿**RED DELICIOUS** are a classic snack favorite. They are crunchy and mildly sweet. They perform poorly in baking and cooking.
- ∿**GINGER GOLD** have crisp white flesh that resists turning brown for hours after being cut or sliced. This makes them an ideal choice for salads and garnishes.
- ∿**GALA** have semisweet yellow flesh. They are crisp and juicy and perfect for snacking or pairing with cheese. They are excellent for sauce as well.
- ∿**ROME** are good for sauce, baking whole or in pies. They are also the apple of choice for cider.
- ∿**GRANNY SMITH** is one of the most popular varieties. These pale green apples are mild to very tart. They are crisp and firm, good for all purpose use.
- ∿**PACIFIC ROSE** are mostly imported from New Zealand. They are rose pink and have an appealing shape that earned them the nickname "the art piece of the apple world". They are crispy, juicy and sweet.
- ∿**GOLDEN DELICIOUS** are mellow and sweet. They are an all-purpose apple that is great for cooking. They are related to Red Delicious in name only.

When buying apples for a pie, 2½ pounds will do, that is about 5 large or 9-10 small apples.

A large apple will yield: 2 cups sliced or chopped, 1¼ cups grated, 1½ cups finely chopped or ¾ cup apple sauce.

A small apple will yield: ¾ cup sliced or chopped, ½ cup grated, ¾ cup finely chopped, or ⅓ cup apple sauce

apple kugel muffins

One beautiful fall day, my friend took her four children apple picking. Fifty pounds of apples later the calls went out to all of her friends and neighbors for recipes that used apples. This was one of her favorites and mine. This recipe can be doubled. It can also be made in a springform pan; just increase the baking time.

3 large eggs
½ cup canola or vegetable oil
1 cup sugar
1 teaspoon cinnamon, plus extra
1 teaspoon almond extract
1 cup flour

½ teaspoon baking powder
2-3 medium McIntosh or Rome apples, peeled and chopped into small pieces
½ cup chopped walnuts or pecans, optional

Preheat oven to 350 degrees. Heavily grease 12 muffin tins with nonstick cooking spray.

In a large bowl, mix the eggs, oil, sugar, cinnamon, almond extract, flour, and baking powder at medium speed, beating until batter is smooth. Do not over-mix.

Place a small mound of apples into each prepared muffin tin. Spoon batter into each tin to cover the apples. Sprinkle with cinnamon and add nuts, if desired. Bake 20-30 minutes or until toothpick in center comes out clean.

Yield: 12 servings

rice pilaf

This very easy side dish can also transform into an almond rice pilaf. Just leave out the mushrooms and once it's finished cooking, mix in 1 cup of slivered almonds and ¼ teaspoon nutmeg.

8 tablespoons (1 stick) margarine
1 medium onion, finely chopped
1 shallot, finely chopped
1 garlic clove, minced
1 cup fine egg noodles, uncooked
2 cups long-grain white rice, uncooked

4 cups chicken broth
8 ounces mushrooms, sliced
   salt
   freshly ground black pepper
   chopped fresh parsley, for garnish

In a large skillet, melt the margarine over medium heat. Add the onion and shallots. Sauté for 6-8 minutes or until golden but not brown. Add the garlic and sauté for 1 minute longer.

Stir in the noodles and sauté until lightly brown. Add in the rice, broth, and mushrooms. Cover the pan and turn the flame down to low.

Cook about 30-40 minutes or until all of the liquid is absorbed. Season with salt and pepper. Garnish with parsley.

Yield: 8-10 servings

cheesy broccoli & cauliflower casserole

Dairy

1 head broccoli
1 head cauliflower
1 large onion, finely chopped
2 tablespoons butter
2 tablespoons flour
1 teaspoon salt
½ teaspoon garlic powder
½ teaspoon dried basil
½ teaspoon freshly ground black
pepper

1¼ cups milk
6 ounces cream cheese
1 tablespoon fresh chives, chopped
¾ cup unflavored bread crumbs
3 tablespoons grated Parmesan
cheese
2 tablespoons butter, melted

Preheat oven to 400 degrees. Remove the florets from the broccoli and cauliflower, discarding the stems.

Place the florets into a pot of boiling water, cook about 10 minutes or until tender. Drain; set aside.

In a medium saucepan, melt the 2 tablespoons butter over medium heat. Add the onion and cook for 5-6 minutes or until tender. Sprinkle on the flour, salt, garlic powder, basil, and pepper. Add the milk. Cook until thick and bubbly. Add the cream cheese and chives, stirring.

Place the broccoli and cauliflower into a large casserole dish. Pour the cream cheese mixture over the vegetables and toss to combine.

In a small bowl, toss the bread crumbs, Parmesan, and 2 tablespoons melted butter. Sprinkle over the vegetables. Bake uncovered for 25-30 minutes or until heated through.

Yield: 10 servings

pecan & sweet potato bake

When it comes to sweet potato recipes, I haven't met one yet that I didn't like. A large can of yams will do in a pinch. But for a chunky, "comfort food" texture and bright orange color, use fresh sweet potatoes. You will find yourself licking the serving dish.

3-4 large sweet potatoes, peeled and
   cut into cubes
½ cup sugar
½ cup plain soy milk or nondairy
   creamer
1 large egg, beaten
3 tablespoons margarine, cut into
   slices

½ teaspoon vanilla
½ cup dark brown sugar
⅓ cup flour
3 tablespoons margarine, melted
½ cup pecan pieces
8-10 pecan halves, for garnish, optional

Lightly spray a 2-quart rectangular or round baking dish with nonstick cooking spray; set aside. In a large pot, bring 2 inches of water to a boil over medium-high heat.

Add the sweet potatoes; cover and cook for 25-30 minutes or until tender. Drain and return to pot. (If using canned sweet potatoes, start by heating the drained sweet potatoes in a large pot for 5 minutes.)

Preheat oven to 350 degrees. Add the sugar, soy milk or creamer, egg, margarine, and vanilla to the sweet potatoes. Using the back of a wooden spoon, gently mix the ingredients; try not to mash the sweet potatoes too much.

Transfer the mixture to the prepared baking dish. In a small bowl, combine the brown sugar, flour, melted margarine, and pecan pieces. Sprinkle topping over the sweet potatoes. Bake uncovered for 25 minutes or until set.

Garnish with pecan halves, if desired. Starting from the center of the dish, set the pecan halves in the pattern of a sunflower.

Yield: 8-10 servings

passover

חזרת ♦ כרפס ♦ חרוסת

מרור

בֵּיצָה

The Family Haggadah

N o one ate alone at the first "Seder" in history. On their last night in Egypt, every Jew was commanded to eat the Passover offering of roast lamb (or goat) along with matzo and bitter herbs. Each household was to consume all of the meat, and if the family was too small, they had to invite a neighbor to join them. And this is the way the Passover offering was eaten in Jerusalem for centuries! This Torah-mandated hospitality is unmatched in its power to guarantee warm camaraderie and national unity.

Today, we still instinctively gather in extended family groups for the Seder. Single friends join families; everyone belongs. Such inclusiveness is only fitting, for in a sense the Seder is a national birthday party. The Exodus galvanized the Hebrew tribes into a full-fledged nation.

A second reason we mobilize several generations around our Seder tables is that a primary *mitzvah* of Passover is to teach our children about the Exodus. This vivid transmission of Jewish heritage began when the Children of Israel left Egypt and continues to this day.

Jews are required to eat matzo for the full duration of the holiday, after ridding their homes of all leavened products, called *chametz*. This includes all products containing grain (including alcohol) that are not especially prepared *chametz*-free for Passover. Matzo is eaten at the Seder as a special

mitzvah. It is called the "bread of affliction," as it nourished the Jewish slaves in Egypt.

At the beginning of the Seder, we eat a vegetable dipped in salt water to remind us of the misery of slavery. Grated horseradish is often used as a "bitter herb," though others can be used. The bitter herb is dipped in *charoset*, a mixture of ingredients combined to resemble mortar used by the Hebrews to build Egyptian cities. At specific intervals, a total of four cups of wine are consumed, symbolizing liberty, in contrast to the matzo.

The ultimate teaching aid, the Seder keeps children (and adults!) involved with its instructions for activity and elaborate storytelling. From the first sip of wine to the last crunch of matzo, its unique tastes, smells, stories and songs create an experience that is — quite intentionally — unforgettable.

passover menu

SOUP:
Chicken Soup
with Stuffed Matzo Balls
pages 62 and 237

SALAD:
Purple Cabbage Salad
pages 79

ENTREE:
Beef Short Ribs with Horseradish
pages 140

SIDE DISHES:
Tzimmes Souffle
page 239
Rosemary Potatoes with
Caramelized Shallots and Mushrooms
page 219

DESSERT:
Lemon Meringues
page 248

M any of us have special memories of our family's Passover Seder. In my family, the night of the first Seder was the culmination of weeks of work. I can picture my Dad on the step stool bringing down the Passover pots and pans. It was a group effort to clean the house, shop for groceries, coordinate the cooking tasks and solemnly search for *chametz*. Grandmothers, grandfathers, aunts, uncles, cousins, neighbors, friends — all were welcome at the Seder in my parents' house. There was not an inch of spare room: a table extended from one end of the living room, through the entryway and ended right at the kitchen door. The excitement was palpable as my Mom and aunt worked feverishly on the Seder meal. I'll always remember smells from the kitchen, laughter from the table, voices of old and young, family melodies: Passover is a holiday you experience with all of your senses. We knew, even as children, that this was a holiday for our memory books.

The Hebrew word *seder* means "order." Even through all of the frenzy of preparation, once the holiday begins there's calmness at the Seder itself. The sense of order derives from a specific set of information slated for discussion, as clearly spelled out in the Haggadah.

For our Seder table we selected a taupe-colored raw silk cloth. The centerpiece is a stunning

Seder plate with all of the requisite items on it. At each place setting rests a Haggadah and wine cups for the four glasses of wine that will be consumed by each participant. Also present is a covered crock holding salt water used for dipping during the Seder. (Salt water symbolizes the tears shed in Egypt.) These crocks later hold chicken soup. Each person is given a small dish to catch the wine that will be spilled off (as a touch of sympathy for the suffering of the Egyptians) when the ten plagues are recounted.

As for flowers, we chose very simple, low-maintenance rose and ivy topiaries. They work well, as the height allows guests to see through them. A low arrangement of roses at the base adds beauty and fragrance.

Use a hot-glue gun to decorate pillowcases with jewel-like leaves and beads that spell out the name of each guest. Stuff a small pillow into each case. The pillows are used for reclining when we recite the Haggadah, drink the four cups of wine and eat matzo. This shows that we are free people; in ancient times, only free people had the luxury of reclining at their meals.

Our menu is a simple one that allows for advance preparation. The multicolored Purple Cabbage Salad can be set out on plates in the kitchen before the guests arrive. The entree, Beef Short Ribs with Horseradish is in keeping with the custom not to serve roasted meat at the Seder. This beef stew is accented with horseradish, another symbolic Passover food. The Tzimmes Kugel

and Rosemary Potatoes with Caramelized Shallots and Mushrooms are delicious complements to this meal. The hour may be late by the time dessert rolls around, so we selected Lemon Meringues. They're light, lovely, and quickly assembled right before serving.

A word about *gebrokts*: Some families do not eat matzo or matzo meal that came in contact with water (or a water mixture). Such "moistened matzo" is known as *gebrokts* (from the Yiddish word meaning broken, as it was common to break matzo and put the pieces into soup). As some of our recipes contain *gebrokts*, they are indicated by ** in this section.

wine list

BARETNURA MOSCATO DI ASTI
CARAMEL EMERALD REISLING/CHENIN

Purple Cabbage Salad pairs well with the Moscato di Asti
because of the wine's mandarin orange blossom flavors.
It will harmonize with the mandarin oranges in the recipe
as well as with other spicy and Asian dishes.

The off-dry refreshing Emerald Reisling with its abundance of fruit flavors
would go well with this salad as well.

BARON HERZOG CALIFORNIA ZINFANDEL
BARKAN MERLOT RESERVE
DALTON CANAAN RED WINE
SEGAL MERLOT RESERVE

The hearty Beef Short Rib Stew with Horseradish Sauce calls out for a flavorful red.
The bold fruit forward Zinfandel, a full-bodied Merlot or the textured blend of the
Canaan Cabernet Merlot will stand up well and are all good choices.

You could alternate these four reds for the four glasses of wine during the seder.

YARDEN HEIGHTS ICEWINE (EISWEIN)

Eiswein goes well with meringue which makes it a natural selection for our Lemon
Meringue dessert.

Stuffed Matzo Balls

passover

To make this book more user-friendly for Passover, I have highlighted those recipes from every section that can be used as is or with minor adjustments for the holiday.

To ensure that ingredients are kosher for Passover, it is advisable to use only new packages and to check each package for Passover certification.

RECIPE	PAGE	CLASS*	ADJUSTMENT
Chopped Liver	23	M	None
Tri-color Gefite Fish	26	P	None
Pistachio Chicken Skewers with Blackberry Sauce	31	M	Substitute potato starch for the corn starch in the blackberry sauce.
Chicken Livers	32	M	None
Veal Loaf**	33	M	Substitute matzo meal for the bread crumbs.
Potato Latkes	36	P	Substitute vegetable oil for the peanut oil.
Portobello Pesto Stacks	38	P/D	None
Antipasto Platter	41	M	None
Braised Artichoke Bottoms	44	M/P	None
Cream of Asparagus Soup	53	M	Use the nondairy creamer.
Creamy Tomato Soup	54	D	None
Emerald Soup	55	M/P	Use the nondairy creamer.
Zucchini Soup	60	M/P	None
Chicken Soup	62	M	None
Parsnip Bisque	65	M/P	None
Candied Almond Pear and Goat Cheese Salad	75	D	None
Health Salad	77	P	None
Purple Cabbage Salad	79	P	None
Chef's Salad**	80	M	Use Passover imitation dijon mustard.
Hearts of Palm Salad	82	P	None
Arugula Salad	83	P	None
Shredded Endive with Lemon Zest Olive Oil Vinaigrette**	87	P	Use Passover imitation dijon mustard.
Red Bliss Potato Salad	88	P	None
New Millennium Waldorf Salad	89	D	None
Pesto Chicken	99	M	None
Chicken Oporto	100	M	None
Balsamic Herb Rubbed Chicken**	102	M	Use Passover imitation dijon mustard.
Olive Chicken	103	M	None
Roast Turkey with Caramelized Onion-Balsamic Gravy	104	M	Substitute potato starch for flour in the gravy.
Poached Chicken in Leek Broth	108	M	None

* Class = meat, dairy or parve *** This recipe is gebrokts.*

RECIPE	PAGE	CLASS	ADJUSTMENT
Chicken Oreganata	109	M	None
Artichoke Chicken	111	M	None
Chicken with Brandy and Mushrooms	114	M	Substitute potato starch for the flour.
Chicken Provence with Cider-Roasted Vegetables	115	M	None
Seared Duck Breast**	118	M	Use Passover imitation dijon mustard.
Honey & Pecan Crusted Chicken with Apricot Chutney**	120	M	Substitute matzo meal for the cornflake crumbs.
Rack of Lamb with Fig Port Shallot Sauce	129	M	None
Herb-Crusted Silver Tip Roast	131	M	None
Sweet and Sour Brisket	131	M	None
Roasted Shoulder of Veal with Mushrooms**	136	M	Substitute potato starch for the flour. Use Passover imitation dijon mustard.
Beef Short Rib Stew	140	M	Substitute potato starch for the flour.
Rosemary Pesto Lamb Chops	141	M	None
Pot Roast	143	M	Omit the flour.
Tuna in Scallion Peppercorn Cream Sauce	159	D	Substitute potato starch for the flour.
Champagne Poached Salmon	160	D	None
Parmesan Crusted Grouper	162	D	None
Blackened Tilapia	164	D	None
Spinach Cheese Lasagne**	178	D	Substitute matzo for the lasagne noodles.
Spinach Cheese Fritatta	190	D	None
Slow Roasted Tomatoes	199	P	None
Shallot Butter Mashed Potatoes	207	D	None
Asparagus Tivoli**	210	P	Use Passover imitation dijon mustard.
Hot and Spicy Barbecue Potatoes	211	P	None
Vegetable Pureé	211	M	Substitute nondairy creamer for the soy milk.
Roasted Caramelized Carrots	212	P	None
Traditional Potato Kugel	217	P	None
Zucchini Tomato Gratin**	218	P	Substitute matzo meal for bread crumbs.
Rosemary Potatoes with Caramelized Shallots	219	P	None
Acorn Squash with Frosted Cranberries	221	P	None
Ebony and Ivory	260	D	Omit cream of tartar.

Class = meat, dairy or parve

**This recipe is gebrokts.*

traditional charoset

5 large Red Delicious apples, cored, peeled, and finely chopped
1 cup walnuts, finely chopped

½ cup sweet red wine
1 teaspoon ground cinnamon

Combine the apples with the walnuts. Slowly add the wine. Mix to combine. Sprinkle with the cinnamon. Stir. Cover and refrigerate until ready to use.

Yield: 10 servings

meichel**

1 (1-pound) box matzo farfel
1 tablespoon vegetable oil
1 tablespoon margarine
1 large onion, finely chopped
1 (10-ounce) box sliced mushrooms

1 (10-ounce) can condensed chicken soup, undiluted
salt
freshly ground black pepper

Place the matzo farfel in a large bowl. Cover with boiling water and let soften for 3 minutes. (Do not let it sit any longer or the end result will be mushy.) Drain the water; set aside.

In a large skillet, heat the oil and margarine over medium heat. Add the onion and sauté for 6-8 minutes or until it begins to turn golden. Add the mushrooms and sauté 3-4 minutes longer.

Add the drained matzo farfel to the skillet and sauté. Slowly add the chicken soup, using as little or as much as you need to reach the consistency of a pilaf. Season with salt and pepper.

Yield: 8-10 servings

stuffed matzo balls**

These matzo balls are unbeatable- light and perfectly fluffy. Use a big wide pot, they really expand! The baking powder is the key ingredient and is now available for Passover.

Don't double the recipe, two batches will not fit in the pot at one time. Sometimes, for a nice twist, I make them "stuffed". Using a vegetable peeler, I scrape off some carrot and celery shavings. When each matzo ball is formed, I poke a small hole, stuff in the shavings, then roll the batter over the shavings. I cook and serve them as the recipe states below. When you bite into the matzo ball you see the color and texture of the vegetables peeking out.

Although the matzo balls can be reheated in your chicken soup, initially cook them separately as indicated below. The starch in the matzo balls will murk up your soup's appearance and soak up a lot of your soup. I tend to make them along side the soup and use 5 cups of the soup with 5 cups of water to boil the matzo balls in so they get the flavor. In a pinch the matzo balls can be made in salted water as well.

For the cooking liquid:

- 5 cups water
- 5 cups chicken soup, broth, or bouillon
- 1 teaspoon kosher salt

Matzo Balls:

- 3 large eggs plus 1 extra egg white, separated
- 1 teaspoon kosher salt
- 1 tablespoon baking powder
- ¼ teaspoon black pepper

- 1⅓ cups matzo meal
- thin carrot shavings (optional)
- thin celery shavings (optional)
- fresh parsley, roughly chopped (optional)

Place the 4 egg whites and salt in a mixing bowl. Let them come to room temperature as you bring the water, chicken soup, and teaspoon of salt to a boil in a large wide pot.

With mixer at medium speed beat the eggs until fluffy white peaks form. Add in the yolks, baking powder, and pepper. Beat on low. Sprinkle in the matzo meal and continue beating. Let the batter sit for 3 minutes to firm up. Wet your hands very well with cold water. Scoop up batter and roll between your wet hands until it forms a golf ball sized ball. Gently place the matzo balls into the soup. Re-wet your hands between each matzo ball. Reduce heat to a simmer, cover and cook for 25 minutes.

If making the "stuffed" option, while rolling each matzo ball, stuff in a few of the shavings and roll the batter back over it. Gently drop into the soup. The matzo balls will double in size, if you would like smaller balls or to get more out of the recipe, roll the balls smaller but cook the same amount of time.

Yield: 6-8 large matzo balls

Quinoa is an interesting food to use at a Passover meal. Choose very light tiny seeds for a higher quality and a more delicate flavor. The large dark seeds are bitter tasting. Store the quinoa in your refrigerator before and after cooking. This is a basic recipe for quinoa, but you can use your imagination to come up with variations.

1 cup uncooked quinoa	2¼ cups chicken stock
1 tablespoon olive oil	½ teaspoon onion powder
1 onion, diced	½ teaspoon garlic powder
3 garlic cloves, minced	1 teaspoon sugar

In a large skillet, heat the uncooked quinoa over medium heat for 2-3 minutes or until you smell a nutty fragrance. Remove from heat and place the quinoa in a fine mesh sieve. Rinse 2-3 times to remove the bitterness. Set aside.

In the large skillet, heat the oil over medium heat. Add the onion; sauté for 6-8 minutes or until it begins to caramelize.

Add the quinoa and the garlic and cook for 3 minutes. Pour in the chicken stock and bring to a boil. Reduce the heat to a simmer. Add the onion powder, garlic powder, and sugar. Cover and simmer for 20 minutes or until all of the liquid is absorbed.

Yield: 4 servings

tzimmes souffle**

My friend gave me this recipe. Though it's really for Passover, we both agree it's almost too good to tuck away in a Passover section. This recipe is great all year-round. For an extra special presentation, make this recipe in individual ramekins for single servings as pictured below.

5 large eggs, separated
2 cups finely grated carrots, about 5-6 large carrots
1 cup sugar
¾ cup matzo meal

½ cup canola or vegetable oil
1 teaspoon lemon juice
2 tablespoons orange juice
1 can crushed pineapple with heavy syrup

Preheat oven to 350 degrees. Spray a 9- by 9-inch square pan with nonstick cooking spray. Set aside.

In a large bowl, beat the egg whites until they are stiff. Using a spatula, fold in the carrots, sugar, and matzoh meal. Fold in the egg yolks, oil, lemon juice, orange juice, and pineapple with the syrup.

Pour into the prepared baking dish. Bake 40-45 minutes or until top is golden. Scoop or spoon out.

Yield: 10-12 servings

vegetable potato kugel**

½ cup vegetable oil
6 large Idaho or baking potatoes
2 medium onions, quartered
2 carrots, peeled and cut into chunks
1 green zucchini, unpeeled and cut
  into chunks

1 tablespoon salt
1 teaspoon freshly ground black
  pepper
2½ tablespoons sugar
½ cup matzo meal
5 large eggs, beaten with a whisk

Preheat oven to 400 degrees. Place the oil in a 9- by 13-inch rectangular baking pan; set aside. Fill a large bowl with cold water and some ice cubes. Peel the potatoes and place them into the bowl of cold water.

Finely chop the onions in the container of a food processor fitted with a metal blade. Add the carrots and process until they are finely chopped. Scoop the onion/carrot mixture into a large bowl.

Cut the potatoes into chunks and place into the food processor; process until almost smooth. Add the zucchini; process until completely grated with the colors flecked throughout. Add the potato mixture to the onion mixture.

Mix the salt, pepper, sugar, and matzo meal into the potato mixture. Using the back of a spoon, press potato mixture to drain out any excess water. Stir in the eggs.

Place the baking pan with oil into the oven. When the oil sizzles, carefully remove from oven and spoon some of it into the potato mixture, mixing well. (This will help make the kugel fluffy.) Pour the potatoes into the oiled pan. Bake uncovered for 1 hour.

Yield: 12-14 servings

popovers**

Serve these huge and light popovers fresh out of the oven. They are wonderful slathered in butter or jam for breakfast. You can also set them out in a basket on the table for other meals. For extra-large popovers, bake the dough in greased oven-proof ramekins.

1 cup water
⅓ cup unsalted butter or margarine
½ cup matzo meal
½ cup matzo cake meal

½ teaspoon salt
2 tablespoons sugar
6 large eggs

Preheat oven to 450 degrees. Generously grease the top and inside cups of a nonstick muffin tin with nonstick cooking spray.

In a medium pot, bring the water and butter or margarine to a boil over medium heat. Add the matzo meal, matzo cake meal, salt, and sugar. Continue cooking, stirring until the dough no longer sticks to the sides of the pot.

Remove the pot from the stove and transfer the dough to the bowl of an electric mixer. Beat the dough at a high speed for 1 minute. Add eggs one at a time; continue beating after each addition. Beat for another 1-2 minutes, scraping down the sides of the bowl.

Divide the dough among 8 of the muffin tins. Bake for 20 minutes. Without opening the oven door, reduce heat to 325 degrees and bake for an additional 30 minutes or until puffed and golden. Remove from pan and serve.

Yield: 8 popovers

zucchini casserole**

butter
3 cups thinly sliced, unpeeled zucchini
2 cups shredded mozzarella cheese
1 small onion, chopped
1 cup dry Passover pancake mix

2 tablespoons Parmesan cheese
4 large eggs, lightly beaten
½ cup vegetable oil
½ teaspoon salt
½ teaspoon dried oregano
freshly ground black pepper

Preheat oven to 350 degrees. Lightly grease a 13- by 9-inch baking dish with butter.

Combine zucchini, mozzarella cheese, onion, pancake mix, Parmesan cheese, eggs, oil, salt, oregano, and pepper in a large bowl, mixing well with a large spoon. Spoon into the prepared dish. Bake 40 minutes or until golden brown.

Yield: 10 servings

baked farmer cheese loaf**

This beautiful cheese loaf offers the sweet taste of blintzes without any of the work. The recipe is great as a dairy side dish or served solo.

4 large eggs
1 cup sugar
1 teaspoon vanilla
1 teaspoon fresh lemon juice

16 ounces farmer cheese
1 matzo board
cinnamon/sugar

Preheat oven to 325 degrees. In the bowl of an electric mixer, beat the eggs until light and fluffy. Add the sugar, vanilla, and lemon juice. Mix in the farmer cheese.

Line a loaf pan with foil or parchment paper, leaving foil or paper hanging over all four sides. Break the matzo in half and place in a double layer in the bottom of the pan. Pour the cheese mixture over the matzo. Sprinkle with cinnamon/sugar.

Bake uncovered for 40-50 minutes or until set in center. Remove from oven. Let cool in pan. Using the foil or parchment, lift the loaf out of the pan and transfer it to your serving platter. Slice and serve.

Yield: 6-8 servings

grandma mollie's compote

Parve

Compote was one of my grandmother's specialties. If someone mentioned that they liked it, she would rush into her kitchen and whip up pounds and pounds for distribution. One afternoon, there was a knock on my husband and father-in-law's office door. They opened it to find Grandma Mollie lugging a wagon twice her size full of compote jars. She had taken a bus and two subways, but like the postal system, neither rain nor snow could keep Mollie from her compote deliveries.

Make sure you use a very large pot to give the liquid space to simmer. You can add dried pears or nectarines to the compote as well. In the summer, Grandma Mollie substituted fresh peeled peaches and whole cherries with their stems removed, for the prunes and apricots. The results were divine. Store the compote in a covered jar or container for up to 2-3 weeks in the refrigerator.

7	pounds large whole prunes	3	lemons, sliced
1½	pounds dried apricots	3	generous cups of sugar

Place the prunes, apricots, and lemons in a large pot. Sprinkle in the sugar. Add water to cover by 3 inches. Bring to a low boil. Reduce heat to a low simmer. Cover the pot.

Heat at a low simmer for 3 hours. Serve in dessert or martini glasses; hang a spiral of lemon zest off the side of each cup.

Yield: 25 servings

best-ever sponge cake**

The week before Pesach had arrived, and Sylvia and her husband Hymie were to be guests at their son and daughter-in-law's home for the holiday. She called her daughter-in-law and said, "Please let me make something to help you out." Not wanting to burden her elderly mother-in-law she replied, "nothing Ma, just come." Sylvia would not take no for an answer and insisted on making her special sponge cake. On Erev Yom Tov, Sylvia and Hymie drove up to their son and daughter-in-law's house and everyone helped unpack their loaded car. When the car was emptied, the daughter-in-law asked, "Ma, where is the sponge cake?" To which Sylvia replied, "Oh, it is a funny story. I made the cake and it smelled so delicious, that we had to have a little sample. So I took a little piece, and Hymie had a little piece, and I had a sliver, and Hymie had a little sliver, and before we knew it the whole cake was gone." Later that evening while cleaning up in the kitchen the daughter-in-law asked Hymie, "So Dad, how was the sponge cake?" To which he said, "Sponge cake, vhat sponge cake, der vas no sponge cake." Sylvia had eaten the whole thing all by herself!

2 large lemons	¼ cup club soda
9 large eggs, separated	½ cup potato starch
2 cups sugar	½ cup matzo cake meal

Preheat oven to 350 degrees. Using a microplane or very thin grater, zest 2 teaspoons of lemon peel from the lemons, making sure to get only the yellow part, not the bitter white pith. Set aside. Cut the lemons and squeeze ¼ cup of lemon juice. Set aside.

Beat the egg whites until stiff; set aside. In a separate bowl, beat the egg yolks, sugar, club soda, and reserved lemon juice for 3 minutes on medium-high speed. Gradually add in the potato starch and matzo cake meal.

Using a rubber spatula, fold the whites into the yolk mixture. Add the lemon zest. Beat for 2 minutes. Pour into an ungreased tube pan. Bake for 1 hour and 10 minutes. Invert untill completely cool. Run a knife around the cake and remove from pan.

Yield: 10-12 servings

This cake can easily transform into a delicious dairy strawberry shortcake. Just cut it in half and fill with fresh whipped cream and strawberries.

flourless chocolate torte

Parve

5 large eggs
8 ounces unsweetened chocolate
4 ounces best-quality semisweet
   chocolate

½ cup water
1⅓ cups sugar, divided
1 cup (2 sticks) margarine

Preheat oven to 350 degrees. Lightly coat a 9-inch springform pan with nonstick cooking spray.

Crack the eggs into a small glass or metal bowl. Place them on the stovetop, but not over a direct flame. You want to warm the eggs, but not cook them. This will allow the eggs to triple in volume when beaten. Set aside.

In a medium pot, melt the chocolates, water, 1 cup sugar, and margarine over medium heat, stirring with a spoon. Remove from heat. Let cool.

Transfer the eggs to a mixing bowl. Add the remaining ⅓ cup sugar to the eggs and beat until tripled in volume. With a rubber spatula, fold the chocolate mixture into the eggs.

Pour into prepared pan. Bake 30-35 minutes; it will be a little loose in center. Serve warm or room temperature with whipped cream and raspberries.

Yield: 10 servings

chocolate sorbet

Parve

1 cup sugar
2 cups water
½ cup cocoa, good quality Dutch
   processed preferred

4 ounces good quality semisweet
   or bittersweet chocolate (not
   unsweetened and not chocolate
   chips)

Prepare a large pan or bowl of ice water (ice cubes and water). Set aside.

Combine the sugar and water in a medium saucepan. Bring to a boil. Remove from heat and whisk in the cocoa and the chocolate. Stir until smooth.

Return the saucepan to the heat and bring to a boil again. As soon as bubbles start to appear, remove from heat and set into the prepared pan of ice water.

Cool for 10 minutes. Pour sorbet into an airtight container. Cover and freeze for 3 hours.

Remove from freezer and transfer to a mixing bowl. Beat the mixture, at a medium-high speed for 1 full minute. Return to the container. Cover and place back in the freezer for 3 more hours. Repeat the beating 2 more times during these 3 hours. Freeze until ready to serve.

Serve in small scoops in martini glasses.

Yield: 8 servings

honey chocolate chip cookies**

Parve

1 (12-ounce) box Passover honey cake mix
1 tablespoon instant coffee granules
1 cup chopped walnuts
1 large egg
2 tablespoons oil, plus enough orange juice to total ½ cup
1 cup chocolate chips

Preheat oven to 325 degrees. Line 2 cookie sheets with parchment paper or lightly grease them.

In a medium bowl, combine the dry cake mix, instant coffee, and walnuts.

In a separate bowl, mix the egg with the oil/orange juice mixture. Add the dry ingredients into the egg mixture. Stir in the chocolate chips.

Scoop out the dough by rounded teaspoonfuls onto the prepared cookie sheets. Bake 10-15 minutes. Remove to a rack to cool completely.

Yield: 3 dozen

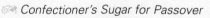

Confectioner's Sugar for Passover

To make 1 cup Passover confectioner's sugar, combine 1 cup minus 1 tablespoon granulated sugar with one tablespoon potato starch. Pulse in a food processor or blender.

praline strips**

A friend gave me a great recipe similar to this one for use during the year. The pralines had a graham cracker base. I tried the recipe substituting matzo and was thrilled with the results, as was anyone who stopped by my house that day in December when I was working on this Passover section. As you can imagine, I had to beg them to taste my Passover desserts, since they are not usually craved out of season. I will say, however, that almost everyone asked for a goody bag to go of this winner!

3-4 whole matzos
1 cup or 2 sticks unsalted butter or margarine
1 cup dark brown sugar

12 ounces chocolate chips or chopped chocolate bars
1 cup finely chopped pecans or chopped almonds

Preheat oven to 325 degrees. Cover a large cookie sheet with aluminum foil. (I like to use a disposable sheet, as the sheet gets very sticky and messy.)

Grease the foil with butter or margarine. Lay the matzos in a single layer, breaking as needed to fill the sheet completely. Set aside.

In a large saucepan, melt the butter or margarine over medium-low heat. Add the brown sugar; boil for 5 minutes, stirring constantly. Watch carefully to make sure it doesn't boil over.

Pour the brown sugar mixture over the matzos, spreading evenly. Bake for 8-10 minutes. Turn the oven off. Remove the pan and sprinkle the chocolate over the matzos. Place it back in the oven for another 8 minutes.

Remove from the oven and spread the chocolate in an even layer. Sprinkle with the chopped pecans or almonds. Refrigerate for 1 hour. Break into pieces. Store in an airtight container in the refrigerator.

lemon meringues

This is a fabulous Passover dessert. The three components: meringues, lemon cream, and chocolate-dipped nuts can all be prepared 2-3 days in advance and assembled right before serving. If not using for Passover, substitute cornstarch for the potato starch, add ¼ teaspoon cream of tartar to the egg whites when whipping them for the meringues, and try using dairy whipping cream and white chocolate-dipped nuts for dairy meals.

Meringues:

2 egg whites
pinch salt
½ cup sugar, super-fine if possible

½ teaspoon vanilla extract
¼ teaspoon almond extract

Lemon Cream:

1½ cups sugar
⅓ cup potato starch
2 cups water

juice of 3 lemons (about ⅓ cup)
3 egg yolks
1 (8-ounce) container whipping cream

Garnishes:

2 ounces semisweet chocolate
1 teaspoon margarine

6 hazelnuts or cashews

Meringues:

Allow the egg whites to stand at room temperature for 30 minutes If you are short on time, place the egg whites in a stainless steel bowl and set it in a bowl of warm water for 2 minutes to bring the whites to room temperature quickly.

Cover two baking sheets with parchment paper. Preheat oven to the lowest possible temperature, 140-175 degrees.

Place the egg whites in the bowl of a mixer. With the whisk attachment, whip the egg whites with the salt about 5 minutes or until soft peaks form; the tips will curl. Gradually add the sugar, beating on high until stiff peaks form; the tips will stand straight and sugar will be dissolved. Fold in vanilla and almond extracts.

Evenly spread the meringues into 12 circles. Flatten slightly so they have a diameter of about 3- to 4-inch circles. Place the two baking sheets in the oven for 4 hours. When they are done, remove from the parchment; if the bottoms are sticky in the center, return them to the oven for longer. You want them completely dried out but not browned. Transfer to a wire rack to cool.

When completely cool, place in an airtight covered container. Store at room temperature for up to 3 days.

Lemon Cream:

In a medium saucepan, combine the sugar and potato starch. Whisk in the water, stirring constantly, until the mixture comes to a boil over medium-high heat. Boil for 1 minute. Remove from heat. Stir in lemon juice.

In a small bowl, stir the egg yolks with a fork. Add a spoonful of the lemon cream to the eggs. Slowly stir the egg mixture into the lemon cream. Continue to cook for 1 minute. Remove from heat. Cool for 15 minutes. Cover the top of the filling with plastic wrap, making sure it touches the cream or a skin will form. Cool to room temperature or refrigerate overnight or up to 2 days in advance.

In a large bowl, with mixer at a high speed, whip the whipping cream. With a rubber spatula, gently fold in ¾ of the whipped cream into the lemon cream. Reserve rest of whipped cream for dollop on top.

Garnishes:

Over a double boiler or in a microwave, melt the chocolate with the margarine. Roll each nut in the chocolate and gently remove with a fork to a sheet of wax paper. Let stand until chocolate is set and shiny; can be put in refrigerator for 5 minutes. Store in an airtight container until ready for use.

To assemble, spread half the meringues with lemon cream. Top with remaining meringues. Place a small dollop of whipped cream on the top of each "sandwich" and top with a chocolate dipped hazelnut or cashew. Serve immediately.

Yield: 6 servings

chocolate chip biscotti**

2 cups sugar
1 cup margarine
6 large eggs
2¾ cups matzo cake meal
¾ cup potato starch

½ teaspoon salt
1 cup walnuts, chopped finely
2 cups semisweet chocolate chips
2 teaspoons sugar
1 teaspoon cinnamon

Preheat oven to 350 degrees. Spray 2 cookie sheets with nonstick cooking spray. Set aside.

In the bowl of a mixer, cream the 2 cups sugar and margarine. Beat until light and fluffy. Add in the eggs one at a time and continue beating.

In a medium bowl, whisk together the matzo cake meal, potato starch, salt, and walnuts. Add to the egg mixture in 3 additions, stirring between additions. Stir in the chocolate chips by hand.

Divide the dough in half and place on the two prepared cookie sheets. Shape each into a large rectangle, approximately 7 by 11 inches. You may need to lightly wet your hands to avoid sticking to the dough.

In a small bowl, combine the 2 teaspoons sugar with the cinnamon. Sprinkle on top of each loaf. Bake for 50 minutes.

Remove from oven and let stand 5 minutes. Cut into individual biscotti while warm. Cool completely.

Yield: 20-24 biscotti

Margarine Substitute

Try this easy replacement for margarine on Passover. Place the desired amount of cottonseed oil in the freezer for 2-3 hours. It will solidify and take on the consistency of soft margarine. You can use it straight from the freezer, and it will work well in many recipes.

You would think that a holiday celebrating something as important as the giving of the Torah would entail elaborate rituals. Yet specific *mitzvot* are noticeably absent on Shavuot, perhaps because all of the observances of the entire Torah are its legacy. As Judaism is a total way of life, how could it be represented by just one symbolic observance?

But we do have delightful customs associated with the holiday. The Midrash tells us that although Mount Sinai is in the desert, it suddenly bloomed with fragrant flowers and grasses on the morning that the Torah was given to the Jewish people. The custom of decorating our homes and synagogues with leafy branches and flowers is based on this miracle.

One of the three major pilgrimage holidays on the Jewish calendar, Shavuot is also known as Chag HaBikurim — the holiday when Jewish farmers brought their first fruits to the Holy Temple of Jerusalem in acknowledgment that their efforts were successful only through God's blessings. Like the farmers and the Jews at Sinai, on Shavuot we affirm that God rules the world and that His blueprint for personal and national success is the Torah.

The Torah has been the mainstay of the Jewish people ever since that awesome day more than 3,300 years ago. It is customary to devote the entire night of Shavuot to its study.

Another Midrash is at the root of this practice: It seems that despite their eager anticipation, the Jews overslept on the first Shavuot morning and Moses had to rouse them to assemble for the great event! To make up for this lackadaisical attitude, we stay awake the entire night of Shavuot, studying the precious Torah that was bestowed upon us.

A popular topic of Shavuot study is the Book of Ruth. Traditionally, this fascinating story is read in the synagogue on the second morning of the holiday. It's an appropriate narrative for Shavuot: it tells of Ruth, a righteous convert to Judaism. She was the ancestress of King David, who passed away on Shavuot. As she chose to follow the God of Israel and all that He stipulated in the Torah with total commitment, she stands as a role model for all Jews.

shavuot menu

BUFFET:
Flower Pot Salad Bar
Basket of Sun-Dried Tomato Pinwheels
and Spinach Artichoke Palmiers
Baby Blintzes
pages 42, 43 and 188

Champagne Poached Salmon
with Champagne Cream Sauce
Shallot Butter Mashed Potatoes
Pasta Pesto with fresh Mozzarella,
Tomatoes and Avocado
Roasted Garlic String Beans with Mango
pages 160, 207, 177 and 202

DESSERTS:
Tiramisu Cheese Cake
Ebony and Ivory
Very Berry Cookies
page 260, 262 and 277

Our outdoor buffet celebrates Shavuot with the fruits and flowers of springtime in cascading abundance. We went wild setting up a Flowerpot Salad Bar. To get this look, use a floral tablecloth covered with purple cabbage-lined terra-cotta pots of all sizes. These pots hold all the makings of an irresistible salad bar, from a huge pot of mixed salad greens to smaller pots of multicolored tomatoes, cucumbers, sprouts, carrots, dried cranberries, chickpeas and various seeds. Matching terra-cotta saucers are used for height, as well as to position some of the pots on a slant. Stick loose roses and greenery in every open space. Two big terra-cotta pots holding floral arrangements flank each side of the table. Little touches, such as using colored enameled gardening tools as serving pieces and watering cans to hold dressing, really made this buffet charming and unique.

Our dining table continues the floral theme by incorporating flowers in every possible place. Suspended from our patio umbrella are floral oasis cages. You can get these from a local florist. Use flowers from your garden or a mixture of hydrangea, delphinium, roses, stock, and bells of Ireland. These spheres of flowers are suspended by multicolored ribbons and are tied

to the spokes of the overhead umbrella. A place mat cut out of banana leaf graces each place setting. Ribbons are knotted through the drainage holes of two-inch flowerpots and little silk flowers are hot glued into them (which keeps them reusable). These flowerpot napkin rings secure fan-folded napkins.

The tradition of eating dairy on Shavuot recalls the Mount Sinai experience: before the Jews received the Torah at Mount Sinai, they were not yet familiar with the dietary rules for meat preparation. After they received the Torah, they realized that they had no meat utensils and no properly slaughtered animals. They ate only dairy foods until kosher meat and utensils were prepared. Another reason for eating dairy is that the Torah itself is compared to milk in the Biblical passage "…honey and milk under your tongue."

We combined the complementary Sun-dried Tomato Pinwheels and Spinach Artichoke Palmiers in a basket. Blintzes, a traditional dairy Shavuot food, appear here in sweet looking baby-size portions. These take the blintz flavor and pack it into cute berry-topped muffins served with a dollop of sour cream. The mainstay of the buffet is Champagne Poached Salmon accented by a cream sauce. Roasted Garlic String Beans with Mango are perfect for a buffet because they taste great at room temperature. Dairy dishes include colorful Pasta Pesto with Mozzarella, Tomatoes and Avocado, as well as Shallot Butter Mashed Potatoes.

Our sumptuous dairy dessert buffet rounds out the festivities. The elegant Ebony and Ivory is a wickedly rich tribute to chocolate. Individual servings are topped with a small pink rose. Tiramisu Cheesecake is a chic spin on a traditional Shavuot dessert. The Very Berry Cookies reflect the fruits of the season.

A buffet frees you to enjoy the holiday meal with your guests in a relaxed atmosphere. With the spectacular array of delicacies on this menu, your family and guests will appreciate sampling small amounts of many varied items. Buffets work for groups of any size: after the easy success of this magnificent meal, you may be tempted to have a larger gathering next year!

wine list

Few people think of champagne as a natural accompaniment to a meal and yet it pairs well with so many foods. We thought a buffet would be a perfect opportunity to show of some of these winning winning bottles. There are some fantastic choices at various price ranges such as: Laurent Perrier Brut or Rose, Nicholas Feuillatte Brut (Mevushal), Hagafen Brut Cuvee and Yarden Blanc de Blanc.

Champagne (and Sparkling Wine) styles range from dry to sweet. Champagnes are labeled: Brut = dry, Extra Dry = less dry, Sec = sweet to semi sweet and Demi Sec = sweet.

For the purposes of the appetizers and main courses, Brut and Extra Dry styles are recommended. For the desserts try sweeter styles and Italian sparklers such as Asti Spumante.

Champagne should be served in a flute or regular tulip shaped glass and not in a coupe, which would dissipate the bubbles.

Chocolate Lovers Truffle Brownies

dessert

white chocolate butterscotch chip cookies   Dairy

2½ cups all-purpose flour
1 teaspoon baking soda
¼ teaspoon salt
1 cup (2 sticks) unsalted butter, at room temperature
1½ cups firmly packed, dark brown sugar

2 large eggs
1 tablespoon light molasses
2 teaspoons vanilla
¾ cup butterscotch chips
¾ cup white chocolate chips

Preheat oven to 350 degrees. In a medium-size bowl, mix the flour, baking soda, and salt. Set aside.

In a large bowl, beat the butter and brown sugar until smooth and creamy. Add the eggs, molasses, and vanilla. Beat well, about 1 minute.

At low speed, beat in the flour mixture. Stir in the butterscotch and white chocolate chips. Turn the dough out onto a large rectangle of waxed or parchment paper. Using the paper to help, roll the dough into a long log. Dough can be frozen or refrigerated at this point and sliced and baked for warm cookies at any time.

Slice the log into ¼- to ½-inch slices and place on ungreased baking sheets lined with parchment paper. Bake 15 minutes or until set. Transfer to a rack to cool.

Yield: 24 large cookies

babe ruth bars   Parve

These bars fall under the same genre as the famous Rice Krispy Treats. Kids and adults will both go for them.

1 cup creamy peanut butter
1 cup light corn syrup
½ cup dark brown sugar
½ cup sugar

6 cups cornflake cereal
1 cup semisweet chocolate chips
⅔ cup peanuts, shelled

Lightly grease a 9- by 13-inch baking pan. Set aside.

In a large pot over medium heat combine the peanut butter, corn syrup, brown sugar, and sugar. Cook, stirring until smooth. Remove from heat and quickly mix in the cornflakes, chocolate chips, and peanuts. Combine until evenly coated.

Press the mixture into the prepared pan. You can use wax paper or parchment to help press it in evenly. Allow to cool completely before cutting into bars.

Yield: 18 bars

chocolate snickerdoodles

½ cup (1 stick) butter or margarine, softened
1½ cups sugar
2 large eggs
1 teaspoon vanilla
1¼ cups all-purpose flour

½ cup cocoa (Dutch processed preferred)
1 teaspoon cream of tartar
½ teaspoon baking soda
¼ teaspoon salt
1 tablespoon sugar
1 tablespoon cinnamon

Preheat oven to 375 degrees. In a large bowl, beat the butter or margarine with the sugar until light and fluffy. Add the eggs and vanilla. Beat well.

In a medium bowl, combine the flour, cocoa, cream of tartar, baking soda, and salt. Add the dry ingredient mixture to the creamed mixture in two parts. Incorporate the first half before adding the second. Mix until a smooth batter is formed.

Shape the dough into 1-inch balls, the size of ping-pong balls or walnuts. In a small bowl combine the tablespoon of sugar with the cinnamon. Roll the balls in the cinnamon-sugar mixture. If the dough is too sticky, wet your hands with warm water. Also, once you roll the ball in the cinnamon-sugar it will be less sticky. Place 2 inches apart on parchment lined or ungreased cookie sheets.

Bake 10 minutes. Immediately remove from the oven. Let cool for 1-2 minutes on the cookie sheet then remove to a wire rack to cool completely.

Yield: 25-30 cookies

☞ *Pie Crust Dough Bonus*
The scraps of dough that are trimmed off from your homemade pie crusts can be turned into delicious cookies. Be creative with the dough; braid, twist, or knot it, then sprinkle with cinnamon and sugar. Bake in a preheated 350 degree oven for 10 minutes.

ebony and ivory

This is by far the most requested and beautiful dairy dessert I have ever made. It has two creamy layers, one of chocolate mousse and one of white chocolate mousse. The two sit one atop the other for a most dramatic presentation. It is very easy to make, especially if using a microwave to melt the chocolate.

My husband teases me that my baking pantry looks more like a plumber's tool box because one of my most valuable possessions is a propane torch. I use it in this recipe to release the sides of the pan. A hot towel also does the trick, but if you are going to buy a propane torch, get the small hand-held versions used for baking. I have come close to melting the countertop on too many occasions to count with my full-size model.

15 ounces good quality semisweet or bittersweet chocolate, broken or cut into bits	6 large eggs, separated
	¼ teaspoon cream of tartar
	3 tablespoons sugar
¾ cup (1½ sticks) sweet butter, cut into small pieces	12 ounces good quality white chocolate, broken or cut into bits
3 teaspoons instant coffee (not freeze dried), dissolved in 3 teaspoons water	⅓ cup plus 1 tablespoon water
	2 cups heavy cream

Ebony Mousse Layer:

Melt the chocolate and butter together in a bowl over a pot of simmering hot water or in a microwave on MEDIUM (50%) for about 2-3 minutes. Stir to hasten the melting and to smooth the mixture. Remove from microwave or stovetop and whisk in the dissolved coffee powder and eggs yolks. Set aside.

In a clean dry bowl, beat the egg whites and cream of tartar at medium speed until soft peaks form. Slowly sprinkle in the sugar, beating at high until stiff but not dry.

Fold the egg whites into the chocolate until completely incorporated.

Using a spatula, scrape the mousse into a 10-inch springform pan, being careful to keep the top half of the pan clean. Place in refrigerator.

Ivory Mousse Layer:

Melt the white chocolate and water in a bowl over a pot of simmering hot water or in a microwave on LOW (30%) for about 2 minutes. Stir to hasten melting and to smooth the mixture. Make sure the chocolate is completely smooth or the mousse will taste grainy.

Whip the cream until soft peaks form, not too stiff. Carefully fold the cream into the melted white chocolate until completely incorporated.

Remove the pan from the refrigerator and immediately turn the ivory mousse on top of the ebony layer. Use a metal spatula to level the top perfectly with the rim of the pan. Don't manipulate for too long because the white mousse starts to set quickly.

Refrigerate for 4-6 hours before unmolding. This dessert can be made two days in advance and refrigerated covered in the pan, or frozen for up to a month.

Before unmolding the dessert, warm the sides of the springform pan ring with a hot, wet, wrung-out towel or a propane torch. Release the sides of the pan. Smooth sides with a metal spatula if necessary for a cleaner look. This can also be done in individual servings as pictured.

Yield: 16 servings

applesauce crumb cake

Parve

1½ cups (3 sticks) margarine, softened for 10 minutes at room temperature
4 cups all-purpose flour
1½ cups sugar
⅛ teaspoon salt

2 teaspoons baking powder
2 large eggs
1 (16 ounce) jar applesauce
2 teaspoons cinnamon, divided
1 teaspoon vanilla
1 teaspoon sugar

Preheat oven to 350. Lightly grease an 8- by 11-inch baking pan. Set aside.

In the bowl of a mixer, beat the margarine, flour, sugar, salt, and baking powder. Remove half of the mixture and set aside.

Add the eggs to the original bowl and beat until combined. Press this mixture into the prepared pan.

In a medium bowl, combine the applesauce with 1 teaspoon cinnamon, and the vanilla. Mix. Spread on top of the batter that is in the pan.

Add the remaining teaspoon of cinnamon and teaspoon of sugar to the reserved dough. Using your fingers, combine until it resembles coarse crumbs. Crumble evenly over the applesauce layer. Bake uncovered for 45 minutes or until toothpick inserted in center comes out clean.

Yield: 12-16 servings

very berry cookies

These moist and pretty cookies remind me of summer. They are a light, colorful, and delicious treat that kids and adults will love.

½ cup pure vegetable shortening, like Crisco or 1 stick butter
⅔ cup sugar
1 egg yolk
½ teaspoon vanilla
1 teaspoon lemon juice
1⅓ cups all-purpose flour
½ teaspoon baking powder

¼ teaspoon baking soda
¼ teaspoon salt
4 fresh strawberries chopped into very small pieces
8-10 fresh strawberries, each sliced into 4 slices
15-20 blueberries, sliced in half

Preheat oven to 375 degrees. In a large mixing bowl with an electric mixer, cream the shortening or butter and the sugar. Add the yolk, vanilla, and lemon juice. Beat well.

In a medium bowl mix the flour, baking powder, baking soda, and salt.

Add the flour mixture to the bowl and mix until combined, it will be dry. Add the chopped strawberries and with a mixer beat for 10-20 seconds or until combined

Drop by rounded tablespoonfuls onto parchment-lined or greased cookie sheets, flatten with slightly wet fingers. Lightly press 1 slice of strawberry and 2 blueberry pieces into each cookie.

Bake 10 minutes. Remove the cookies to a rack to cool.

Store in a single layer.

Yield: 24-30 cookies

hamantasch

This is an old family recipe. It is a very easy dough to make and work with. The egg glaze and cinnamon/sugar on top give the cookies a beautiful color. My Mom and Aunt make these in advance and freeze them. Do this at your own risk. At a group confession, every one of my cousins and siblings admitted to sneaking hamantasch and eating them frozen weeks before Purim.

¾ cup vegetable oil
3 large eggs
2 teaspoons vanilla
¾ cup cold water
1 cup sugar
3 teaspoons baking powder

6 cups all-purpose flour
flour for dipping
apricot butter or prune butter
1 large egg, beaten
cinnamon/sugar

Preheat oven to 350 degrees. Cover 2 baking sheets with parchment or foil.

Either by hand or in a mixer combine the oil, egg, vanilla, water, sugar, baking powder, and flour. Knead until it forms a soft dough. Roll the dough out into a very thin layer.

Dip the rim of a 3- to 4-inch cup or glass in flour. Use the glass like a cookie cutter to cut out circles. Re-roll the scraps of dough and reuse.

In the center of each circle, drop a teaspoon of apricot butter or prune butter. Shape into a triangle by folding 2 sides of the circle to the center and pinch together at the corners. Fold remaining side up to the center and pinch together at the corners.

Place hamantaschen 1 inch apart on the baking sheet. Brush with beaten egg. Sprinkle with cinnamon/sugar. Make sure corners are tightly pinched so they don't open during baking. Bake 20 minutes. Can be made in advance and frozen.

Yield: 4 dozen

✍ *This cookie dough is great for all year round: After cutting the dough into flat circles or any shape, transfer them to the baking sheet and put a dallop of the thickest all-fruit preserves you can find, in the center. Sprinkle with cinnamon/sugar and bake as indicated.*

chocolate lovers truffle brownies

My family is tough to please when it comes to parve chocolate desserts. The worst criticism is when I ask how a dessert tastes and the answer is, well, parve. These brownies are the answer to the parve problem. They transcend the world of brownies. They are so fudgy and incredible, they are without a doubt the best you will have ever eaten. Their elegant three layers make them perfect for children and adults.

Brownie Layer:

- 8 ounces best quality semisweet or bittersweet chocolate (not unsweetened), chopped
- ¾ cup (1½ sticks) butter or margarine
- 2 teaspoons espresso powder dissolved in 1 teaspoon boiling water
- 1½ cups sugar
- 2 teaspoons vanilla
- 4 large eggs
- 1 cup all-purpose flour
- ½ teaspoon salt

Crust:

- ⅔ cup light brown sugar
- ⅔ cup butter or margarine
- 1⅓ cups all-purpose flour, sifted
- 1 cup finely chopped pecans

Glaze:

- 6 ounces best quality semisweet or bittersweet chocolate (not unsweetened)
- 2 tablespoons butter or margarine
- ½ cup heavy cream or nondairy creamer

Brownie Layer:

Preheat oven to 350 degrees. Grease and flour a 9- by 13-inch baking pan.

Melt the chocolate, butter, and espresso mixture in a metal bowl set over a pan of simmering water. Stirring until smooth. Remove the bowl from heat and cool 10 minutes.

Stir the cooled chocolate mixture. Whisk in the sugar, vanilla, and eggs one at a time until batter is smooth. Stir in the flour and salt until just combined. Set aside.

Crust:

Cream the brown sugar and butter or margarine until light and fluffy. Slowly add flour and continue to mix until blended and smooth. Add pecans. When completely combined, press crust into bottom of prepared pan. Set aside.

Spread brownie batter evenly over the crust and bake in the middle of the oven until top is firm and tester inserted in center comes out clean, about 25-27 minutes. Remove from oven and place immediately into the refrigerator. Set aside.

Glaze:

Heat all the glaze ingredients in a large metal bowl set over a saucepan of simmering water until chocolate and butter are melted and glaze is smooth. Remove from heat and cool glaze to room temperature, stirring occasionally, about 10 minutes.

Pour glaze evenly over the brownie layer and return to the refrigerator. Cut into 20 bars and serve cold. You may top each brownie with a blackberry, raspberry, or strawberry.

Yield: 20 brownies

bakery cookies   Parve

Cookies:

1½ sticks margarine	2 eggs
1½ cups sugar	1 teaspoon salt
3 teaspoons vanilla	3½ cups flour

Glaze:

6 ounces chocolate chips
2 tablespoons pure vegetable shortening
   sprinkles or non-pariels

Cookies:

Preheat oven to 350 degrees. In a large mixing bowl, cream the margarine with the sugar. Add the vanilla, eggs, and salt. Beat until smooth. Slowly incorporate the flour, beating until dough forms. Shape into thin flattened 3-4 inch logs. Place on a parchment-lined or lightly greased baking sheet. Bake 12-15 minutes. Remove from oven and let cool.

Glaze:

Place chocolate and shortening in a small glass bowl. Microwave at 70% for 1 minute. Stir. Microwave at 70% for 20-second intervals, stirring in between to melt chocolate.

Dip the very ends of each log into glaze and immediately into sprinkles or non-pariels. Let sit on wax paper to dry; you can freeze for 3-4 minutes to speed the process.

Yield: 48 cookies

🍰 *Cake Design*
For a cool geometric design, scatter slivers of paper over your platter or cake. Sift confectioner's sugar or cocoa over the arrangement. Carefully remove the pieces of paper. The results are delightful.

castaway cake

Even when made parve, you will never believe that this cake is not full of butter and cream. It is so simple and delicious. The cake makes an 8- by 8-inch square. You can use deep cookie cutters to cut out circles or triangles for individual presentations. You won't get a lot of servings out of it, but it makes for a special look.

Cake:

- 2 large eggs
- 1 cup sugar
- 1 cup unbleached all-purpose flour
- 1 teaspoon baking powder
- ½ teaspoon salt
- ½ cup milk or nondairy creamer
- 1½ tablespoons butter or margarine

Topping:

- 4 tablespoons butter or margarine
- ½ cup plus 2 tablespoons dark brown sugar
- 4 tablespoons milk or nondairy creamer
- 1 cup sweetened, flaked coconut

Cake:

Grease and flour an 8- by 8-inch square or 9½ inch round baking pan. Preheat oven to 350 degrees. Place the eggs in a mixing bowl and beat on low until frothy. Add the sugar and beat on high until the mixture is creamy and lemon colored. Stir in the flour, baking powder, and salt.

In a small saucepan, heat the milk or creamer with the butter or margarine until boiling. Add to the batter, beating to combine. Pour batter into prepared pan and bake for 30 minutes. Remove from oven to cool for about 10 minutes, leaving the cake in the pan. Preheat the broiler to high.

Topping:

Melt the butter or margarine in a saucepan. Add the brown sugar, milk or creamer, and coconut. Stir to combine. Pour over the warm cake.

Place the cake under the broiler for about 1 minute, watching the whole time carefully to make sure the topping gets caramelized but not burnt. Rotate as necessary. When topping is golden, remove from oven and cool completely. Carefully remove cake from pan.

Yield: 6-8 servings

ginger crinkle cake

My neighbor and I love ginger crinkle cookies, so I was determined to find a cake with this kind of flavor. This cake fits the bill; it's moist and not too sweet. Its flavors blend nicely and are not too strong. Make sure to use a mild molasses, not a robust one. This cake is parve, which is great, but I love it with a cold glass of milk. The color is dark, so don't use it to determine doneness. Follow cooking times and don't overbake or it will not be moist.

Cake:

3 cups all-purpose flour	1 cup (2 sticks) margarine
2 teaspoons cinnamon	½ cup packed dark brown sugar
2 teaspoons ground ginger	2 large eggs
1 teaspoon baking powder	1 cup mild flavored molasses
1 teaspoon baking soda	1 cup water

Glaze:

1 cup sifted confectioner's sugar
½ teaspoon vanilla
1 tablespoon water

Cake:

Preheat oven to 350 degrees. Grease and flour a 10-inch bundt pan and set aside.

In a medium bowl, stir together the flour, cinnamon, ginger, baking powder, and baking soda. Set aside.

Place the margarine in a large mixing bowl and beat it for 30 seconds on medium speed.

Add the brown sugar and beat until light and fluffy. Add the eggs and molasses and beat for 1 minute. Slowly add the flour mixture alternating with the water. Beat after each addition until combined. Pour into the prepared pan. Bake 45-50 minutes or until toothpick inserted in center comes out clean. Cool in pan. When completely cooled, prepare the glaze.

Glaze:

In a mixing bowl, combine the powdered sugar, vanilla, and water. Mix thoroughly with a spoon. You want to be able to drizzle it, but keep it as thick as possible for a nice heavy glaze. If you must, add ½ teaspoon of water at a time to thin as needed. Spoon over cake.

Yield: 12-16 servings

chocolate palmiers

When you've only got a few minutes to make a great dessert, this cookie is perfect. When served warm out of the oven, they taste a little like chocolate croissants. I prefer an Israeli cocoa spread. It has a pure chocolate taste. If you like a nutty flavor, use the chocolate hazelnut spread. You can even sprinkle ½ cup chopped nuts of your choice over the spread before you roll up the dough.

1   (17.3-ounce) box puff pastry
    sheets (2 sheets)

12 tablespoons cocoa spread or
    chocolate hazelnut spread, divided

6   teaspoons superfine or regular
    sugar, divided

Lightly grease a large cookie sheet or line it with parchment paper. Roll out each pastry sheet into a 15- by 9-inch rectangle.

Using a knife, spread 6 tablespoons of the cocoa spread evenly over the pastry. Sprinkle with 3 teaspoons sugar. Tightly roll one of the long sides into the center of the rectangle; stop when you get to the middle. Roll the other long side into the center. Repeat process with second pastry sheet, remaining 6 tablespoons cocoa spread, and remaining 3 teaspoons sugar.

Using your sharpest knife, cut into ¾- to 1-inch slices. Lay the cookies flat on the prepared baking sheet. Bake for 15-18 minutes or until golden.

Yield: 26-30 palmiers

marble fudge cookies

Many of you will recognize these as Chinese cookies. Taste these and you'll agree that these melt-in-your-mouth, puddle-of-fudge delights deserved a better name.

Cookies:

3 cups all-purpose flour
1½ cups pure vegetable shortening, like Crisco (no substitutes)
1½ cups sugar

1¼ teaspoons baking soda
1 large egg
¼ cup chocolate chips (about 1 ounce)

Fudge Glaze:

6 ounces chocolate chips
3 tablespoons vegetable shortening

1 tablespoon confectioner's sugar

Cookies:

In a large mixing bowl, with mixer at medium speed, mix the flour, shortening, sugar, and baking soda. Add the egg. Mix until dough forms.

Place the chocolate chips in a glass bowl and melt in the microwave for 1 minute at 70%; stir to hasten melting. With a knife, cut the melted chocolate into the dough, swirling as best you can.

Using parchment or waxed paper, roll the dough into 3 logs, each about the size of a salami or 2½- to 3-inch in diameter. Freeze for ½ hour-1 hour to make the slicing neater and easier.

Preheat oven to 350 degrees. Spray 2 cookie sheets with nonstick cooking spray or line with parchment paper. Slice each log into 12-15 cookies. Bake 15-20 minutes. Let cool on a rack.

Glaze:

Either in a double boiler or in the microwave, melt the chocolate chips with the shortening and confectioner's sugar. Stir till smooth and shiny. Put a puddle in the center of each cookie. Place in refrigerator for 10 minutes to set the chocolate. Store in a single layer so chocolate doesn't smudge. Alternatively, for the shiny center you can use 8 ounces of melted Shufra baking chocolate, puddled in the center of each cookie.

Yield: 30-34 cookies

sunken apples & honey tart

This cake is perfect for Rosh Hashana. Its apples, honey, and round shape represent the holiday's symbols. As the cake bakes the apples and batter intertwine for a beautiful presentation.

⅓ cup honey

2 tablespoons fresh lemon juice

3 medium Granny Smith or Rome apples, peeled, cored, and cut into 8-10 wedges

¾ cup sugar

6 tablespoons margarine, softened

¼ cup packed dark brown sugar

1 teaspoon vanilla

2 large eggs

1 teaspoon grated lemon rind, (only yellow not white pith)

1 cup all-purpose flour

1 teaspoon baking powder

¼ teaspoon salt

1 tablespoon sugar

½ teaspoon ground cinnamon

Preheat oven to 350 degrees. Coat a 9-inch springform pan with nonstick cooking spray. Combine the honey and lemon juice in a large nonstick skillet. Bring to a simmer over medium heat. Add the apples; cook 12-14 minutes or until almost tender, stirring occasionally to coat the apple wedges. Remove skillet from heat and set aside.

In the bowl of a mixer, combine the ¾ cup sugar, margarine, brown sugar, and vanilla. Beat on medium until well blended, about 45 seconds-1 minute. Add the eggs and beat. Beat in the grated lemon rind.

In a separate bowl, combine the flour, baking powder, and salt. Stir with a whisk to combine. Gradually add the flour mixture to the batter. Beat on low until blended.

Pour the batter into the prepared pan. Remove the apples from the skillet with a fork or slotted spoon, discarding liquid.

Arrange the apple slices in a concentric spoke-like design on top of the batter.

Combine 1 tablespoon of sugar with the cinnamon. Sprinkle evenly over the tart.

Bake for 1 hour. Cool completely and release the sides of the springform pan.

Yield: 8-10 servings

270 ‰ KOSHER BY DESIGN

blueberries & cream cake

This is a delicious vanilla cake with a tunnel of blueberries running through the center. Use a 12-ounce jar of good quality preserves. It will have whole berries in it for a fresher taste than blueberry jelly.

2 cups all-purpose flour
1 tablespoon baking powder
½ teaspoon salt
2 sticks butter or margarine, softened
1½ cups sugar

2 large eggs, at room temperature
1 cup dairy or parve sour cream
1 tablespoon vanilla
1 cup blueberry preserves, plus 3 tablespoons preserves
   confectioner's sugar

Preheat oven to 350 degrees. Grease and flour a 10-inch bundt pan.

In a large bowl whisk or sift the flour, baking powder, and salt together. With a mixer on high, beat the butter or margarine until light and creamy. Add the sugar and beat until fluffy. Beat in the eggs, sour cream, and vanilla. Slowly add in the flour mixture. Remove ½ cup of the batter. Spread the rest into the prepared pan.

Using the back of a spoon, make a trough in the batter all the way around. Mix the 1 cup preserves with the ½ cup reserved batter. Spoon it into the trough.

Bake for 1 hour. Let the cake cool in the pan for ten minutes and then flip onto a wire rack to cool completely.

Heat the 3 tablespoons of preserves until just melted. Drizzle over the cake. Dust the top of the cake with a sprinkle of confectioner's sugar; you can use a sifter.

Yield: 12 servings

warm apple & pear fruit beggars purse Parve

This is a Foremost Caterer's signature dessert. Warm phyllo bundles are filled with sautéed apples and pears, a touch a cinnamon, and have a hint of warm chocolate sauce running through the center. It can be made with any combination of fruit of that season. I have tried a mixture of plums, peaches, and nectarines in the summer with delicious results. With this combination, leave the skins on and don't sauté the fruit as long as apples; you want the fruit pieces to keep their shape.

Use good quality chocolate that you would eat as a snack. For parve meals, use a good bittersweet chocolate bar and use their score marks to separate into squares. Store phyllo dough in your refrigerator so it will be thawed when ready for use. You can keep it there for up to 5 days. Phyllo dough sheets are paper thin, so work gently with them.

2 tablespoons margarine, for sautéing	5 tablespoons brown sugar
3 Granny Smith apples, peeled, cored, and cut into ½- to ¾-inch chunks	cinnamon
	3 tablespoons cornstarch
2 Bosc or Anjou pears, peeled, cored (use 1 more if the pears are small), and cut into ½- to ¾-inch chunks	1 box phyllo dough, defrosted
	1 stick margarine or more, melted
2 large oranges, cut in half, divided	6 small squares good quality bittersweet chocolate bar

Preheat oven to 320 degrees. In a large skillet, heat the margarine over a medium flame. Add the apples and pears. Sauté for 3 minutes. Squeeze the juice of 1 orange half directly into the skillet; continue sautéing. Add the brown sugar to the pan. Mix with the fruit. Sprinkle with a few shakes of cinnamon.

In a small bowl, combine the cornstarch and the juice of the remaining 1½ oranges. Stir vigorously until smooth.

Slowly add the cornstarch mixture to the pan, stirring or whisking continuously. The mixture will start to thicken and caramelize. You want the brown sugar to be sticky and thick, not runny. Remove from heat.

Unwrap the phyllo dough, laying out the sheets horizontally in one stack in front of you. Cut the layered stack of dough lengthwise and width-wise to make 4 equal rectangular quarters.

Take one phyllo rectangle and brush all around the edges with melted margarine. Lay the next rectangle of phyllo directly over the first but at an angle. Brush with margarine. Do this 4 more times for a total of 6 sheets.

Place a small mound of the caramelized fruit in the center. Add a square of chocolate.

Lift one edge of the phyllo dough towards the middle, gathering and pleating the dough as you go around, pulling all the edges to the middle to form a purse. Make 8 purses this way.

Brush and drizzle each purse with melted margarine. Place on a parchment-lined cookie sheet. Bake for 10 minutes, this will finish cooking the fruit. Raise the heat to 350 degrees. Bake an additional 15 minutes, this will turn the phyllo nice and golden.

When golden brown remove from oven. Serve warm. If made in advance, rewarm for a few minutes in the oven to warm the fruit and melt the chocolate.

Yield: 8 servings

chocolate & vanilla rope cookies

Parve

¾ cup (1½ sticks) margarine
¾ cup sugar
1 large egg
2½ teaspoons vanilla
2 cups all-purpose flour

½ teaspoon baking powder
¼ teaspoon salt
3 tablespoons good quality
unsweetened cocoa

Lightly grease 2 cookie sheets or cover them with parchment paper. With a mixer on high speed cream the margarine with the sugar. Add the egg and vanilla, blend well.

In a small bowl mix the flour, baking powder, and salt. Add to the creamed mixture and blend well.

Remove half the dough from the bowl. Wrap this half in plastic wrap and refrigerate. Add the cocoa to the other half of dough. With the mixer, blend until the dough becomes uniformly chocolate. Remove from bowl and wrap in plastic wrap. Refrigerate. After 3 hours, or when dough is very firm, remove both from refrigerator.

Preheat oven to 325 degrees. Break off a small piece of chocolate dough and roll into a thin log. Break off a piece of vanilla dough and roll into a thin log. Use a knife to trim them to the same length, about 3 inches each. Twist the rope together by crossing chocolate over vanilla and winding it around to form a rope shape.

Transfer to a cookie sheet. Repeat with remaining dough. If the vanilla gets too soft, put it in the freezer for a few minutes. The chocolate dough should stay firm.

Bake for 13-15 minutes. Let the ropes cool slightly on the sheet and then remove them to a rack to cool completely.

Yield: 24-30 cookies

chocolate cookies & cream trifle

Cake:

1¾ cup all-purpose flour
2 cups sugar
¾ cup cocoa
1½ teaspoon baking soda
1½ teaspoon baking powder
1 teaspoon salt

2 large eggs
1 cup nondairy creamer or milk
½ cup vegetable oil
2 teaspoons vanilla
1 cup boiling water

Chocolate Cream:

1 cup nondairy creamer or milk
1 (2.8-ounce) box instant chocolate pudding

1 (8-ounce) container whipping cream

Vanilla Cream:

1 (8-ounce) container whipping cream
Crushed cookies, either chocolate chip or chocolate sandwich

Chopped up peanut chew-type candies (optional)

Cake:

Preheat oven to 350 degrees. Grease and flour 2 (8½-inch) round baking pans, or same diameter as your trifle dish, as the chocolate cakes will be placed whole into the trifle bowl.

Place the flour, sugar, cocoa, baking soda, baking powder, and salt into a large mixing bowl. Whisk or stir until well blended. Beat in the eggs, creamer or milk, oil, and vanilla. Beat until smooth. With a spoon or spatula, fold in the boiling water. Pour the batter into prepared pans. Bake for 50 minutes. When cake is done, cool completely.

Chocolate Cream:

Mix the creamer or milk and pudding mix together. Whip the container of whipping cream. Fold it into the chocolate pudding mixture. Set aside, can be covered and refrigerated.

Vanilla Cream:

Whip the cream. Set aside. Can be covered and refrigerated.

Place one of the cake layers in the bottom of a trifle dish. Add a layer of chocolate cream, layer of vanilla cream, layer of cookie crumbs, layer of candy if you are using. Repeat.

Yield: 12-14 servings

mascarpone-stuffed strawberries over cinnamon chips

This is a beautiful light dairy dessert that is great for a spring lunch table. Mascarpone is a wonderfully rich and creamy Italian cheese that is the magic ingredient in tiramisu. It is usually found with the fancier cheeses and comes in 8-ounce containers. If you can't find kosher Mascarpone, you can substitute by whipping 8 ounces softened cream cheese with ¼ cup heavy cream and 2½ tablespoons sour cream.

The cinnamon chips are terrific as well. I always make an extra tortilla or two because the chips make a great snack and tend to "disappear" from the cooling rack.

3 large soft flour tortillas
butter-flavored cooking spray
cinnamon and sugar
½ cup Mascarpone cheese
3 ounces cream cheese (not whipped), softened

3 tablespoons fine sugar
16 large strawberries (with stems intact)

Preheat oven to 350 degrees. Coat one side of each flour tortilla with the cooking spray. Using a pizza wheel or sharp knife, cut each tortilla into eight wedges.

Place the wedges in a single layer on a large baking sheet. Sprinkle the wedges with cinnamon sugar. Spray again with cooking spray.

Bake in the preheated oven for 8-10 minutes. Repeat with any remaining tortilla wedges. Allow wedges to cool approximately 15 minutes.

Meanwhile, with a mixer on medium speed, beat the Mascarpone, cream cheese, and sugar until whipped and smooth.

With a small melon baller cut a cavity into the "belly" or middle of each strawberry. Using a pastry bag fitted with a star tip, or with a small spoon, pipe Mascarpone mixture into each berry.

Sprinkle the Mascarpone lightly with cinnamon sugar. Cover and refrigerate the strawberries until ready to use.

To serve, place 6 wedges, like a pizza pie missing slices, on each plate. In the center of each plate lay 4 stuffed strawberries.

Yield: 4 servings

tiramisu cheesecake

A light fluffy change from the traditional cheesecake. You will love the slight espresso flavor mixed with the creamy cheese. The preferred ladyfingers are the soft sponge-cake kind. I have seen them in many supermarkets near the fruit section. If you can't find them, don't panic, you can use the hard ladyfinger cookies, cut in half to line the outside. Don't forget the grated chocolate for the top; it looks very pretty. You can freeze this cake in an airtight container or well wrapped in foil. To thaw, loosen the covering and leave in the refrigerator for at least a day.

14 chocolate sandwich cookies	1 (8-ounce) package Mascarpone cheese, softened
2 tablespoons butter, melted	1 cup sugar
12-14 soft sponge ladyfingers (3-ounce package)	1 tablespoon cornstarch
1 teaspoon instant espresso powder or instant coffee	1 teaspoon vanilla
2 tablespoons whole milk	3 large eggs
2 (8-ounce) packages cream cheese, softened	1 (8-ounce) container sour cream milk chocolate bar, for grating

Preheat oven to 350 degrees. In the bowl of a food processor fitted with a metal blade, process the cookies until they are finely crushed into crumbs. Add the butter and mix to moisten.

Press the crumbs into the bottom of an ungreased 9-inch springform pan. Cut the ladyfingers in half, crosswise. Line the ladyfingers around the sides of the pan, rounded side out and cut side down.

In a small cup or bowl mix the espresso powder in the milk, stirring to dissolve. Set aside.

In a medium mixing bowl beat the cream cheese and Mascarpone until combined and fluffy. Gradually add sugar. Beat on medium-high until smooth. Turn the speed to low and beat in the cornstarch, vanilla, and eggs until just combined. Stir espresso mixture into the batter.

Pour the batter into the ladyfinger-lined pan. Place the pan on a baking sheet. Bake for 45-50 minutes. Center will appear nearly set when gently shaken. Remove from oven. Immediately spread the sour cream on top, starting at the center and going almost to the edges.

Cool in pan for 15 minutes. Use a small knife or spatula to make sure the ladyfingers are not sticking to the sides of the pan. Cool at least one hour. Cover with plastic wrap and chill in the refrigerator for at least 5 hours. Sprinkle grated chocolate over the top of the cheesecake.

Yield: 12 servings

ultimate cheesecake

I have never tasted a better cheesecake. It's so creamy and rich that I guarantee some of the batter will not make it into the crust. The slow heat cooking method keeps this cake beautiful, with no cracks or fallen tops. Just leave yourself plenty of time. Once I didn't plan well and ended up chatting with my husband until 2:30 in the morning waiting for the cheesecake to be done. But yes, the cake was worth it. The caramel topping is optional for an easy change.

1½ cups graham cracker crumbs
6 tablespoons (¾ stick) unsalted butter, melted
¼ cup dark brown sugar
5 (8-ounce) bars cream cheese, softened for 20 minutes
5 large eggs
2 large egg yolks
1⅓ cups sugar

1 teaspoon vanilla
⅛ cup all-purpose flour
¼ cup heavy whipping cream
caramel topping (store bought, usually in ice-cream section), optional
3 chocolate-covered toffee candy bars (like Skor or Heath bars), broken into pieces, optional

Preheat oven to 200 degrees. Spray a 10-inch springform pan with nonstick cooking spray, coating the bottom very well.

In a medium bowl, combine the graham cracker crumbs, melted butter, and brown sugar. Press into the bottom of the prepared pan. Set aside.

In the bowl of an electric mixer, combine the cream cheese, eggs, and egg yolks. Beat at medium speed until smooth. Add the sugar, vanilla, flour, and heavy cream. Blend until smooth.

Pour the batter into the prepared crust. Bake for 3 hours and 10 minutes. Turn the oven off, open the door a crack, and leave the cake in the oven for another hour. Refrigerate at least 8 hours or overnight.

If desired, pour caramel sauce over the top of the cake and sprinkle with the chopped toffee bars. Or drizzle the caramel sauce on the plate, lay a slice of the cake down, and sprinkle with the toffee pieces.

Yield: 14 servings

beignets

Beignets are fried dough balls, similar in taste to funnel cakes. Nothing pleases children more than this simple-to-make dessert. Their powdered sugar faces are the best indication of their powdered-sugar-coated thumbs up review. When I make a batch of these, I will cut up a firm banana into ½-inch slices and make half of the batch plain and half with bananas.

4-6 cups vegetable or corn oil	1 teaspoon salt
1 cup milk	4 teaspoons sugar
1 cup water	1-2 firm bananas, cut into ½-inch slices
1 large egg	(optional)
3 cups all-purpose flour	confectioner's sugar
2 tablespoons baking powder	

Pour the oil into a deep pot to a depth of 3-4 inches. Heat the oil to 370 degrees.

Meanwhile, in a large bowl with the mixer at medium-high speed, combine the milk, water, and egg. Add the flour, baking powder, salt, and sugar. Mix until the batter is smooth.

Using a ⅛ cup measure, drop the batter into the hot oil and fry about 3-4 minutes. Don't make them much bigger or the inside won't cook properly. The beignets will float to the surface; turn them a few times until the beignets are golden on both sides. Drain on paper towels and either roll in or use a strainer to sprinkle on confectioner's sugar. Serve hot.

To make banana beignets, fill the ⅛ cup measure halfway full. Add a slice of banana, fill the rest of the way with batter. Fry as directed above. Roll in confectioner's sugar.

Yield: 20-24 beignets

strawberry lemon tart

A microplane (see page 87) is a must for grating the lemon rind. Just make sure to get only the yellow zest and not the bitter white pith. The tart shell can be baked the night before and then filled and decorated before serving. Some people like to blind bake the tart shell, which means filling it with pie weights or a piece of parchment filled with dry beans and then baking it as directed. The purpose of this is to keep the shell nice and flat. You can do this on this tart, but most often, I skip this step. The bottom of your shell will not be as flat, so you may end up with extra filling which you can discard. But the end result looks just as great.

Tart Dough:

- 2 cups all-purpose flour
- ½ cup sugar
- ½ teaspoon baking powder
- ¾ cup margarine or butter, frozen and cut into chunks
- 1 egg yolk
- 2 tablespoons fresh lemon juice (juice of 1 lemon)

Lemon Cream:

- 6 large lemons
- 6 large eggs, room temperature
- 1 cup plus 6 tablespoons sugar
- 6 tablespoon butter or margarine, cut into small pieces
- 15-20 strawberries, evenly sliced

Tart Dough:

Preheat oven to 400 degrees. Combine the flour, sugar, and baking powder in the container of a food processor fitted with a dough blade; pulse 3-4 times until combined. Add margarine; pulse until mixture is crumbly. With machine running, add the egg yolk and lemon juice; process until pastry begins to form a ball. This dough can also be made by hand or with an electric mixer with a dough hook.

Press the dough into the bottom and up the sides of an 11-inch tart pan with a removable bottom. You can use a 9-inch tart pan as well, just discard any extra dough. Prick the tart all over.

Bake for 10 minutes; reduce heat to 350 degrees and bake 10 minutes longer. Remove from oven and set aside to cool.

Lemon Cream:

Grate the lemon rind until you have 6 tablespoons of zest. Place it in a medium saucepan. Juice the lemons into the saucepan. Cook over medium-low heat. Add about ¼ cup of this hot liquid to the eggs in a separate bowl and stir, to temper them so they don't scramble.

Whisk the eggs, sugar, and butter or margarine into the saucepan until the mixture is smooth. Remove from heat.

Place the prebaked tart shell on a baking pan. Fill the shell with the lemon filling. Bake in a 325 degree oven for 10-12 minutes or until center is just set. Remove to rack. Cool.

Starting around the outer edge, garnish with strawberry slices in concentric circles. You can leave the center empty so that the lemon cream peeks out.

Yield: 8-10 servings

fresh peach or plum torte

Dairy or Parve

½ cup (1 stick) butter or margarine	1 teaspoon baking powder
1 cup sugar	5 peaches or 6 plums, pits removed,
1 teaspoon vanilla	thinly sliced, unpeeled
2 large eggs	½ lemon
1 cup all-purpose flour	1 tablespoon sugar
pinch of salt	cinnamon

Preheat oven to 350 degrees. Spray a 9- or 10-inch springform pan with nonstick cooking spray.

In a large mixing bowl, cream the margarine and the sugar. Add the vanilla, eggs, flour, salt, and baking powder. Press the dough into the prepared pan, wetting your hands if necessary.

Arrange the peach or plum slices in concentric circles. Lightly squeeze the lemon over the tart. Sprinkle with the sugar and the cinnamon. Bake 1 hour, uncovered.

Yield: 10 servings

lemon delight bundt cake

This recipe came to me from the owners of The Peppermill in Brooklyn. The Peppermill is the ultimate store for any kosher gourmet cook and baker. This cake is fabulous in a regular bundt pan, but they recommend trying it in a fancier version like a Bavarian pan that has dramatic ridges all over for detailed presentation, a fleur-de-lis pan which has elegant swirls along the bottom edge, or a rose pan that has a gorgeous rose petal design.

Cake:

2½ cups all-purpose flour
1½ cups sugar
 3 teaspoons baking powder
¾ cup orange juice

¾ cup vegetable oil
1½ teaspoons lemon extract
 4 large eggs

Glaze:

¾ cup confectioner's sugar, plus more for dusting
⅛ cup lemon juice

Cake:

Heat oven to 325 degrees. Grease and flour a bundt pan. You can use the can of flour and oil spray. Combine the flour, sugar, and baking powder in a large mixing bowl. Add the orange juice, oil, lemon extract, and eggs. Beat 3-4 minutes at medium speed. Pour into the prepared pan.

Bake 45-50 minutes or until cake tester inserted in center comes out clean. Remove the cake from the oven. Using a long thin skewer, poke deep holes into the cake at 1-inch intervals.

Glaze:

Mix the ingredients for the glaze until smooth and well combined. Spoon the glaze over the hot cake allowing it to run into the holes. Allow the cake to cool.

Remove the cake from the pan and sprinkle with confectioner's sugar.

Yield: 10-12 servings

⌘ Personalized Dessert Plates
Decorate your dessert plate with a personalized message. Melt chocolate in a saucepan over low heat. Cool slightly, then pour into a small zip-lock bag. Cut off a tiny corner from the bag. Gently squeeze to pipe designs or your message along the rim of the plate. Set aside to harden.

---

chocolate banana cake

Have some extra bananas? This cake is for you. You can try the parve sour cream to make it a nondairy cake. Either way, use the best Belgian or Israeli chocolate bar you can find. This cake can also be made without the glaze.

Cake:

- 1 cup pure vegetable shortening
- 2 cups sugar
- 2 large eggs
- 2 ripe (not brown) bananas, mashed
- ⅓ cup sour cream
- 1 teaspoon vanilla

- 2½ cups all-purpose flour
- 2 teaspoons baking soda
- ⅓ cup cocoa
- ¼ teaspoon salt
- 1 cup boiling water

Decadent Chocolate Glaze:

- 6 tablespoons unsalted butter, or margarine
- 6 tablespoons heavy whipping cream, or non-dairy whipped topping

- 3 ounces milk or semi-sweet chocolate
- ¼ cup semisweet chocolate morsels
- 1¼ cup confectioner's sugar, sifted
- 1 teaspoon vanilla extract

Cake:

Preheat oven to 350 degrees. Grease a 10-inch tube or a bundt pan; set aside.

In a large mixing bowl, cream the shortening and sugar until fluffy. Add the eggs, one at a time. Add the bananas, sour cream, and vanilla, mix until all are incorporated.

In a separate large bowl combine the flour, baking soda, cocoa, and salt. Add the dry ingredients to the banana mixture in 3 parts, alternating with the boiling water. Mix. The batter will be runny. Pour into prepared pan. Bake for 1 hour.

Decadent Chocolate Glaze:

Combine butter or margarine, cream, chocolate, morsels, sugar, and vanilla in a heavy saucepan over low heat. Cook whisking constantly, until smooth. Cool slightly. Pour over cake; let it run over the sides. Try not to manipulate glaze too much, let set. Cake can be refrigerated, bring to room temperature before serving.

Yield: 12 servings

nut coffee layer cake Parve

This is an unusual and beautiful dessert. A real celebration cake. It feeds a lot of people, so it's great for a party or an occasion when you have a lot of company. The garnish is simple to do yet is a real show stopper. A tip for this cake (and any cake that you frost between layers): After the cakes cool in the pan, make sure they are not stuck in the pan, but don't remove from pans. Cover the pans and place the cakes in the freezer for a few hours or up to 10 days ahead. Frost the cakes while they are frozen to keep crumbs from getting into the frosting.

Cake:

9 large eggs, separated
1½ cups sugar, divided
1 cup all-purpose flour
3 teaspoons baking powder
2 tablespoons cocoa

7 ounces ground hazelnuts or walnuts
1 cup orange juice
½ cup vegetable or canola oil
1 teaspoon vanilla

Coffee Crème:

2½ cups (5 sticks margarine), room temperature
5 egg yolks
2⅓ cups confectioner's sugar

4-5 tablespoons instant coffee or espresso granules dissolved in a little water

Garnishes:

10-12 ounces good quality semisweet chocolate, grated
1 (8-ounce) bag chopped walnuts

3-4 chocolate leaves (brush melted chocolate on lemon leaves, when dry gently peel back leaf) or a few hazelnuts

Cake:

Spray 2 (10-inch) cake pans very well with nonstick spray. Parchment paper cut into circles works even better; place the parchment into the pans and spray with nonstick spray. Preheat oven to 350 degrees. In a medium bowl, with the mixer at medium speed, beat the egg whites, gradually add ½ cup sugar. Beat until stiff peaks form. Set aside.

In a large bowl with a mixer, combine remaining cup of sugar, flour, baking powder, cocoa, and nuts. Add the egg yolks, orange juice, oil, and vanilla. Beat until smooth.

Fold the egg whites into mixture. Divide evenly between the two prepared pans. Bake for 25 minutes or until toothpick inserted in center comes out clean.

Remove cakes from oven. Cool cakes in pan. Cover and put pans in the freezer for a few hours or up to a few days ahead.

Coffee Crème:

With a mixer at a high speed, cream the margarine and egg yolks together. Combine the dissolved coffee with the sugar and add this mixture into the margarine. Beat well.

Turn the cakes out of the pans. Place one cake layer, bottom-side-up on cake plate or platter.

Spread a layer of the creme evenly over the layer. Place the second layer of cake top-side-up on the icing. Spread a thick layer of creme around top and sides of the cake. Divide the top of the cake into ⅛ths (like a pizza) by indenting lines on the frosting with a knife.

Garnishes:

Arrange the garnishes, alternating chocolate and nuts, in the pre-indented sections on top. You can cut a triangle wedge out of a paper plate and hold it in the indentation while you sprinkle. This helps keep you in the lines, or you can just hold one of your hands on the line as a way to keep the garnish in the line.

Continue until you have 4 nut sections and 4 chocolate sections. Smooth the frosting on the sides. You can mix a little bit of the chopped nuts and grated chocolate and press into the bottom of the cake for a finished look. Lay 3-4 chocolate leaves or a small pile of shelled hazelnuts in the center of the cake.

Yield: 16 servings

☞ Frost or glaze your cakes without frosting your cake plate. Arrange four strips of wax paper under the edges of the cake to cover the edges of the plate. Slather on the frosting. When you're done, carefully pull out the paper strips.

peanut butter-chocolate mousse terrine Parve

Peanut Butter Layer:

2 cups confectioner's sugar

¾ cup plus 2 tablespoons jarred creamy peanut butter

8 ounces nondairy cream cheese

3 tablespoons parve whipping cream

2 large egg whites

Chocolate Layer:

8 ounces good quality semisweet chocolate, chopped

1½ teaspoons instant coffee

2½ tablespoons water, room temperature

3 egg yolks

1 cup parve whipping cream

Glaze:

⅔ cup parve whipping cream

6 tablespoons margarine

5 ounces semisweet chocolate

Peanut Butter Layer:

Line a 6-cup loaf pan with plastic wrap, letting some hang over the sides. Set aside.

In a large bowl with mixer at medium speed, mix the sugar, peanut butter, parve cream cheese, and whipping cream.

In a medium bowl beat the egg whites until soft peaks form. Fold the egg whites into the peanut butter mixture.

With the pan in front of you horizontally, tilt the pan to a 45-degree angle. Spoon the mouse into it; the mousse will form a 45-degree angle with the pan. Place the pan in the freezer, propping it up to keep this angle.

Chocolate Layer:

Melt the chocolate in top of double boiler or in a pan set over a pot of simmering water. Stir until smooth. Remove from heat and set aside to cool for 10 minutes. Dissolve the coffee in the water in a small bowl. Whisk the egg yolks into the coffee.

Add mixture into the warm chocolate and stir until smooth. Beat the cream until soft peaks form. Gently fold the cream into the chocolate until fully incorporated.

Set the pan with the peanut butter mousse flat in front of you. Spoon chocolate mousse over the frozen peanut butter mousse. Smooth the top. Cover the pan. Freeze until chocolate layer is firm, 6 hours or overnight.

Glaze:

Heat the cream and margarine in medium saucepan over low heat until cream simmers and margarine is melted. Turn off the heat. Add chocolate and whisk until mixture is smooth. Let cool until thickened, but still able to be poured. If making in advance, place in an airtight container with lid, but do not refrigerate or it will be too thick to pour and spread.

Remove the terrine from freezer 15 minutes before serving. Invert onto cake platter. Remove plastic wrap. Pour glaze over mousse and smooth.

Yield: 8-10 servings

chocolate pecan pie Parve

This fudgy and delicious pie is a snap to make with a purchased pie crust, and it's done all in one pot. It's an ultimate indulgence without a huge commitment of time.

2 tablespoons margarine	3 large eggs, lightly beaten
1 cup semisweet chocolate morsels, divided, or 8 ounces semisweet chocolate, broken into bits, divided	¼ cup firmly packed light brown sugar
	1 cup light or dark corn syrup
	1 teaspoon vanilla
1 (9-inch) deep dish unbaked pie crust, if frozen, do not defrost	1½ cups pecan halves

Heat oven to 350 degrees. Place the margarine in a medium pot over a medium heat. Melt the margarine and add half of the chocolate pieces. Stir until smooth and melted. Remove from heat.

Brush the bottom of the pie crust with a little of the beaten egg. Add the brown sugar, corn syrup, vanilla, and remaining beaten eggs into the chocolate mixture. Stir until combined very well and the eggs are no longer visible.

Blend in the pecans and remaining chocolate morsels. Pour into pie crust and bake for 55 minutes or until knife inserted 2 inches from edge comes out clean. Cool on wire rack.

Yield: 8 servings

caramel pear rolls

Parve

This melt-in-your-mouth dessert looks like a tray of cinnamon buns. Similar to a cobbler, it is a biscuit-like pastry, rolled around a shredded pear filling and drenched in a caramel sauce. It's just incredible right out of the oven.

2 cups sugar
2 cups water
¼ cup margarine
½ teaspoon cinnamon
2 cups flour
2 teaspoons baking powder
½ teaspoon salt
¾ cup pure vegetable shortening, like Crisco

⅔ cup vanilla soy milk or nondairy creamer
¼ cup sugar
½ teaspoon cinnamon
4 medium Bosc or Anjou pears, peeled and shredded or grated in a food processor

Preheat oven to 350 degrees. In a large saucepan combine sugar, water, margarine, and cinnamon. Bring to a boil and continue to boil for 5 minutes. Remove from heat and set aside.

In a large mixing bowl, combine the flour, baking powder, and salt. Using a pastry blender, or your fingers in a pinching motion, cut in the shortening until pieces are pea-sized. Make a well in the center of the flour mixture and pour in the soy milk. Stir until just moistened.

Lightly flour your surface and knead the dough gently for 10-12 strokes. Roll the dough into a 12- by 10-inch rectangle.

In a small cup or bowl combine the sugar and cinnamon. Sprinkle the shredded pears evenly over the dough. Sprinkle on the cinnamon/sugar mixture.

Roll the dough into a spiral, starting from the long side. With a sharp knife, cut into 12 (1-inch-thick) slices.

Arrange the slices in an ungreased 13- by 9- by 2-inch rectangular pan. Pour sauce over the rolls. Bake for 50 minutes. Best when served warm.

Yield: 12 servings

☞ *Pear Pointers*

BARTLETTS are good for snacking and cooking. They have a definite pear flavor.

COMICES are sweet and juicy. Though they're perfect for poaching, don't use them in pies or bake whole.

BOSCS are crisp and slightly tart. They hold their shape well when baked or sautéed.

ANJOUS are all-purpose pears with a smooth texture and mild flavor. They also hold their shape well.

SECKELS are nice for garnishes, but too small to make peeling them worth using in a recipe.

index

my favorite recipes